PRAYING DOCTORS – Jesus in the Office
A Foreword for Rene Pelleya-Kouri, M.D.

This is NOT a book for ordinary physicians. This book was written through an EXTRAordinary physician from the heart of the GREAT physician. This book should NOT be limited to those in the medical practice, but ALL of us who call upon the Name of the Lord who want to see His healing power manifest in the lives of people for whom we are praying.

Dr. Rene, as I call him, humbly but boldly began by sharing his personal testimony. The life experiences of this man accomplish for the reader what a face-to-face encounter accomplish. You learn that this is a doctor unlike <u>any</u> you have ever visited. His encounters with Our Lord have removed the God complex awarded with many M.D. Degrees. Through his writing, and his demeanor, Dr. Pelleya-Kouri demonstrates the exciting relationship available to 'any man' with our Lord and Savior, Jesus Christ.

The testimony is interwoven through the teaching, which is never far from its Biblical base. (The Word is quoted at every juncture.) The teaching is practical for physicians and lay people alike. AND it is so full of power, the reader is repeatedly drawn into the confrontation between the kingdom of darkness and the Kingdom of Light.

I recommend this book to anyone in the Medical Profession, but also anyone who is a seeker of the Truth. I caution you to have Hi Liter and pen at your side, as there are many nuggets you will want to recall later. I also encourage you to be prepared to have some of your own 'personal truths' assaulted by the Sword of Truth as wielded by this Daring Doctor, who has turned his life AND his practice over to the Lord, Our Healer, Jesus, The Christ.

HEALING WORDS MINISTRIES
www.healingwordsmin.org

Cheryl B. Williams
Email: cherylwilliams@healingwordsmin.org
Phone: 904-378-1546

PRAYING DOCTORS

"JESUS IN THE OFFICE"

TESTIMONY AND BASIC TRAINING MANUAL

Rene Pelleya-Kouri, M.D.

Unless otherwise noted; scripture quotations are taken from:

The Holy Bible
Authorized King James Version
Results Publishing
International Christian Publishers

Holy Bible
New International Version (N.I.V)
Zondervan 1990

The Amplified Bible
Zondervan 1987

Holy Bible
New Revised Standard Version
With Apocrypha
Oxford University

Order this book online at www.trafford.com
or email orders@trafford.com

Most Trafford titles are also available at major online book retailers.

Note for Librarians: A cataloguing record for this book is available from Library
and Archives Canada at www.collectionscanada.ca/amicus/index-e.html

Printed in Victoria, BC, Canada.

ISBN: 978-1-4251-8783-5 (soft)
ISBN: 978-1-4251-8784-2 (e-book)

*We at Trafford believe that it is the responsibility of us all, as both individuals
and corporations, to make choices that are environmentally and socially sound.
You, in turn, are supporting this responsible conduct each time you purchase a
Trafford book, or make use of our publishing services. To find out how you are
helping, please visit www.trafford.com/responsiblepublishing.html*

*Our mission is to efficiently provide the world's finest, most comprehensive
book publishing service, enabling every author to experience success.
To find out how to publish your book, your way, and have it available
worldwide, visit us online at www.trafford.com*

Trafford rev. 7/17/2009

 **Trafford** PUBLISHING® www.trafford.com

North America & international
toll-free: 1 888 232 4444 (USA & Canada)
phone: 250 383 6864 ♦ fax: 250 383 6804 ♦ email: info@trafford.com

Acknowledgments

To my Father Abba, to His Son, my dear Lord Jesus and to the Holy Spirit that dwells in me.

To my family in heaven and in earth: Papi, Mami, Fifi and her family, Maria and her family, Roberto, Rene, Cristina, Lacy, Eddie, Lucas, and Isabel Maria. To all my Christian family.

To the physicians: many more than we could imagine are bringing salvation and healing in their practices.

To so many ministries and ministers that have helped me so much. I can only mention a few: to Maria Vadia, my little sister on fire, who has been training me since the beginning. To Cheryl Williams, my wise and annointed mentor from Christian Healing Ministries. To Todd Bentley, Fresh Fire Ministries and the Lakeland Revival. During this revival I wrote this book, was ordained minister of the gospel and got appointments to the nations! Such grace and blessings! To Frank and Jill Marzullo from Christian Covenant Fellowship who ordained and blessed me as minister of the gospel. To the one and only Patricia King.

To the prophets and friends: K.K Chin, Norman and Margie Spencer from Prophetic People Ministries International and Randy and Kathy Lechner from Covenant Ministries.

Father Tom Dilorenzo, Father John Fink, Father Dan Doyle, Father James Fetscher, Jim and Mary Horvath, Scott and Carolyn Kaldall, Randy Clark, Bill Johnson, Heidi Baker, Dominick Avello, Francis and Judith MacNutt, Greg and Lydia Trainor, and to many more that have been such a blessing along the way.

And a special thanks to God for my newly found, Holy Spirit-ruled Church, Miami International Covenant Church, with Pastors Hector and Esther Jordan, their anointed offspring Sarah and Aaron, and every saint there.

I want to also bless my place of work MCCI and my old friends Stephen Gallegos, Richard Allen, Roberta Racaniello and Poldi Orlando.

To Rosie Lopez who patiently typed my handwritten manuscript. Thank you and blessings to all.

Table of Contents

Introduction I

When I came to Jesus I knew that part of my ministry would be in the marketplace- at the medical office- and possibly training physicians. People thought that I should write a book and received spontaneous prophetic words about it.

While sharing with my mentor from Christian Healing Ministries, Cheryl Williams, how I loved to visit the Lord in heaven and that my heart was not into writing Praying Doctors she grabbed my hands tightly and said, "Bring the things of heaven into the earth. Start writing a practical book to help many who need it."

That immediately changed my direction. I was convicted and the Holy Ghost in me got activated to write Praying Doctors. Soon after leaving Jacksonville I went to the second Patricia King's growing in the Supernatural conference in Arizona, and as Paul Keith David ministered, the window of seeing opened broadly, and I received from the Spirit, permission to see. This seeing began to also feed the practicalities of in a way a rational book. So the following visions are the beginning of Praying Doctors.

Hurt eagle, big eagle, grieving in midair;
My children are hurt;
Groaning, cryings, explosions of pain;
A dying, a new birth.
This is a new arena of the spirit.
You have been born of the spirit.
You are a son of light.
You have been born into the light.
Your father is Abba, God himself.
You grabbed salvation.
Salvation grabbed you.
I am being torn open.
The pain of humanity is too much.
There is a burden, there is travail;
I have to be broken, undone;
The birth of compassion is painful;

All birthings are painful;
Wait upon the Lord;
He is your strength;
He is your defense;
At vulnerable times, at sensitive times;
When you are shedding your skin;
He will protect you.
I am going through the pains of birth under the shadow of the almighty.
I groan.
I am a chick trying to break through the egg.
I am going through the birth canal.
I can only make it with your help, oh mother;
Oh I am letting go of all;
The old passes away;
Regressions pull back;
The whole world groans;
I am dying Lord;
You came alive in me;
I decrease so you increase;
In my weakness there is your strength.
Cleanse me Jesus from whatever gets in your way;
Lord I need a revelation of you;
My skin is falling;
I am undone;
The egg is breaking;
I peek out of the birth canal;
I am hurt and bloody;
The eagle groans;
My child be born;
I surrender. I let go;
Then there is a breakthrough;
Now I stand nude and bare before my Lord.
The chick cries for his mother;
He is hungry;
Just went through birth;

Loose me Father, cries eagle;
The eagle of ministry is loosed;
It is loosed and it looks, searches, finds, and feeds its offspring.
Jesus you are my food so feed me Lord;
I see the cross;
Out of the cross food and drink came for all;
Jesus is my food and my drink;
I eat the bread, drink the blood;
Such honor, such grace, such mercy, such love, such blessing.
I am blessed, so blessed;
He chose me since the beginning of times to make His abode in me.
Rest my son.
You are now the eagle that feeds himself;
The Kingdom is in you;
Life is in you;
Resurrection power is in you;
We move as one;
Sound the alarm;
Call the band of eagles;
The anointing comes.
Healing is released for the Doctor's hearts
Eagles groan, angels come;
The Father and the Son release, loose the anointing for the doctor's office;
This is your purpose and your destiny;
To call upon the band of eagles;
Eagles with a burden;
Eagles that travail;
We will change medicine;
Sozo will flourish in the medical office;
The man with the torch sets offices on fire.
The river of life will flow at the office.
Water will fall.
From the office it will go to the hospital, and from the hospital it will go to the universities.

Open heavens and the glory of God will direct the course of medicine.

Large eagle eyes and the heart set on the Lord will be the mark of the physician.

The healers will represent The Healer.

God is opening a direct pathway. A major highway into the things of heaven.

Impartation, revelation, healing hands;

Room of the organs;

Specific knowledge of the mechanisms of disease;

Power over illness, disease, infirmity;

Anointing for inner healing;

Miracles, signs, wonders;

Whole offices converted;

Whole hospitals converted;

Whole universities converted;

It is the power of the cross and the blood of Jesus.

He said: it is done;

Eagles now perch and rest right near the Lord;

New assignments will soon come.

Introduction II

Healing flows from the heart of God. God is healing. I am the God that healeth thee. The word, Jesus, healed all that approached Him. Today, it is the same. He is the same yesterday, today, and forever. In the cross He did it all: Isaiah 53:4-5, Matthew 8:17, 1 Peter 2:24. Our minds need to be renewed and transformed. Romans 12:2.

We need to shatter our limited carnal mental unbelief strongholds. We invite the mind of Christ to rule in our lives. We cast down imaginations... 2 Corinthians 10:4-5. We set our affections in Him. Colossians 3:1-2. We let the old man be buried and the new man be alive. Our transformation, change, and sanctification is usually a process. We get actively involved. We are saved when we repent, accept, believe in our heart, and confess Jesus as our Lord and savior. We have a place in heaven; but I want the Kingdom now. I don't want anything to separate me from my King.

Romans 8 says that nothing can separate me from the love of Christ. We were saved by grace. We need to fight for our salvation-sanctification with fear and trembling. The whole man needs to be involved: spirit, soul, and body. The power of the Spirit of God is always waiting with open arms for us prodigals to return home. Joy, freedom, peace, victory, love, hope, are too awesome.

The love of God, our relationship with Him is the highest treasure. Healing is an ongoing flowing happening activity of the spirit within. God is always showing aspects of our humanity that need Him. It is the relationship that we need. Seek you first the Kingdom of God and all else will be added unto you. When He said love God above all things it is not just saying it but living it.

I trained at the University Of Miami School of Medicine, completed medical school, three years of internal medicine and two years of nephrology. I loved medicine but I was not a happy camper. I was unsaved and had festering inner wounds that held me back in many ways. I was very interested in illnesses, healing, and in trying to help my patients. While working long hours at the medical wards, it began to down on me that there were vital areas in some patients related to their sickness and recovery that we were not even approaching or touching. Purely allopathic scientific medicine was not the whole answer. Today it is a completely different story. I practice allopathic internal medicine with the best standard of care and I am also intensely involved in the spiritual, mental, emotional well being of my patients.

I found the truth: Jesus, and the truth has set me free. I want the same for my patients. He wants to pour Himself upon all flesh. This is such a time. A week after the baptism in the Holy Ghost (that's when my new life in Christ began to express itself) a woman came for preoperative clearance. She was to have resection of a pancreatic mass thought to be cancer. We had evidence of the mass on the ultrasound and the CT scan; she had abdominal pain, anorexia and weight loss. I had never prayed for anyone in the Christian way. I thought I am nobody and I don't know anything but Jesus is! So I just said let this tumor be gone in Jesus name. When she went to surgery they did several tests, and there was no evidence of any mass whatsoever! Praise the Lord. So we have scans before prayer and scans after prayer. Mass and no mass! She came back to the office healed, full of joy and praising the Lord.

Zeal for prayer and healing invaded me and I began to pray for everybody. Attacks soon came from all angles; even from people who had been very close to me, but I knew that we wrestle not against flesh and blood, but against principalities, against powers, against the rulers of the darkness of this world, against spiritual wickedness in high places. Ephesians 6:12.

In one occasion in which I was going to be confronted in a meeting I went to the bathroom and spoke in tongues and the Lord said I'll speak for you. I did not know what I was going to say. I thought is this my last day here? I trusted the Lord and ended giving a lecture on the proven benefits of prayer. I mentioned Benson's Harvard mind body institute in which prayer has definitely been proven to be beneficial. Francis MacNutt's studies of the effect of prayer on rheumatoid arthritis that showed very positive results, even total healing in some patients. I even quoted Larry Dossey who said that we will reach a day when if you don't pray for your patients you could be sued. The attacks diminished greatly after that meeting. Praise the Lord.

Praying in the medical office is a tremendous challenge. Obviously you need the basic Christian training and equipping. The daily early morning God time: scriptures, praise and worship, tongues, soaking, the glory. Prayers of protection, prayers of cleansing and deliverance, prayers of decreeing, prayers of being set free at the end of the day. I always daily include Francis MacNutt's prayer of protection and prayer to be set free.

At the office I am very focused on my allopathic medical responsibilities: from head to toe. I don't want to miss anything at all. I strive for the best medical management of my patients; then comes the need for prayer, salvation, physical healing, inner healing, and deliverance. I learned that I have to be absolutely respectful and not intrusive so I had to learn to hold my horses. I am under the authority of the work place and the medical system. I have to ask the patient very clearly if they would like me to pray for them. Some patients do not want prayer and that is perfectly ok. I treat them well in a purely allopathic way. I am convinced that God is releasing a powerful anointing for the physicians so they can accomplish His work upon many patients in a matter of minutes in the office.

There is something dramatic and special occurring in the doctor's office. People come expecting and God used that expectation in a supernatural way. I would honestly say that the vast majority of people we pray for, receive significant benefits. Some get healed immediately and for others it is a process. It is very rare that nothing happens.

Even today 09/27/07 a patient with chronic deteriorating Alzheimer's disease came to see me with his wife. He is a very quite man without memory. He just sits there staring at space kind of lost. Today I felt that we needed to intensely pray. I asked the Holy Ghost to show us the root cause of his problem. I declared the presence of God upon him and to let his healing begin. Suddenly the man exploded with tremendous anger, then hurt; he wept inconsolably for a long time saying how his children had totally abandoned him. He became totally clear and alive in the expression of this hidden pain. He had hurt, abandonment, rejection, humiliation, unforgiveness, even dating back to his own childhood. We did inner healing and mini deliverance of the spirits of unforgiveness and accusation. I believe that part of his loss of memory developed as a result of all the longstanding pain and suffering, and his inability to cope with it. He hid in his own very quiet world. His wife said that he had never cried and that for years she had not seen him so alive, so expressive, and so clear. I believe the healing of his loss of memory began for him today. We will keep on praying. Amen.

I remember an elderly lady that came to see me for respiratory failure. She was using supplemental oxygen and was carrying her oxygen tank. I asked the Holy Spirit to guide me. We went to the time when her lung problem began. It was three years earlier when her husband died. We investigated the circumstances related to her illness. My patient had been in conflict with her husband. She had unresolved issues with him when he died that were never healed. She never grieved as she had to "take care of everything". The first thing we were guided to do was the grieving of her husband's death. She wept for the first time since he had died. She repented for judging him and forgave him. She received forgiveness from God and made Jesus her Lord and savior. She forgave herself. She renounced judgment on the doctors and forgave them. The presence of the Lord was available to us right there in the office. She felt healed in her spirit, emotions, mind, and body. We also did deliverance and cast out spirits of unforgiveness, bitterness, rage, hate, accusation, condemnation, rigidity, and stuckness. We invited an infilling of the Holy Ghost and commanded those spirits never to return. We declared her lungs healed. I could literally see her chest expanding as she became filled with the Holy Ghost. I took her oxygen tank off and told her to walk. She had no shortness of breath and her oxygen saturation was higher now without the supplemental oxygen! Hallelujah, thank you Jesus. All has been done at the cross. The whole visit took about half an hour.

This is an example of Sozo salvation: forgiveness of sins and spiritual rebirth, healing of the soul: mind and emotions. Healing of the body. Deliverance- casting out devils. She was saved completely and became whole. Thank you Jesus. This was a wonderful day at the office. God gives us all good things. All good things come from above.

We absolutely save lives with allopathic medicine. I believe that medicine is given to us by God, but we don't need to limit God. Many times he wants more for our patients. He is ready and available to pour healing into the doctor's office. He created us and loves us even in the market place.

This is an awesome prayer that honors physicians from the deuterocanonical scriptures:

Sirach 38
1-Honor physicians for their services, for the Lord created them;
2- for their gift of healing comes from the Most High, and they are rewarded by the king.
3- the skill of physician makes them distinguished, and in the presence of the great they are admired.
4- the Lord created medicines out of the earth, and the sensible will not despise them.
5- Was not water made sweet with a tree in order that its power might be known?
6- And he gave skill to human beings that he might be glorified in his marvelous works.
7- By them the physician heals and takes away pain;
8- The pharmacist makes a mixture from them. God's works will never be finished; and from him health spreads over all the earth.
9- My child, when you are ill, do not delay, but pray to the Lord, and he will heal you.
10- Give up your faults and direct your hands rightly, and cleanse your heart from all sin.
11- Offer a sweet-smelling sacrifice, and a memorial portion of choice flour, and pour oil on your offering, as much as you can afford."
12- Then give the physician his place, for the Lord created him; do not let him leave you, for you need him.
13- There may come a time when recovery lies in the hands of physicians,
14- for they too pray to the Lord that he grant them success in diagnosis and in healing, for the sake of preserving life.
15- He who sins against his Maker, will be defiant toward the physician."

Thank you Lord that we are really your physicians and that you love us and consider us an important part of you church.

Chapter One

"TESTIMONY"

I was born on Mother's Day in Havana, Cuba, May 12, 1946.

Psalm51:5
Behold, I was shapen in iniquity; and in sin did my mother conceive me.

I almost died at birth, and soon after birth, my mother had a nervous breakdown. She needed to go away to recover. As a child I was very introverted, shy, timid, and fearful. I went to LaSalle Catholic School, and during retreats I would experience the presence of God. These were times of ecstasy and deep communion with the Lord. I could not move, talk, or respond to the environment as I was filled by His Presence. Important spiritual times where also when I sang at the choir. There was a song that I have never forgotten:

Amemos al amor de los amores,
Amemos al senor,
Dios esta aqui, venid adoradores,
Adoremos al Cristo redentor
Gloria a Cristo Jesus
Cielos y tierra
Bendecid al Senor
Honor y Gloria a ti rey de la Gloria,
Amor por siempre a ti Dios del amor.

Little did I suspect that my life would go into a path of destruction.
One of my family's characteristics was that of professionalism. My mother was a physician and my father an attorney. Several of my aunts and uncles were also physicians and attorneys. Every Sunday my family would meet and it was an incredible potpourri of worldly knowledge and wisdom. A character that was above all others was my maternal

Grandfather, Juan Bautista Kouri, a professor of medicine at the University of Havana. A remarkable physician, surgeon, and an innovator in medicine. He was also a Grade 33 Freemason and general inspector, a new age pioneer involved in Hinduism, Eastern mysticism, yoga, meditation, different philosophies, free thinking, moral relativism, no sexual limitations etc.

I know that generational curses affected me severely and that demons infected me through such sins of the fathers.

Exodus 20:5
I am a jealous God, visiting the iniquity of the fathers upon the children unto the third and fourth generation of them that hate me.

I had to repent and renounce such sins of my ancestors.

Leviticus 26 (A.B)
40- But if they confess their own and their father's iniquity in their treachery which they committed against Me- and also that because they walked contrary to Me.
41- I also walked contrary to them and brought them into the land of their enemies- if then their uncircumcised hearts are humbled and they then accept the punishment for their iniquity.
42- Then will I [earnestly] remember My covenant…, and [earnestly] remember the land.

Thank God for the Lamb of God that if we repent and accept Jesus as our lord and savior we are forgiven.

Galatians 3:13
Christ has redeemed us from the curse of the law, being made a curse for us: for it is written, Cursed is everyone that hangeth on a tree.

The years I lived in Cuba 1946-1960 were very dry spiritual years. There was overall ungodliness in my family, and I would say in most families at that time. The Holy Spirit had not fallen in the Catholic Church then. We did not talk about Jesus or have a bible. We were lost and totally set up for the activities of the kingdom of darkness.

I would say that the event that I will mention next was a setup of the devil. When I was about 12 or 13 years old a catholic brother expelled me from the Lasalle chorus for naively laughing with my peers about a foolish situation. I felt hurt, rejected, and humiliated. I went outside the school to get an ice-cream, and the vendor not only gave me the ice-cream but also gave me a pornographic booklet! The moment I saw those pictures and read the booklet, a demon of lust came into my life and affected me for over 40 years.

It did not help that about the same time I received "growth injections" that greatly stimulated my sexuality. My first emotional sexual romantic love relationship was with a prostitute when I was 13 years old. Love became totally contaminated with sex. Sex tried to fill a bottomless place of hurt. I had become a sex addict. I lived with feelings of rejection, abandonment, shame, insecurity, fear, worthlessness, self pity, self hate, etc. There were many strongholds that needed to be destroyed, such as the shame fear stronghold.

Jeremiah 1:10
See, I have this day set thee over the nations and over the kingdoms, to root out, and to pull down, and to destroy, and to throw down, to build, and to plant.

But there was the other side of the coin: arrogance, rebellion, disobedience, lust, witchcraft, stubbornness, iniquity, idolatry.

1 Samuel 15:23
For rebellion is as the sin of witchcraft, and stubbornness is as iniquity and idolatry. Because thou hast rejected the word of the Lord, he hath also rejected thee from being king.

In 1960 I came to Miami, FL at the age of 14 and depression hit me really hard. I began to drink alcohol to relieve the pain. In 1970 a realization came that there was something really wrong with me, that I needed to find God and receive healing. At that time I connected to a Hindu Guru and began intense meditation practices to seek the presence of God. Only by the grace of God I went to medical school and trained at the University of Miami for 7 years. I completed trainings in internal medicine and nephrology.

In 1982 I had a dialysis unit and a large practice of medicine and nephrology. I was in my second marriage and had a second child.

Romans 6:23
For the wages of sins is death; but the gift of God is eternal life through Jesus Christ our Lord.

Rapidly I became totally addicted to cocaine and lost everything. I left Miami and went to a treatment center in Mississippi by the name of Copac. There I suffered the worst feelings, moods, and emotions. The self hate was intense and consumed me. The sense of grief, regret and loss overwhelmed me. I had lost my wife, my daughter, my house, and my practice of medicine.

I was under the control of total cravings and obsessions. I was convinced that I could never recover and I was planning my next relapse, thinking that I for surely would die, but had no other alternative. I felt totally hopeless.

That day I walked into the woods and found a small pond. I could not take it any longer, and asked God to please kill me. I was totally broken down, and fell weeping into the humid earth. A new idea came then into my mind. I said to God that if he did not want to kill me to please take all the negativity, cravings, and hell that were inside of me.

Joel 2:32
Whosoever shall call on the name of the Lord he shall be delivered.

Suddenly, a gust of wind came, there was the sound of the leaves being shaken, the waters of the pond were stirred, and in a moment God took away all that was killing me. He absolutely took away the cocaine addiction, the cravings, the self hate, the depression, the negativity, and the darkness. I was filled with light, love, joy, peace, beauty, clarity, and happiness. It was an event that I still clearly remember. I never used any drugs again. God sovereignly healed my cocaine addiction in one moment in 1983. As I went back to the housing complex, I began to declare of how God can heal addiction in an instant. They thought that I had taken drugs so they did a urine test on me and the results were negative. I kept telling people that God healed me at a pond in the woods. I called it God's pond.

Genesis 28
16- And Jacob awaked out of his sleep, and he said, Surely the Lord is in this place; and I knew it not.
17- And he was afraid, and said, How dreadful (awesome) is this place! This is none other but the house of God, and this is the gate of heaven.
19- And he called the name of that place Bethel.

I stayed a whole year in Mississippi, went to Alcoholics Anonymous, did The Twelve Steps, had a sponsor, and confessed my sins in a Catholic Church. The drug addiction was totally over, but the issues of relationship, love, sex, and deep hurt, were not healed. I brought my two children to Mississippi, because I knew that they had been deeply hurt, but they were young and rejected any therapy. I renewed my efforts to find the God that had healed me.

Exodus 15:26
… I am the Lord that healeth thee.

I talked to priests and ministers from different denominations, but then went on in a more profound way into esoteric spiritual psychologies, the new age, Buddhism, Hinduism, eastern and native American practices, spirit guides, the totem pole process, gestalt therapy, breath work, regression therapy, reincarnation. I had many gurus and teachers for many years. I went to India and had many spiritual experiences. I was in Jungian analysis twice a week with a catholic priest for several years.

By the year 2000 I was losing hope of finding God and being healed. I had three marriages, three divorces, and multiple relationships. I would ask myself "why do my soul mates become hate mates?" I even called it as Freud called it, repetition compulsion in hell.

1 Corinthians 6

13- ... Now the body is not for fornication, but for the Lord; and the Lord for the body.

18- Flee fornication. Every sin that a man doeth is without the body; but he that committeth fornication sinneth against his own body.

16- ... For two, saith he, shall be one flesh

No amount of therapy, religion, spirituality, meditation, mantra, etc was healing my relationship problems. I also had two very hurt children, and tons of negative feelings in me. Maria and Fifi, my two new born again sisters were always praying for my salvation. They would tell me. I was full of rage and very reactive.

In 2001 my mother had triple coronary bypass surgery; postoperatively she had severe gastrointestinal bleeding that would not stop. My mother was bleeding to death. I saw my sister Maria placing her hands on my mother's belly and making strange loud noises. The bleeding immediately stopped.

Romans 8:26

Likewise the Spirit also helpeth our infirmities: for we know not what we should pray for as we ought: but the Spirit itself maketh intercession for us with groanings which cannot be uttered.

I felt the power of God in the room and was very impressed. I liked it. It was the first time that I saw the manifest power of God in a Christian. I did not know that nice Catholic women would do such things. I saw Jesus healing my mother. In that vision Jesus said to me. I am happy that you are here. Later I wept. I was being touched by the kingdom of God, by the King himself. I was witnessing the healing power of God. Love in action.

My mother recovered from the coronary bypass surgery and the postoperative bleeding and was able to go home. Later that year she went to glory with the Lord. We had a Catholic charismatic mass as part of the wake presided by father Dan Doyle. Maria, my sister, invited everybody to do the prayer of salvation. I thought to myself, I have done all kinds of prayers, and today I am going to say this prayer. So I repented of my sins and accepted Jesus as my Lord and savior at my mother's funeral. The most important event in my life.

Romans 10:9-10
That if thou shalt confess with thy mouth the Lord Jesus, and shalt believe in thine heart that God hath raised him from the dead, thou shalt be saved. For with the heart man believeth unto righteousness; and with the mouth confession is made unto salvation.

In February 1, 2003 my sister Maria invited me to an event. She had written a book, There Is Power in Your Tongue. It was a charismatic mass of Thanksgiving in celebration of the publication of her book, again presided by Reverend Doyle. The mass was given in the backyard of a private home. It was a beautiful day. Suddenly, everybody began to sing in a way that I had never heard before. I wanted to leave, but I could not move. I did not understand what they were saying. As I was listening, I realized that it was the most beautiful sound that I had ever heard. The music went deep into my heart, and tears began to flow. Darkness left me and the heavenly music began to come out of my mouth as well.

Acts 2
1- And when the day of Pentecost was fully come, they were all with one accord in one place
2- And suddenly there came a sound from heaven as of a rushing mighty wind, and it filled all the house where they were sitting.
3- And there appeared unto them cloven tongues like as of fire, and it sat upon each of them.
4- And they were all filled with the Holy Ghost, and began to speak with other tongues, as the Spirit gave them utterance.

Joel 2:28
...I will pour my Spirit upon all flesh...

The same thing that happened to me in Mississippi, in which I was healed from my cocaine addiction, happened again twenty years later at the mass. This time it was a profound deep healing of all the things that I worked so hard to heal for so many years. The light that came in me created will, discernment, boundaries, wisdom, and discrimination. At that moment I was healed of sexual addiction and old woundings. I knew in my deepest place that this God that came into me in Mississippi in 1983 and then again in 2003 is the one true God.

Exodus 15:26
I am the Lord that healeth thee.

Exodus 18:11 (A.B)
Now I know that the Lord is greater than all gods. Yes in the [very] thing in which they delt proudly [He showed himself infinitely superior to all their gods].

I was again at the right place, the awesome place, the house of God the gate of heaven.

Acts 1:8
But ye shall receive power, after the Holy Spirit is come upon you: and ye shall be witnesses unto me…

2 Corinthians 3:17
…Where the spirit of the Lord is, there is liberty.

I felt free for the first time in my life.

John 8:36
If the Son therefore shall make you free, ye shall be free indeed.

This time I was not going to let go of him. I held tight to my savior. He had called me when it pleased him, Galatians 1:15.

I cried for a long time grieving and trying to understand why it took me such a long time to find Jesus. The father of lies does blind and deceives, 2 Corinthians 4:4.

For three months I underwent daily intense deliverance. Every morning the Holy Ghost would take me to a place, in which I had to repent, renounce, forgive, and cast out demons in the name of Jesus that would come out through heaving, coughing, and throwing up foam or phlegm.

Acts 10:38
How God anointed Jesus of Nazareth with the Holy Ghost and with power: who went about doing good, and healing all that were oppressed of the devil, for God was with him.

Hebrews 13:8
Jesus Christ is the same yesterday, and today, and forever.

1 John 3:8b
For this purpose the Son of God was manifested, that he might destroy the works of the devil.

I had certain knowledge of the demonic realms as for many years I dwelled in their environment.

It is clear in the scriptures that there are two kingdoms.

Matthew 10:7
And as ye go, preach, saying, The kingdom of heaven is at hand.

Luke 4:5
And the devil, taking him up... showed unto him all the kingdoms of the world...

Luke 4:6
And the devil said... for that is delivered unto me.

Luke 11:18a
If Satan also be divided against himself, how shall his kingdom stand?

Whosoever is not in the kingdom of light belongs to the kingdom of darkness.
I am referring to the Light as Jesus Christ.

John 8:12
I am the Light of the world…

John 1:9
That Jesus, the true Light, which lighteth every man that cometh into the world.

The Anointed One, the Messiah, the Savior, the only Son of God, a part of the trinity that came to earth being God and man, taking no recognition of His Godhead, Philippians 2:6-12, who gave his life for us and for our salvation that includes the forgiveness of sins, the opening of our relationship with God our Father, the healing of our bodies, minds, and emotions, the defeat of the evil one, the gift of eternal life, the gift of the Holy Spirit, and all our provision, peace shalom, wholeness etc.

There are absolute supernatural realms. There are true angels of light. Angels that are part of the kingdom of God. They are sent to help us.

Hebrews 1:14
Are they not all ministering spirits, sent forth to minister for them who shall be heirs of salvation?

And there is also the other kingdom with its fallen angels and demonic entities whose function is to steal, kill, and destroy, John 10:10.
Satan is a liar and the father of lies. John 8:44.
He usually comes as an angel of light, 2 Corinthians 11:14.

I was fully involved in the new age movement. In 1973 I went into an identity crisis. I realized that I had been acting very robotically throughout my life. I felt I needed to take control of my life. I wanted to be a better person guided by spiritual principles. I wanted to find God.

I hooked up then to Hinduism. I met my first Guru, received mantras, began meditating, and received powerful experiences. For thirty years I practiced other religions and occultic ways. I met many gurus and teachers from different spiritual branches. They all talked about God and the ways to God. It really excited me. Even the mantras were "The names of God".

In the midst of my spiritual quest I lived from crises to crisis, from hell to hell. I remember on one occasion in which I spent two weeks with the Dalai Lama practicing the Kalachakra Tantra in which we had to visualize and merge with 720 deities. I had gone there expecting to grow deeper in my spirituality. I also wanted to obtain healing of my relationship with the opposite sex.

Lo and behold a beautiful European woman sat beside me and rapidly we became involved romantically and everything else. These events were very painful and began creating a sense that I could not get healed of my inappropriate sexuality. I had permanent open doors to the demonic.

I was actively practicing 1 Samuel 15:23. For rebellion is as the sin of witchcraft, and stubbornness is as iniquity and idolatry.

I was immersed in occultic practices, other religions, and sexual immorality. I attempted to heal myself also with psychospiritual methods. I became an expert in imagery and visualization. Specifically, in the Totem Pole Process. For fifteen years I worked intensely with inner spiritual animal guides. I acquired vision, power, and knowledge and attempted to heal myself and others. I continued to be enslaved to my past.

I believe that all the above unchristian practices enslaved me to progressive sexual immortality. They all fed to the new age relativism, moral relativism, the "We are God" principle, all is consciousness, etc.

In 1987 my life was destroyed again and I went to India seeking enlightenment. I went to a mountain by the name of Arunachala in which "Shiva abided". I immersed myself in Ramana Maharshi's who am I method of enlightenment. It was pure hell. The demons simply abused me.

I believe that psychological supernatural spiritual dimensions, apart from Jesus, are controlled by Satan and his demons; unless you have accepted Jesus as your Lord and savior and have the Holy Spirit actively living in you, you are a sitting duck, defenseless and available for the works of the devil. Jesus came to destroy the works of the devil. 1 John 3:8b.

The world was ours but we lost it in our pride and rebelliousness. All hell broke loose in the earth after the fall of man. Our lord Jesus came to restore our world. There is an ongoing spiritual conflict. We have been redeemed, delivered, forgiven, cleansed, justified, and sanctified. Evil has no power over us, because of the power of the blood of the everlasting covenant of the lord Jesus Christ our savior.

It is written in Revelations 12:11, I overcome by testifying to what the word of God says the blood of the covenant of the Lord Jesus Christ does for me. I don't care if I die in the process.

1 Peter 2:9
We are royal priesthood.

Ephesians 1:13
We have been sealed with the Holy Ghost.

Ephesians 2:6
We are sitting together in heavenly places.

Romans 8:2
Christ Jesus has made us free from the law of sin and death.

Colossians 2:15
He spoiled principalities and powers

1 John 4:4
He who lives in us is more powerful than the one in the world.

Deuteronomy 28:13
We are the head and not the tail. We are above and not below.

Ephesians 1:3
He has blessed us with all spiritual blessings in heavenly places in
Christ Jesus.

1 Corinthians 3:16
We are temples of the Holy Ghost.

Romans 8:11
The spirit of resurrection lives in us.

Romans 8:39
Nothing can separate us from the love of God.

1 John 4:8
God is love.

1 Corinthians 13:8
 Love never fails.

Romans 8:31
If God is with us who can be against us.

2 Timothy 1:7
For God has not given us the spirit of fear; but of power, and of
love, and of a sound mind.

James 4:7
Submit yourself therefore to God. Resist the devil, and he will
 flee from you.

Matthew 28:18, 19
All power is given unto me in heaven and in earth.
19- Go ye therefore...

I am a new Christian but many Bible verses rapidly took root in
me. By the grace of God I have two sisters who were instrumental in my

salvation, Fifi and Maria. Maria Vadia is a Catholic evangelist totally dedicated to the Lord. She is Holy Spirit filled and flows in the gifts and fruits of the spirit. She trains and equips saints all over the world; as I write today 7/29/07, she is on a ministry trip to Tanzania and Zambia. I have been blessed; after I was saved I hooked up with her and swelled up like a sponge receiving from her atmosphere and the river flowing from her.

She had been praying for me for over fifteen years. She might have felt a bit frustrated by my persistent abiding in the kingdom of darkness. As she interceded more violently, the Lord showed her a man bound in a tomb just like Lazarus was. She pressed on until the man got up and began to move into the opening of the cave; at the same time my heart began to change toward my sisters. I had also taken a sabbatical from all Gurus and teachers as I needed to be in isolation to write a book, "Seeds of Enlightenment: Death, Rebirth, and Transformation through Imagery". It is not a Christian book! It is an abomination. Do not get it!

I was now alone looking at the chaos and corruption in me. I wrote daily from 4a.m-7a.m. I wept constantly as I went deep into myself seeking images to produce the book. All the hidden pain came to the surface; the self hate, the bondage, the failure of relationships, and the deep sadness. I lived a double life, an M.D and a drug addict. Seeking God and doing things of hell.

The last thing I wrote and felt in "Seeds of Enlightenment" is that underneath all the chaos, destruction, and rubble was unconditional love. God is love. I believe that God was leading me to Himself.

Through deadly mazes and labyrinths, through sins and death, He protected me in my search for Him. When I went into a sabbatical and separated from all the teachers, an evil grip was broken. I went deeply into my pain and He showed His Face, the Face of Love.

An access was opened to the prayers of the people of God. The sickness and death of my mother was a key time too, in which I began to get close to my sisters. Before she died she had said that I would receive Jesus as my Lord and savior. Did she continue to intercede for me in Heaven? What I sought all my life came when Jesus became my Lord and savior. Love, the love of God, unconditional love, right love, and freedom. A lot of the rubble that separated me from God has been removed.

When I was young, even before my adolescent years this is what I wanted. This was my innermost desire, to know God, to love God, to have a relationship with God. It took me fifty years to find the pearl of great price, to find the highest treasure hidden in the field, to find love underneath the rubble, to find my God.

So much deception. The kingdom of darkness is about counterfeit. Thank you my King that you finally rescued me. Hallelujah.

These are new pages now, new pages in my new book, new pages in my life, and tears of joy and gratitude flow from my eyes. He is about miracles and wonders, grace and mercy. His love is fathomless and is available to all. He who is forgiven much, loves much. My life was a search for healing and healing came, Jesus came. Today if you are reading these pages and have never done it repent, change direction, change the way you think and receive Jesus Christ as your Lord and Savior. Proclaim it out loud with your mouth and believe in your heart. Invite the Healer now into your life and be totally healed. Spirit, soul, and body. That's who He is- Jehovah Rapha.

Exodus 15:26
I am the Lord that healeth thee.

Run to Him, let Him hold you in His embrace.
I was set free in 2003.

John 8:36
If the Son therefore shall make you free, ye shall be free indeed.

2 Corinthians 5:17
Therefore if any man be in Christ, he is a new creature: old things are passed away; behold, all things are become new.

I then had the revelation that it is only the cross of Jesus: His blood, death, and resurrection that achieve true healing and wholeness. I had been intensely involved in many spiritual psychotherapies and other religions with failure after failure. It was all about repentance, forgiveness, salvation, healing, and deliverance that is only available through Jesus

Christ.

Acts 4:12
Salvation is found only in Him.

Luke 24:49
And, behold, I send the promise of my Father upon you: but tarry
ye in the city of Jerusalem, until ye be endued with power from
on high.

2 Timothy 3:5
Having a form of godliness but denying the power.

Luke 5:17
… The power of the Lord was present to heal them.

I soon began training at Christian Healing Ministries under Francis
and Judith MacNutt and built a prayer room in my house in which there
are ongoing salvation, healing, deliverance, prophetic, and intercession
services.

My two children were very hurt. I accepted my mistakes and how I
had hurt them. God had forgiven me.

Psalm 51:7
Purge me with hyssop, and I shall be clean: wash me, and I shall
be whiter than snow.

Isaiah 1:18
Come now, and let us reason together, saith the Lord: though
your sins be as scarlet, they shall be as white as snow; though
they be red like crimson, they shall be as wool.

I asked my children for their forgiveness. The Lord of miracles is
always doing miracles. He imparted to me the spirit of fatherhood,
something that was never in me. My son told me, this is the first time that
you are a father. The lord has also given me many children to protect and

guide, they are such joy.

My practice of medicine has become a healing and revival center of the Holy Spirit. Everyday of my life I see miracles of salvation, healing, deliverance, baptisms of the Holy Ghost with evidence of speaking in tongues, and prophetic utterances. The kingdom of God is manifesting in the office. I will give you a few testimonies of healing.

<u>Revelations 19:10b</u>
The testimony of Jesus is the spirit of prophecy.

A new patient came to the office to be evaluated. She was very sad and told me that her daughter, who lived in a country in South America, was diagnosed with terminal metastatic breast cancer. She was given three months to live, already had bought a coffin, and was waiting for the end lying in bed filled with oppression and depression. I hate the devil and I hate cancer!

Faith came into the doctor's office. The beautiful Lord came. My patient and I were filled with the Holy Ghost, and the assurance that her daughter would be healed. We prayed, interceded, and commanded the evil spirit to leave her and declared her totally healed and whole. I wanted to pray through the phone, but we could not reach her. I told the mother to reach her later to declare her healed. I also told her that she needed to go to the doctor so he would document her healing.

That event left my mind as I have a busy practice and see many people throughout the day, but lo and behold a woman came running, crying, full of joy and hugged me intensely. I didn't know what was going on. She then tells me, don't you remember? We prayed for the healing of my daughter. She went to the doctor and she was declared cancer free. She sold the lot at the cemetery and the coffin. The Lord cancelled that funeral! Hallelujah, praise you Jesus.

A man came with intractable ulcers in his forehead and neck. The ulcers were reaching his eyes. Nothing was working, neither cortisone nor antibiotics. I sent him to the university where he had biopsies and studies, but no treatment seemed to help. I prayed one time and nothing happened. The next time he came I prayed again over his forehead, and most of the ulcers disappeared instantly without leaving any scars. I said I can't believe this! I called his wife and asked her what do you see? She said, "You prayed and the ulcers are gone". I said this is too much. I really had to repent to the Lord for my unbelief.

Romans 12:2
I asked for more and more renewal of my mind.

This type of event really confronted the scientific mechanical intellectual doctor's mind. I have seen psoriasis totally gone in a day.

A man came with a history of chronic frozen shoulders and knees. He had to use a walker to get around. He told me that his family had to make up a device that would reach his body so he could bathe himself as he had become so frozen and rigid that he could not reach and touch his body anymore. Also there was no way that he could flex his knees; he could not squat at all.

He had become very frozen and rigid, felt very uncomfortable, and had a strange appearance. We asked the Lord to loosen him, and immediately he could touch all of his body and squat perfectly well. He became wild, continuously touching his whole body, and squatting. He called the nurses and other patients so they could watch him. Hallelujah, thank you Jesus. That was a very joyous moment in the office.

A woman came to the office with a history of intractable abdominal pain for twenty years. She seemed very oppressed, depressed, and could only talk of her pain. She had upper and lower endoscopies, ultrasounds, and scans. Multiple treatments by gastroenterologist had failed. I prayed intensely but nothing happened.

In the next visit I asked the Lord to give me a word of knowledge. This is the word He gave me, San Lazaro. I cast out the spirit of San Lazaro. She yelled, coughed, and cried. I saw something leaving her abdominal area. She shared with me that she worshiped San Lazaro above Jesus, and that it was a secret thing and that for years she wanted to change, but that she had not been able to do so. When I mentioned San Lazaro and cast him out, she knew that God was freeing her. She was filled with joy and reaccepted Jesus in her life. The pain was totally gone.

San Lazaro is often used in the Cuban Santeria religion. The African name is Babalu Aye, and any relationship to this spirit is incompatible with true Christianity. It is a spirit from the kingdom of darkness. It had bound this woman for many years. The pain went with him as he was cast out, hallelujah. I praise you Lord.

Many people are ignorant of the evil effects of such syncretism (fusion of different systems of belief). Santeria falls under the occultic: divination, spiritism, witchcraft, seeking knowledge, contact, or power from forbidden spiritual realms which is an abomination to our Lord and carries generational curses and demonization. There are full blown Santeros or priests that lead ceremonies, initiations, prayers, etc. But there are many people who have visited Santeros and are under curses, and need deliverance. True conversions would deal with such issues.

A while after Hurricane Katrina, I was invited to evaluate the cleaning crew in New Orleans for evidence of lung disease. We were working at a room in a casino. The power of God manifested with many salvations, words of knowledge, and miracles. I remember a man who had a blood pressure of 240/130. He had left his medicines in another town. I always have medicines in my office that rapidly lower the blood pressure, but there I had no pills whatsoever. I recommended that he would go to an emergency room to get medicines, but we first prayed. Instantly his blood pressure became normal, 140/80. I said, "Wow. This is unbelievable", and the man said, "But I have faith". I prayed God help my unbelief. We have an awesome God!

A woman with advanced diabetes nearly blind from diabetic retinopathy said that she had not been able to read the Bible for a year due to the failure of her vision. We prayed and I placed my Bible (Isaiah 53:4-5) in front of her and told her to read. There are still the marks of her tears and mascara that stained the pages of the bible as she could clearly see, read and weep.

A very ill old man was brought by his wife who was now very sad and frustrated, because he had totally lost his vision. The ophthalmologist told her that there was nothing they could do. We prayed for him, stood in front of him, and asked him what do you see? He said, "I see a strange Doctor with a white coat, a stethoscope around his neck, and a really bad hair-do". We cracked up laughing and praised the Lord. He saw clearly. His vision returned and stayed. Hallelujah.

A young man came to see me as his Doctor was on vacation. He needed certain meds. The Holy Spirit influenced me in pursuing a conversation. He said that he was in a church, but that he was held back by shame. He admitted that he was homosexual, and that the urges and cravings would take him to have sexual relationships that he considered inappropriate. He admitted that he had been violated as a child. He became willing to go through salvation, healing, and deliverance right there in the office.

He accepted Jesus as his Lord and savior. We cast out the demons of abuse and homosexuality that entered him when he was abused as a child. It came out through heaving, coughing, and burping. We called upon the Lord to heal that wound and to break all soul ties. He forgave the perpetrator. He became filled with the Holy Ghost and spoke in tongues.

I gave him an appointment and saw him at the prayer room in my house a month later. He came with his mother and cousin. My sister Maria was with me. He said that all the cravings were gone and that he felt like a man for the first time in his life. He was now participating at church. We rejoiced and praised the Lord.

Six months later I saw him at a church. He had gone through a three day retreat and seemed full of the joy of the Lord, truly born again. A miracle that happened in twenty minutes at the Doctor's office. The goodness of the Lord is overwhelming. God wants to heal all illnesses.

Another patient came as an emergency to see me, because his Doctor was not there. He was totally out of control. He was screaming and complaining of multiple symptoms. The chart said that he was a schizophrenic. I prayed that the peace of Jesus would come upon him and it did. He closed his eyes and became very peaceful. I ordered some tests and kept on seeing my other patients. The nurses suddenly called me saying that he was having a heart attack. I went to the room where he was at and found him holding his chest and crying. I asked him what's going on. He said. "The Lord Jesus came into my heart and I am healed. I am crying, because I never felt such love before." The nurses began praising the Lord. He did not have a heart attack, but a Jesus attack. Oh, the love of God.

This man Jose now comes once a week to my office just wanting me to lay my hands on him, and it's ok. So a while back I had a whole family in my office. I was having trouble reaching them in the area of salvation, but suddenly Jose storms into the room with his walker. He asked me to pray for him so I did. I got out of my chair and laid hands on him and prayed. The presence of the Lord comes, and he leaves full of joy. Then the head of that family in my office says, "I want you to do that to us". So we all hold hands, and do a powerful prayer of salvation. They all got saved and blasted. Oh our Lord works in wonderful and mysterious ways.

Many of these people have no transportation, and have trouble going to churches. So the office is kind of a church for them. We give them Bibles and instructions. I am praying for a bus to take groups to anointed meetings nearby. Thank you Lord.

A lady brings me her husband in a wheelchair. She states that her husband has advanced Alzheimer's disease. He has seen psychiatrists and neurologists, and he is on the latest meds. He is now not walking, talking, or eating and on top of that they had told her that he also probably has prostatic cancer as his prostate is indurated, and the PSA is very high, but they didn't want to do a biopsy, because of his condition. We prayed for the healing of Alzheimer's disease, and a week later he came walking, and talked to me fluently. The wife said that it was a miracle. That he was now eating well and that a lot of his memory had returned. I did a blood test to check on his prostatic antigen, and it had gone down from twenty to three. Thank you Lord. Some days the presence, power, love, and faith of God inundates the room.

A man that I had never seen before, and that I didn't know anything about came through the door. I told him "the Lord healed you"! He walked into the room and said, "You don't understand, my rotator cuff tendon has totally ruptured, and I can't move my arm. I come for a clearance as I am schedule for surgery tomorrow". I told him, "but I understand that the Lord has totally healed you". He says, "How can that be". I asked him to please raise his arm. He had not even sat down yet. So he raised his arm which is completely normal. Then he seems worried and says, "How can this be. This is impossible". He keeps raising his arm up and down, up and down.

This man in the midst of a miracle, something in him could not believe. He never sat down. He was healed instantly without prayer. The last thing that he said was that he was going to the orthopedist right away so he would explain to him what had happened.

We had WOW (Women of Worship), a Catholic Charismatic conference in Chicago, on July 7, 2007 in which we had greatly anointed priests and ministers. We had available a healing room and a prophetic room. I was at the healing room and a woman comes who says that she had progressive fibromyalgia. She could barely stand or walk. She had seen multiple specialists and received multiple treatments without any results. Immediately we discerned a spirit of fibromyalgia. I explained to her that this was a spirit that I was sensing and seeing. That we wanted to cast it out. She agreed. We commanded it out and immediately it came out with heaving, coughing, and spitting. We then did other emotional healings. In the afternoon she was dancing powerfully, for the Lord had absolutely healed her. She gave testimony in front of everyone. Hallelujah.

The office is a wonderful place in which we can have immediate evidence of healings through tests. A woman came with a blood sugar over 300 mg/dl, and after a short prayer the blood sugar was lowered to 80 mg/dl. The oxygen saturation of the blood always goes up with prayer. We have a simple device, an oxymeter, that we place in the finger and we can see the number going up. There is nothing impossible for God. Again, God wants to heal all illnesses. He has already done it at the cross.

Isaiah 53

4- Surely he has borne our griefs, and carried our sorrows: yet we did esteem him stricken, smitten of God, and afflicted.

5- But he was wounded for our transgressions, he was bruised for our iniquities: the chastisement of our peace was upon him; and with his stripes we are healed.

Matthew 8

16- When the even was come, they brought unto him many that were possessed with devils: and he cast out the spirits with his word, and healed all that were sick:

17- That it might be fulfilled which was spoken by Esaias the prophet, saying, Himself took our infirmities, and bare our sicknesses.

<u>1 Peter 2:24</u>
Who his own self bare our sins in his own body on the tree, that we, being dead to sins, should live unto righteousness: by whose stripes ye were healed.

I read these scriptures to my patients and pray with them that the revelation would come, that they would fully understand that all healings are included in the atonement. Jesus was wounded that I might be healed. Jesus said at the end: it is done. Amen.

It is a mystery sometimes when some saints do not get healed. I believe that in general we have to persist in seeking God, praying, interceeding, pressing on, and going for the breakthrough. Jesus healed all that came to him. He was obedient to the Father.

<u>John 5</u>
20a- For the Father loveth the Son, and showeth him all things that himself doeth...
19b- For what things soever the Father doeth, these also doeth the Son likewise.

This is the basic prayer that Jesus taught us in Matthew 6.

I will focus on Matthew 6:10.

<u>Matthew 6:10</u>
Thy kingdom come. Thy will be done in earth, as it is in heaven.

With the kingdom comes the King. The manifest presence of God. We know that there are no illnesses in heaven. We know the Father's will. Jesus healed all. Hallelujah.

Declare your own healing in the name of Jesus. Lay hands on someone and declare them healed. It is the will of God. Amen.

After Jesus was tempted in the dessert he returned in the power of the Holy Ghost into Galilee. In a synagogue in Nazareth, he declared the meat of his ministry:

Luke 4:18
The Spirit of the Lord is upon me, because he hath anointed me to
preach the gospel to the poor; he hath sent me to heal the
brokenhearted, to preach deliverance to the captives, and
recovery of sight to the blind, to set at liberty them that are
bruised.
19- To preach the acceptable year of the Lord.
21- This day is this scripture fulfilled in your ears.

This is our ministry. Receive the anointing of the Spirit of God.

Hebrews 13:8
Jesus Christ the same yesterday and today, and forever.

1 Corinthians 3:16
Know ye not that ye are the temple of God, and that the Spirit of
God dwelleth in you?

Matthew 10:1
And when he had called unto him his twelve disciples, he gave
them power against unclean spirits, to cast them out, and to heal
all manner of sickness and all manner of disease.

Matthew 10:7, 8
And as you go, preach, saying, the kingdom of heaven is at
hand. Heal the sick, cleanse the lepers, raise the dead, cast out
devil: freely ye have received, freely give.

Mark 16
15- And he said unto them, go ye into all the world, and preach
the gospel to every creature.
16- He that believeth and is baptized shall be saved; but he that
believeth not, shall be damned.
17- And these signs shall follow them that believe; in my name
shall they cast out devils; they shall speak with new tongues----,

they shall lay the hands on the sick, and they shall recover.

Luke 10:19
Behold, I give unto you power to tread on serpents and scorpions, and over all the power of the enemy: and nothing shall by any means hurt you.

Matthew 28
18b- All power is given unto me in heaven and in earth
19- Go ye therefore, and teach all nations...
20b- Teaching them to observe all things whatsoever I have commanded you: and, lo, I am with you always, even unto the end of the world. Amen.

John 14:12
Verily, verily, I say unto you, he that believeth in me, the works that I do, shall he do also; and greater works than these shall he do; because I go unto my father.

John 14:14
If ye shall ask anything in my name, I will do it.

John 14:23
If a man love me, he will keep my words: and my Father will love him, and we will come unto him, and make our abode with him.

Romans 12:2
And be not conformed to this world: but be ye transformed by the renewing of your mind, that ye may prove what is that good, and acceptable, and perfect, will of God.

I pray right now over you so you will receive a powerful revelation and anointing from our Father God. So you can go right now, lay hands, and heal the sick. This is the will of God for you. Thank you Lord. My life has been totally and absolutely changed in a miraculous way by the grace, mercy, and power of God. Jesus has really set me free. I prayed that He would open a way so I could minister, and He did it right away. This is for all who believe. Thank you Lord.

I began my testimony with Psalm 51:5, and I am lead to end it with Psalm 139:13-16 from the amplified bible.

Psalm 139:13-16

13 For You did form my inward parts; You did knit me together in my mother's womb.

14 I will confess and praise You for You are fearful and wonderful and for the awful wonder of my birth!
Wonderful are Your works, and that my inner self knows right well.

15 My frame was not hidden from You when I was being formed in secret [and] intricately and curiously wrought [as if embroidered with various colors] in the depth of the earth [a region of darkness and mystery].

16 Your eyes saw my unformed substance, and in Your book all the days [of my life] were written before ever they took shape, when as yet there was none of them.

Thank you Lord. Amen.

CHAPTER TWO

"FUNDAMENTALS FOR PRAYING IN THE OFFICE"

I. SALVATION

This is the major miracle. The wonder of wonders. This is the reason the Father sent Jesus. He loved us so much that he sent his only son to die for us so that we could be back in relationship with Him.

John 3:16
For God so loved the world, that he gave his only begotten Son, that whosoever believeth in him should not perish, but have everlasting life.

Jesus explained it to the teacher Nicodemus that we must be born again.

John 3
5- Jesus answered, Verily, verily I say unto thee, Except a man be born of water and of the Spirit, he cannot enter into the kingdom of God.
6- That which is born of the flesh is flesh; and that which is born of the Spirit is spirit.
7- Marvel not that I said unto thee, ye must be born again.

Nicodemus was an expert in religious traditions, laws, rituals and the scriptures, but he did not understand Jesus.

Salvation can be a dramatic healing moment. In my case I made a choice and repeated a prayer accepting Jesus as my Lord and savior. Two months later my life did dramatically change after the baptism of the Holy Ghost with evidence of speaking in tongues.

Many of my patients are churchgoers but when I ask them where would they go after they die, I hear a lot of different answers like I was dust and will be dust, or I am a good person and I don't hurt anybody, or I have been a catholic all my life. Some even say that they will probably go to hell, that they just don't care or that they don't believe in the afterlife etc.

We have to be sensitive, careful, and compassionate when dealing with the sick and the wounded. These are the people that Jesus is looking for: the lost sheep, and we don't have to be rigid in our approach.

I have a patient who was into the new age, Buddhism, yoga, meditation syndrome. She mentioned that she considered Jesus a historical figure, a prophet with wonderful teachings. She would not accept him as the Son of God, the Messiah. We did not fight about it and kept loving her, but lo and behold she developed a cough and upon investigation we found a mass in the lung. She then had a lung biopsy that was positive for an atypical neoplasia. The pulmonologist, the thoracic surgeon, and the radiologist all were sure that she had lung cancer and recommended surgery to resect the mass. During the preoperative clearance (by the way this an excellent time to pray. People are worried, fearful and there are always wonderful results when we bless the surgeon, the anesthetist, the nurse, and the equipment, when we bind the enemy, when we call upon ministering angels to be present during the whole ordeal, when we decree excellent results and postoperative period.)

I told my patient that I wanted to pray for her healing and she agreed. We prayed and declared total healing of the tumor, mind you that she was not even saved! After the surgery she called me from the hospital very excited to tell me that they opened her up but did not find any tumor at all. Praise Jesus! After she was discharged from the hospital she ran to my office asking me to do the prayer of salvation. She believed Jesus did a miracle for her and she wanted Him for her Lord and savior. Hallelujah.

We need to be daily prayed up and in the presence of the Lord. Paul in Ephesians 6:18 said to pray always with all prayer and supplication in the Spirit.

An older man came to see me as his doctor was not available that day. He had the freemason's ring and was declaring his believes about the great architect of the universe. He did not want to deal with the true Jesus, the word, the way, the truth, and the life, our only hope for salvation. I gave him the medicines that he needed and he left.

Six months later he came back to me as his doctor again was not available. He appeared very weak and his blood pressure was low. I did a rectal exam and found that he was bleeding from the GI tract. A stat CBC showed a hemoglobin of 6 mg/dl. He was critical. I called an ambulance to take him to the hospital. This time he wanted me to pray for him and I did. The word of God came alive. I told him to make a choice right then and there. Live or die. The grace and conviction of God came upon him. He renounced sins and freemasonry. He tried to pull out the cursed ring but could not. When he declared that Jesus was his Lord and savior the ring fell from his finger and he was filled with the Holy Spirit. He had life now, real life and he would not die. At the hospital a bleeding ulcer was found; he was transfused and did well. When he came back to our medical center he proclaimed Jesus as his Lord and savior and that He had saved him. Everybody said that his personality had totally changed.

When the kingdom of God comes upon you in such a dramatic fashion there is an obvious transformation in who you are. You are translated from the kingdom of darkness into the kingdom of light. We are kingdom people. We carry the kingdom of God within us and we need to always be ready to act in the ways of God at any time and everywhere. The first and deepest kind of healing that Christ brings is the forgiveness of sins. Our repentance and God's forgiveness. In general this is the first and basic place to go. I have had hundreds of patients who have received Christ in the office through a short powerful spiritual prayer. I explain to them the basic gospel of salvation and when they believe in their hearts and proclaim with their mouths that God raised Jesus from the dead a profound experience occurs. The Holy Spirit always touches them. This is also a very good moment to pray for healing and prophesy.

We would like to deepen the context of salvation. I learned about the spiritual areas or laws at Christian Healing Ministries during a teaching on salvation by Norma Dearing[1]; also on conferences by Greg Trainor[2] of the Holy Spirit missionary association and definitely in the writings of Dr. Bill Bright, founder and president of Campus Crusade for Christ International. [3]

Principles of Salvation:
I. God loves you and has a wonderful destiny and purpose for you here in earth and eternity in heaven.

John 3:16

For God so loved the world, that he gave his only begotten Son, that whosoever believeth in him should not perish, but have everlasting life.

John 10:10b

I am come that they might have life, and that they might have it more abundantly.

II. The problem: Sin is in man and separates him from God and God's love and plan for his life.

Romans 3:23

For all have sinned, and fall short of the glory of God.

Since the beginning man rebelled and went his own way. A way that leads to death (separation from God).

Romans 6:23

For the wages of sin is death (spiritual separation from God).

III. The only solution is Jesus Christ.

Romans 5:8

But God commendeth his love toward us, in that, while we were yet sinners, Christ died for us.

1 John 1:7b--and the Blood of Jesus Christ his Son cleanseth us from all sin.

1 Corinthians 15:3-6

...Christ died for our sins according to scriptures; he was buried and rose again the third day according to the scriptures and that he was seen of Cephes, then of the twelve. After that, he was seen of above five hundred brethren at once...

John 14:6
Jesus said to him. I am the way, the truth, and the life: No man cometh unto the Father, but by me.

IV. How to do it. How to receive salvation. How to be washed clean from sin. How to be born again. How to have eternal life: we must repent and receive Jesus Christ as Lord and Savior.

1 John 1:9
If we confess our sins, he is faithful and just to forgive us our sins, and to cleanse us from all unrighteousness.

Ephesians 2:8-9
For by grace are ye saved through faith; and that not of yourself: it is the gift of God:
Not of works, lest any man should boast.

John 3:3
Jesus answered and said unto him verily, verily, I say unto thee, Except a man be born again, he cannot see the kingdom of God.

Revelations 3:20
Behold, I stand at the door, and knock: if any man hear my voice, and open the door, I will come in to him...

Roman 10
9- That if thou shalt confess with thy mouth the Lord Jesus, and shalt believe in thine heart that God hath raised him from the dead; thou shalt be saved.
10- For with the heart man believeth unto righteousness; and with the mouth confession is made unto salvation.
13- For whosoever shall call upon the name of the Lord shall be saved.

John 1:12
But as many as received him, to them gave he power to become

the sons of God, even to them that believe on his name.

Salvation Prayer:

You can receive Jesus right now by faith through prayer. The following is a suggested prayer:

Today is a most special day as I am going to confess that you Jesus are the son of God, that came in the flesh, suffered, died in the cross, resurrected after three days, and are sitting at the right hand of the Father. Thank you Lord that you came for my salvation- to open my life to God.

I repent of all my sins and receive your forgiveness. You also came to totally heal me mentally, emotionally, and physically; you took it all into your body in the cross. Thank you Lord that you destroyed death and ended the ruling of evil and curses over my life. Today Lord I open my heart totally to you. Please come in Lord and live in me. I declare that you are my Lord, savior, redeemer, healer, and deliverer. Thank you Lord that I am now born again. I will walk in the ways of your kingdom from now on, praise you Lord Jesus.

To summarize: salvation refers to the process or result of being converted or saved. This process usually includes the following steps.

To believe that Jesus is the son of God.

To believe that Jesus died on the cross to take punishment for sin that we deserve, and thus to save us from our sins.

To repent of our sins, and

To confess Jesus as the Lord of our life.[4]

Π. Baptism in the Holy Spirit

It is Jesus who baptizes us with the Holy Ghost.

John 20:22

He breathed on them, and saith unto them, Receive ye the Holy Ghost.

Matthew 3:11

I indeed baptized you with water unto repentance: but he that cometh after me is mightier than I, whose shoes I am not worthy to bear: He shall baptize you with the Holy Ghost, and with fire.

We need the power of the Holy Ghost for our own revelation, healing, deliverance, all truth, comfort, and to minister effectively.

Luke 24:49
And, behold, I send the promise of my Father upon you: but tarry ye in the city of Jerusalem, until ye be endued with power from on high.

Act 1:5
For John truly baptized with water; but ye shall be baptized with the Holy Ghost not many days hence.

Act 1:8
But ye shall receive power, after that the Holy Ghost is come upon you: and ye shall be witnesses unto me…

John 16:7
Nevertheless I tell you the truth; It is expedient for you that I go away: for if I go not away, the Comforter will not come unto you; but if I depart, I will send him unto you.

John 16:13
When the Spirit of truth is come, he will guide you into all truth…

Act 2:1
And when the day of Pentecost was fully come, they were all with one accord in one place.

Act 2:4
And they were all filled with the Holy Ghost, and began to speak with other tongues.

Paul tells us not to be ignorant concerning spiritual gifts [1]

Corinthians 12:1.

1 Corinthians 12
7- But the manifestation of the Spirit is given to every man to
profit withal.
8- For to one is given by the Spirit the word of wisdom; to
another the word of knowledge by the same Spirit.
9- To another faith by the same Spirit; to another the gifts of
healing by the same spirit.
10- To another the working of miracles; to another prophecy; to
another discerning of spirits, to another divers kinds of tongues;
to another the interpretation of tongues.

I am amazed at all the different opinions many of my Christian
patients have about the Holy Spirit and the gifts of the spirit. The immense
majority have not received the baptism of the Holy Spirit with evidence of
speaking in tongues and do not seem to know the importance of it. The
power of the Holy Spirit active in me is what changed my life. Many
immediately bring 1-Corinthians 13 "without love I am nothing". Why
would there be a conflict between power and love? Some do have
religious spirits that need to be cast out! It seems that they have not really
read 1-Corinthians 12 and 1-Corinthians 14.

1 Corinthians 14:1
Follow after charity and desire spiritual gifts.

Mark 16:17
And these signs shall follow them that believe; in my name shall
they cast out devils; they shall speak with new tongues… they
shall lay hands on the sick, and they shall recover.

2 Timothy 1:7b
For God has not given us the spirit of fear; but of power, and of
love , and of a sound mind.

In 1 Corinthians 2:4 Paul talks about the demonstration of the spirit and of power. In 1 Corinthians 2: 12-16 Paul explains how we need the living Holy Spirit inside of us to know the things of God. We cannot really do what God wants us to do without the activation of the Holy Ghost within us. Paul was very clear about the need to receive the Holy Ghost.

Acts 19:1
… Paul finding certain disciples.
2- He said unto them, Have ye received the Holy Ghost since ye believed? And they said unto him, We have not so much as heard whether there be any Holy Ghost.
6- And when Paul had laid his hands upon them, the Holy Ghost came upon them; and they spake with tongues, and prophesied.

When Peter visited Cornelius this is what happened.

Act 10:44
While Peter yet spake these words, the Holy Ghost fell on all of them which heard the word.

Act 10:46
For they heard them speak with tongues and magnify God.

Receiving the Holy Ghost

Galatians 3:13-14
Christ has redeemed us from the curse of the law… that we might receive the promise of the Spirit through faith.

In John 7:38 Jesus said he that believeth on me, as the scripture hath said, out of his belly shall flow rivers of living water.
39- (But this spake he of the Spirit, which they that believe on him should receive: for the Holy Ghost was not yet given; because Jesus was not yet glorified.

I received the Holy Spirit by being at the right place at the right time.

In my office, under the power and guidance of the Holy Spirit many patients have been baptized with the Holy Ghost with evidence of speaking in tongues. There is always a period of instruction that could be several minutes to several visits. We discuss that when Jesus walked in the earth with the apostles they worked in his anointing. We read Acts 1:1-8, Acts 2, John 15:26, John 16:7-15, Acts 19:1-6 and other verses.

So when in the spirit I get the ok, I pray over my patients so they receive the Holy Ghost with the gift of tongues. I lay hands and pray a simple prayer such as:

> Lord Jesus my Lord and savior I confess that you
> baptize us in the Holy Ghost,
> I thirst for the living waters,
> I love you my Lord,
> I ask for the promise of the Father,
> I believe that if I ask I will receive,
> Thank you Lord, come Holy Ghost,
> I receive the prayer language that you give me,
> Help me release it.

I then pray in tongues and suggest that they open their mouths and do the same. It is all by faith. At times I ask them to speak a word from the Lord and often they do. I encourage them to use their new prayer language every day to build up their most holy faith, Jude 20, and to edify themselves 1 Corinthians 14:4, also when we don't know how to pray we use tongues Romans 8:26-27.

The descent of the Holy Spirit at Pentecost signified God's presence in the disciples in a new dimension. The gift of tongues immediately came forth. I do ask God for all the gifts to minister to the people with the utmost effectiveness.

GIFTS OF THE HOLY GHOST

The nine gifts are readily divided into three groups of three, under the heading of revelation gifts, power gifts, and vocal gifts.

Revelation Gifts: A word of wisdom, a word of knowledge, discerning spirits.

Power Gifts: Faith, gifts of healing, working of miracles.

Vocal Gifts: different kinds of tongues, interpretation of tongues, prophecy.[5]

The Word of Knowledge:

The word of knowledge is a supernatural revelation of information by the Holy Spirit. Paul received many of his revelations through words of knowledge.[6]

1 Corinthians 2
12- Now we have received, not the spirit of the world, but the spirit which is of God; that we might know the things that are freely given to us of God.
13- Which things also we speak, not in the words which man's wisdom teacheth, but which the Holy Ghost teacheth; comparing spiritual things with spiritual.

The Holy Spirit often gives us a revelatory word of knowledge concerning the need of a person for healing. This is an indication that God wishes to heal that person. God gives us his revelation in many ways:

Thoughts

Impressions

Body impressions: ex: a pain in a place in your body.

Feelings or emotions: you could feel the shame, fear, anger of the person you are praying for.

Seeing, visions: it is not uncommon for me to get a vision, even a story that will lead to the healing of the person.

A 78 year old lady with chronic severe osteoarthritis of the knee with marked pain and trouble walking came into the office. I prayed for physical healing and nothing happened. I then asked God for a word of knowledge and received a vision. I saw my patient when she was about 13 years old. She was involved in a sexual encounter in her own house in her bed! I asked the Lord, is this from you? How would I share such an event? Gently and nonjudgementally I told her what I had seen, what the Lord had shown me. Immediately she reacted with intense emotions and said yes, that was Carlos, who took away my childhood and never saw me again. This trauma that happened 65 years earlier was still affecting her. We dealt with the deep wounding, betrayal, and sin. She received forgiveness and forgave, and the knee got healed. Hallelujah. I love Jesus. Thank you God for your mercy and grace.

Another lady had a large herniated disc in her back causing nerve compression, spinal stenosis, and severe sciatic pain. As I was praying for physical healing, the Lord gave me a vision of an infant boy that had died. I told her what I saw and she broke down. She said oh, that was my angel that died of meningitis when he was five months old. That pain and grief was still embedded in her body. We prayed and released the child and the whole situation to Jesus. She received a profound emotional healing and the healing of her back. Hallelujah.

Healing is as mysterious and profound as God is. On one occasion I am giving a teaching on healing at the church and I see a very large angel that guides me into bringing the sick to where he is. I stopped the teaching and invited the sick to come to the place where the angel was. I didn't even mention the angel, not to scare them. I just began to lay hands and to declare healing; they were getting healed before I reached them. The presence and the healing anointing just fell on the people. Thank you Lord.

Other ways of receiving revelation are:
The still small voice 1King 19:12, 1 Samuel 9:15-16
Trances. Acts 11:5.
The word of God.
Angels.
Speaking: unpremeditated words just come out.
Dreams.
While having a nap before a prayer meeting I saw someone being healed on the left eye. Later on while in the meeting I shared the dream

and immediately a person at the meeting received a total healing of her left eye. There are probably innumerable numbers of ways that God can reveal himself to you, give you a revelation or teach you something. I had a burden for certain friends that had stopped growing in the spirit and were at the door of full backsliding. I grow bamboos and the Lord focused my attention on two new babies and told me to watch them. For several weeks I watered them; one grew several inches everyday and is now blossoming. The other stopped growing and died. We cannot stop growing in the Lord.

There are many studies on the gift of the spirit. See the references[7]. It is not the purpose of this manual to do a teaching on it. I will go more in depth in some of the gifts when it is appropriate in other areas of the book.

Faith-Aspects of Faith- Definitions
Different Kinds of Faith and Healings

Hebrews 11:1
Now faith is the substance of things hoped for, the evidence of things not seen.

Roman 4:17b
God, who quickeneth the dead, and calleth those things which be not as though they were.

Romans 12:2
And be not conformed to this world: but be ye transformed by the renewing of your mind, that ye may prove what is that good, and acceptable, and perfect, will of God.

Mark9:23
Jesus said unto him, if thou canst believe, all things are possible to him that believeth.

Luke 1:37
For with God nothing shall be impossible.

Hebrews 11:6
For without faith it is impossible to please God.

Romans 14:23b
For whatsoever is not of faith is sin.

Romans 10:17
So then faith cometh by hearing, and hearing by the word of God.

Romans 12:3b
God hath dealt every man the measure of faith.

Mark 16:20b
The Lord confirms the word with signs following.

Job 22:28a
Thou shall decree a thing and it shall be established unto thee.

James 5
15b- And the prayer of faith shall save the sick…
16b- The effectual fervent prayer. ..
17- Elijah prayed earnestly.

Luke 18:1-8
The persistent widow crying day and night, the continual coming.

This is the prayer of faith:
James 5:14-18 and Luke 18:1-8
It is fervent, earnest, continuous, long and God will respond.-
Luke 18:8
And the Lord shall raise him up. James 5:15.

Sometimes we have to really fight for a breakthrough. Sometimes a word of knowledge will do the same thing in an instant. At other tines the gift of faith comes in a powerful way with the conviction of healing. It is the faith of God, and healing will occur. Sometimes only by hearing the word of God someone will receive a healing or a miracle. At other times the release of the glory of God and the healing anointing at a meeting, conference, or crusade will heal many.

A great friend of mine, a missionary to the poor suffered an acute catastrophic brain event. He bled massively into his brain requiring total vital support at the ICU. The neurosurgeon showed me the scans and the MRI that showed that the left brain was totally destroyed. He was absolutely convinced that my friend could not ever wake up, move, or talk. He talked to the family to stop all life support. My sister Maria, myself, and a small group began earnest, fervent, relentless, intense prayer of faith. His wife was in our ranks. The neurosurgeon did not seem friendly. We took over the atmosphere of that room in the ICU. My friend eventually woke up walked and talked. One day while still in the ICU after he had just woken up the neurosurgeon came for his rounds and he could not believe his eyes. My friend held up a cross with the arm that would never move! It was awesome! We do have an awesome Lord. My friend went home with his family and he continued his recovery.

Several months later while in my office I received a phone call that he had suddenly died. He had been preparing himself to go and see his boat. I was in shock and confusion. I asked the Lord what's going on. My nurse called me to tell me that there was a patient that came from very far away without any appointment and that she needed to talk to me. Millie is an African American woman that I dearly love. She uses a wheelchair as she is overweight. I met her in an extensive care facility for gravely ill people. We prayed and she did not need to stay in such a facility any longer.

She has definite prophetic gifts. She did not know anything about my friend. She said, the Lord told me to come to see you. He knows your grief. The Lord says that your friend, the one you truly love, the one that He brought back to life, that it was only for a moment. He needed to conclude certain things in his life. The family and friends needed to prepare themselves and that he is now in the glory with our Lord Jesus Christ. I wept feeling such great love from my Lord and from my Father and From the Holy Ghost. The Lord sent his messenger and transformed the whole situation.

I later met with the family and friends and gave them the word of the Lord. Life and peace came into our midst, thank you Lord.

Now, Millie is another miracle story. Her life, her adoption of sick children, her recovery from terminal illnesses!

On one occasion she had developed elephantiasis of the leg due to lymphatic occlusion; nothing worked, her leg was humongous. A group of us prayed and the leg shrank right in front of our eyes. It has never swollen up again.

But even more impressive was a problem that was really affecting her. Her daughter was in the streets doing the worse imaginable activities. I told her that I really felt that the Lord was involved in her case. I told her to find her daughter, get her and bring her to me.

One day while in a small church praising and worshiping, I was on call and had my cell phone on vibrating. I received a call and it was Millie calling to tell me that they had her daughter and that they were going to bring her to me. I said bring her, and gave them the address. Soon, an individual came in asking for me and said Millie is outside. So I walked out and there was this large old Cadillac full of people, and Millie yelling we got her, here she is. So they brought her out of the car and held her in front of me, and I prayed help me oh Lord. I began immediately to cast out demons and she began to manifest right there in the parking lot of the church. Stuff came out of her and there were puddles on the floor. They had paper towel in the car that was very helpful. She stopped heaving, coughing, and throwing up and peace came upon her. We held hands and said the prayer of salvation. They all received the Holy Ghost and spoke in tongues. This was a miracle. Millie's daughter has been home now for over a year going and participating in church. Hallelujah.

Several years ago a friend sent me a DVD from Toronto Airport Fellowship Church showing evangelist revivalist Todd Bentley from Fresh Fire Ministries healing people through the cell phone. The Holy Spirit grabbed a hold of me and I knew that at that moment whoever I would reach through the phone would be healed. I believe an impartation of the gift of faith came upon me as I watched that DVD! I reached several of my patients and they all got healed. I simply told them what I was watching and that God wanted to heal them and to receive their healing. I saw them at the office during the next several days and documented their healing.

One man had atrial fibrillation and it converted to normal sinus rhythm. One had a cardiomyopathy with an ejection fraction of 25% and it came up to 45%, normal being 55%. A lady had severe crushed vertebra and was on a wheelchair, and she ended running through the house after our prayer. Another was healed of longstanding depression. There have been many other healings through the phone or sending the word through a family member or friend since then.

<u>Matthew 8:8-10</u>
The centurion asked Jesus to speak the word only, and my servant shall be healed... Jesus marveled and said verily, I have not found so great faith in Israel.

<u>Psalms 107:20</u>
He sent his word, and healed them, and delivered them from their destructions.

I already mentioned the young woman with metastatic cancer that got healed in Brazil through the cell phone.

One of my patients told me that his grandson had been sick with lung disease since the 9-11 terrorist attack in New York City. He was living in New York then and was not even one year old at the time of the attack. He got sick and was never cured. He was followed by pulmonologists requiring the use of steroids etc. We prayed and broke the power of evil over him and declared his lungs totally healed. The grandfather came back to the office to tell me that since the day we prayed his grandson has been totally healed.

Another grandfather told me that his grandson still in the womb was found to have severe heart disease and would require seven surgeries and the doctors were not sure if he would make it. We prayed for total healing of the heart. After he was born the cardiologist explained to the family that he did not understand what happened as they had an ultrasound showing the diseased heart, but that now all had been corrected and that he might need only a simple closure of a defect and that definitely he would live and be ok. Hallelujah. Thank you Jesus.

So the phone ministry is now a normal part of my medical Christian practice. There have been innumerable healings, prophetic words and blessings through the phone. Every time I see a phone I see Todd Bentley wildly calling and healing, and I covet to do the same and do it. Hallelujah. Thank you Jesus. In Mark 11 and Matthew 21 we learn about faith. It all begins with the fig tree that had no fruit and Jesus saying let no fruit grow on you ever again.

Mark 11
21- And Peter calling to rembrance saith unto him, Master, behold, the fig tree which thou cursedst is withered away.
22- And Jesus answering saith unto them, Have faith in God. The literal translation of Jesus statement is HAVE THE FAITH OF GOD.
23- For verily I say unto you, That whosoever shall say unto this mountain, Be thou removed, and be thou cast into the sea; and shall not doubt in his heart, but shall believe that those things which he saith shall come to pass; he shall have whatsoever he saith.
24- Therefore I say unto you, What things soever ye desire, when ye pray, believe that ye receive them, and ye shall have them.
25- And when ye stand praying, forgive, if ye have aught against any: that your Father also which is in heaven may forgive you your trespasses.

We see some important aspects of faith
 Faith is of the heart.
 Faith has to be released,
You have to speak it and you have to act it out.
 You have to forgive.

Other gifts of the spirit that I will briefly mention are:

A Word of Wisdom

Knowledge gives us facts and wisdom shows us what to do about those facts.

Prophecy

<u>1 Corinthians 14</u>
1- Follow after charity and desire spiritual gifts but rather that ye may prophesy
3- But he that prophesieth speaketh unto men to edification and exhortation and comfort.

This is a great instrument the Lord has placed at the disposal of all believers 1 Corinthians 14:31. To overcome condemnation, unworthiness, failure, and discouragement.

For the regular saint like me who does not have the office of the prophet, the gift of prophecy is to build up and encourage. It is a blessing; it is coming from the heart of the Father. I truly love this gift.

Gifts of Tongues

The prevalent way is to get this gift with the baptism of the Holy Ghost. Then we use it privately for edification and to build our most holy faith.

As we develop this gift, with practice, we learn about different kinds of tongues that can include praise, intercession, rebuke, exhortation, healing, etc. and at times it is used in public assemblies 1 Corinthians 12:28. If an individual starts speaking in tongues in a public assembly, **the gift of interpretation of tongues** should be used by the individual or someone else with the gift of interpretation of tongues so the church may receive edification 1 Corinthians 14:5.

Discernment of spirits

The word discern may be defined as "to recognize and distinguish between." Discernment is a form of direct perception[8].

The first chapter of the bible emphasizes the importance of being able to discern evil when it is present. It is a supernatural ability to identify the nature and character of spirits. In general we mostly refer to it when talking about deliverance but it is really much broader. Ex: The Holy Spirit, the spirit of God, good angels, fallen angels or demons, human spirits. It is of vital important that we learn to discern the Holy Spirit when He manifests.

Randy Clark mentions a time when a visible tubular cloud manifested and he tasted of it but soon kept preaching and the cloud left. The manifest presence of God, the glory of God brings the nature of God: healing, miracles, deliverance, love, provision, etc. Randy said, "Next time it comes I know better". We will abandon our agendas and totally get into His presence. This is our priority, His presence. When it comes we follow it. Amen.

The way we discern the spiritual realm is very diverse. We already discussed how God gives us his revelation in different ways. This applies to all spiritual areas, for example: Elijah seeing the angelic army and opening the eyes of his servants who then saw the mountain full of horses and chariots of fire round about Elijah! 2 Kings 6:16-18.

Wow, I pray that I see such an army. The servant received an impartation so he would see in the supernatural but we also need to train.

Hebrews 5:14
But strong meat belongeth to them that are of full age, even those who by reason of use have their senses exercised to discern both good and evil.

The Holy Spirit knows. We have to be sensitive, yielded, and submitted to the Holy Spirit. Once in a large church meeting a known speaker began to preach about "The True Church". Most people began to cheer. I fell back into my chair sensing an arrogant, divisive, controlling spirit. I later shared my feelings with other spirit filled mature Christians and they had felt the same.

Right in our midst, in Holy Spirit filled congregations, we have discerned bitter spirits, power, control, domination, intimidation spirits, nasty spirits, religious spirits, and it is a hard situation as these saints have annointings and are ministering and many times their ministry is contaminated and many times they reject help.

The Holy Spirit has revealed to me the realm of evil spirits in a myriad ways:

Seeing the spirit with our spiritual eyes:

A face, a shape, a form, a whole being, sensing the spirit, feeling the spirit, an intuition- a knowing of the spirit, a word of knowledge, a thought, seeing the spirit in the eyes of the person.

It seems that Francis MacNutt gets very sleepy.

Some people can smell demons etc.

At Christian healing ministries, Francis and Judith MacNutt center, there is a powerful anointing for healing and deliverance. The Lord seems to activate the saints and powerfully release the giftings. On one occasion I served in the ministry of deliverance and the Lord clearly showed me the strongman above each individual that we prayed for. The discernment was right on target and totally effective.

A young beautiful woman came to my office dragging her right leg. She said that she had a neurological illness and needed to be referred to the university. I sensed a powerful evil spirit in her and began taking her history. Eventually I shared that Jesus could heal any illness. She immediately manifested the demonic. Defiance and rage erupted. I had not talked about my denomination, but she screamed, the Catholics do not speak in tongues. I had not spoken in tongues. The only thing I had said was that Jesus can heal. I felt a chill inside of me. This was a time when I was not going to create a wild show at the office. I just calmed the situation and completed the history and physical exam. I wanted to know where did she become infested and asked her if she had ever seen a healer. She admitted that in Europe she had seen a sorcerer. I felt that this evil spirit was different than all that I had dealt with before. Something like of the old country? I gave her my card and blessed her and told her that if she needed any help to call me but I never saw or heard from her again.

It is very remarkable that my grandfather was a freemason and that I never learned anything about it, but I wrote a book about the inner world, imagery and visualization, and in my book there are certain symbolisms and philosophies that seem related to freemasonry. To me it means that there was spiritual transference of evil into my inner world. I mention this because I have a sensitivity, a knowing that arises when I am in the presence of a freemason or someone with the freemason curses. It is something about the head, something about arrogance and grandiosity. I just sense, feel, perceive, intuit, know that the spirit is present and I ask if they are freemasons or if someone in their family is a freemason or has been a freemason and they say yes. Many times I sense occultic spirits as a blockage, a wall, a denseness, something that I cannot get through.

So there are many ways that the Holy Ghost uses to expose evil.

Today at work a man came to me with what appeared to be a spirit of infirmity.. very atypical pains with negative tests, but I also perceived a heaviness, a denseness, a wall, and this is what I relate to occultic spirits so I asked him " have you ever been involved with the occult such as horoscopes, Ouija boards, palm reading, cards, spiritual readings etc." and he said yes, I had a girlfriend and his mother was a witch that would read my hands; I had a daughter with my girlfriend and soon we broke up. They have not allowed me to see the child and I have been sick since then. So here we have sin, occultic spirits, infirmity spirits, and a downhill course. He agreed and set up a meeting for salvation, healing, and deliverance in the prayer room in my house.

Gifts of Healing and the Works of Miracles

A man was brought in a stretcher to my office. He had advanced Parkinson's disease and had not been able to walk any more. We cast out the spirit of Parkinson's and commanded healing of his brain. We then said get up and walk. He was willing and we helped him get out of the stretcher and he walked on his own. He's been walking ever since. Instantaneous-A Miracle.

I am praying for another man with advanced Parkinson's disease and he is showing gradual progressive improvement: that is the healing process. Healing and miracles can overlap. The whole bible is a supernatural book filled with signs, wonders, healing, and miracles.

Keep the word in your heart that will give you life and health Proverbs 4:20-22.

Chapter Three

"HEALING"

The deaf man- A 91 year old totally 100% deaf man came to see me. He could not hear me yelling right into his ears. I laid hands on both ears and commanded the spirit of deafness to leave him. I also commanded full healing of his auditory system. I moved away fifteen steps and gently spoke to him. He repeated everything I said. He received miraculous total healing of his deafness; but! He then said, "I did not come here for this. I came to see you because I am totally deaf and I want to see the ear specialist so I could get a hearing device." Immediately he was totally 100% deaf again. He could not hear me as I yelled into his ears. Wow!

I had a vision of Bill Johnson grimacing, and then staring in silence, then commenting I don't think that he has read 'The Supernatural Power of a Transformed Mind". Please, read that wonderful, powerful, magnificent, revelatory book[9].

Romans 12:2
And be not conformed to this world: but be ye transformed by the renewing of your mind, that ye may prove what is that good, and acceptable, and perfect, will of God.

This event stayed with me. He did not know that I was praying for him. He received a miracle from God and totally rejected it. Is this the prevalent state of affairs? Many patients don't want prayer!
Isn't unbelief a sin?

John 16
8- And when he is come, he will reprove the world of sin, and of righteousness, and of judgment:
9- Of sin, because they believe not on me.

The spirit of unbelief and the deaf dumb spirit made him deaf again. Like the man at the pool of Bethesda, Jesus sovereignly healed him and later told him not to sin again. Maybe that sin was unbelief.

I commanded the spirit of deafness to come out in the name of Jesus and the spirit came out. It obeyed the command, but the man had no faith plus other issues, so when he heard, he rejected the word, he rejected Jesus, he rejected healing, he went into his old ways.

Matthew 13:15
For this people's heart is waxed gross, and their ears are dull of hearing, and their eyes they have closed; lest at any time they should see with their eyes, and hear with their ears, and should understand with their heart, and should be converted, and I should heal them.

He was bitter, stubborn, hard.

Ezekiel 12:2
Son of man, thou dwellest in the midst of a rebellious house, which have eyes to see, and see not; they have ears to hear, and hear not: for they are a rebellious house.

He needed only to believe.

Mark 9:23
Jesus said unto him. If thou canst believe, all things are possible to him that believeth.

The wonderful thing about the office is that people come back and that God always loves them; so for the next visit with him I am planning to give him a sheet of paper with a salvation prayer that will start by saying, pray it out loud! Believe in your heart!

Who knows, Jesus might snatch him then.

I will continue to intercede. At times the Lord sets ambushes. I love you God.

Jesus has already taken care of everything at the cross. We need to know that God's desire is to heal every sick person. It is like salvation. His death, shedding of blood and resurrection allows salvation for all humans but many have not appropriated this gift of grace.

The Greek word for salvation, Sozo, means saved completely, restored into wholeness. It includes forgiveness of sin and salvation from eternal punishment for sin, eternal life, all blessings and provisions, victory over the power of sin, deliverance from demonic oppression, power over sickness and disease, including emotional and mental disorders, the breaking of curses, etc. The provision for salvation, healing, and deliverance has been accomplished at the cross and we have been given power and authority to accomplish such work of the kingdom of God.

Matthew 18:11
For the Son of man is come to save that which was lost.

John 20:21b
As my Father hath sent me, even so send I you.

Matthew 10:7-8
As you go, preach, saying, the kingdom of heaven is at hand, heal the sick, cleanse the lepers, raise the dead, cast out devils: freely ye have received, freely give.

In the office we need to always ask the person if they would like prayer. It is important to have relationship with the patient and as much trust as possible. As part of the history and physical exam I ask all of my patients about their religious beliefs, the church they go, their Christian development etc. Occasionally a Holy Spirit believer on fire comes and we bask on the glory or they even pray and prophesy over me! How beautiful is the Church of Jesus Christ! To the doctors is relatively easy to obtain information about the illness. That's what we do all the time, characterize symptoms and give a diagnosis. Naturally we go back to the family history, the surgeries and traumas they had, their childhood and development, relationships, marriages, children etc. We have what we call the review of systems in which we investigate the person from head to toe, and we do the same in the physical exam.

The Holy Spirit has already ingrained in me an approach to the different areas that could be involved in the sickness of the patient. I train at Christian healing ministries under Francis and Judith MacNutt. In his book "Healing" Francis MacNutt describes the four basic kinds of healing[10].

A.) Sickness of our spirit- caused by our own personal sin requiring prayer of repentance.

B.) Emotional sickness- caused by the emotional hurt of our past requiring prayer of inner healing called also emotional healing or healing of the memories.

C.) Physical sickness- in our bodies requiring prayer for physical healing.

D.) Demonic oppression- requiring prayer for deliverance.

There are many healing schools, all wonderful parts of the wholeness which is Jesus. In Chester and Betsy Kylstra's Restoring the Foundation school there is an emphasis on the integration of four areas of ministry[11]. These areas of ministry are-

Sins of the fathers and resulting curses also called generational curses.

Ungodly believes similar to what John and Paula Sandford call inner vows in their wonderful book the transformation of the inner man[12].

Soul spirit hurts of past emotional traumas.

Demonic oppression.

It is a fact that everybody needs salvation. I believe that most Christians need breaking of generational curses and healing of emotional wounds and that many need deliverance. We will detail further these areas of prayer always knowing that all has been accomplished at the cross and that we need to be guided by the Holy Spirit.

Medicine is not just the mechanical scientific aspects of the patient. These human beings have spirit, soul, mind, emotions. As trained scientific physicians many times we do not know the real cause of an illness. Many patients have longstanding hidden issues, hurts and traumas that need transformation of the mind, healing, and deliverance.

There are root causes of illness embedded deep within the person. These issues are the cause of physical illnesses as all of our parts are intimately connected: spirit, soul, (mind, emotions, will,) and body. Many times I tell a patient the root cause of your physical ailment is not in your body; usually the body does not just get sick!

We have been trained to focus on the body in a "scientific way" that could be interpreted as a soulless way. I have practiced medicine in a robotic fashion, seeing the patient as a mechanical object. If you have pain I'll give you an analgesic, if you are depressed I'll give you an antidepressant etc. and many patients want only that, and I have to respect that. Some are very defended, hostile, and resistant to any spiritual emotional investigation but some want to go for the gold. Hallelujah.

We have extraordinary textbooks of medicine; as an internist I use the Harrison's and the Cecil and Loeb's textbooks of medicine, but at times we need to investigate areas of the soul and spirit where the origins of the illness lies. The medical office setting is a very sensitive environment. We see many sick people with many different personalities and agendas. We need to learn not to react and respond in the wrong manner. Remember, our enemy wants to create separation, blame, attack etc. He is the accuser of the brethren and our warfare is not against people but against evil.

God has his plans for the patients and I have to tune in to Him. I have to be ready and available at all times to allow the Holy Spirit to bring the love of the Father to the sick and wounded. We know what the Father wants for his children. Jesus healed all that approached Him. I'll keep repeating it throughout this book. Our healing was already accomplished at the cross. Decree it over your patients!

Our ministry is one of compassion. I pray that the compassion of Jesus rule in your life and your practice. The Lord gives us all grace, knowledge, wisdom, revelation, truth, power, authority, support, comfort, love to go to our deepest recesses, and bring full salvation there. He will do the same to our patients through us. He is the healer of the broken heart. We are now His temple.

The Holy Ghost lives in us.

We sit in the throne.

Nothing can stop us, Hallelujah. Amen.

PHYSICAL HEALING

I try to pray for everybody and the more I pray for people the more they get healed. The more they get healed the more testimony we have and the more faith, boldness and increments in healing. I speak to them Isaiah 53:4-5 and other healing scriptures. I praise, worship, and thank the Lord. I lay hands appropriately. I call for the presence, the glory, and the Holy Spirit. I really want God to be in the room. I call upon the river of life to inundate the patient. I call upon the love of the Father. Most of the time I use a prayer of command, declaration, decreeing. We always have to be guided by the Holy Ghost; even though I am addressing physical healing, many times I brake generational curses, call for inner healing of wounds, and cast out demons.

Even today, a woman came who appeared to be bitter and depressed with multiple aches, pains, and a severe migraine. She agreed for prayer. I used a simple prayer that I learned from Bill Johnson from Bethel Church in Redding, California. I called for the presence of God to fill her completely. I called the kingdom of God to come and the will of God to be done right in her as it is in heaven. There are no illnesses in heaven! I commanded healing and that everything that was not of God to leave her now in Jesus most Holy name. She was filled with The Holy Spirit and said excitedly, something came up from deep in my belly and left through my left nostril. I am healed. I have no pain or headache, what happened? What came out of me? I said a spirit of infirmity, aches and pains, migraine, bitterness, oppression, and depression. I commanded that spirit never to return and called upon the Holy Ghost to fill her house completely. She felt totally healed and full of joy and strength. Thank you Lord.

I have seen in my practice permanent healing of migraines, retinal damage, blindness, hearing difficulties, deafness, neck pain, swellings, adenopathies, arthritis, rotator cuff tears, longstanding sciatic pains and dysfunction from the herniated discs, asthma, irritable bowel syndrome, insomnia, acute diverticulitis, polymyalgia, fibromyalgia, lupus, peptic ulcers, heartburn, reflux, lung disease, improved oxygenation, healing of masses and tumors in different parts of the body such as lung, pancreas, breast, neck, cervical cancer, illnesses that were considered malignant prior to surgeries then found to be benign, heart disease, healing of cardiomyopathies, healing of arrhythmias, healing of rashes like psoriasis, healing of colds, healing of depression, schizophrenia, manic depression, reconciliation of couples, repentance, forgiveness and healing of hurts and woundings, repentance and healing of abortions, healing of all kinds of abuses in childhood, even in the womb. Renunciation and deliverance of freemasonry and witchcraft. Release of constricted hands after forgiveness prayer, economic blessing upon a prophetic word. Healing of family members, healing of carpal tunnel syndrome, improvement in Parkinson's disease, and healing of osteoarthritis of the knees and other parts of the body, and many other things that I never recorded and that I don't even remember.

With a simple prayer, most people receive an instantaneous total miraculous healing or a progressive healing. We always listen to the Lord as at times there is unforgiveness, hidden sins, emotional trauma, and occult and generational issues. A lot of people have been involved in the occult, for example: Ouija board, horoscopes, palm reading, etc.

I know that in my community there is significant Santeria witchcraft issues and freemasonry which are causes in itself of illness, disease and infirmity, and major blocks to healing.

As I pray for healing of physical pain I lay my hands in the area and declare healing in the name of Jesus. Many times I pray specifically, for example: at the knee, I declare healing of the total knee, articulation, joint, the capsule, the tendon and muscles, the cartilage, the patella. I could even call for a creative miracle: a totally new knee and sometimes In the name of Jesus I cast out spirits of pain and infirmity.

For herniated discs at the lumbosacral spine, at times, I guide them to sit well into the back of the chair and then I hold their feet and tell them to relax. I love it when there is a very pronounced short leg as it always grows when we pray and it brings faith and joy to the patient. I declare that the herniated discs are to go to their right place. I declare that the nerves have been released, that the tendons, muscles, cartilages, bones and all tissues are healed. I command the spirit of pain to leave in the name of Jesus. It works beautifully most of the time, but even a simple prayer when they are even standing can work as well. God is the healer, not a technique.

There are many great resources for specific prayers:
Joan Hunter's book- "Healing the Whole Man Handbook".[13]
"A More Excellent Way, Be In Health" Henry W. Wright.[14]
Healing Rooms- how to minister to specific diseases, healing room ministries.[15]
Ministry training manual Randy Clark global awakening.[16]
Probably the most complete and excellent manual that I have laid my hands on.

We pray guided by the Holy Ghost and with what we know. Some people seem to have a special anointing for certain illnesses. Sometimes we have revelation for certain mechanisms of disease. Like for example, migraine headaches. I believe that there is a conflict in the mind of the people that suffer migraines- specifically a conflict with a parent, and if we go deeper we find judgment, resentment, bitterness, and an inability to express such emotions and it all turns inward as an inner attack. Actually many illnesses are that: self hate and other components. So if I see a patient that suffers migraines in the prayer room in my house I probably go for the resolution of the inner conflict- the exposure, acknowledgment, the expression of feelings, the repentance, and the forgiveness. Then I would also pray for the wholeness and healing of the brain, the neurons and the brain vessels, and the normalization of the neurotransmitters like serotonin, and I would cast out the spirit of migraine with any other involved spirit.

The kingdom is God is so fantastic. We have said a word of knowledge regarding migraines in a meeting and a person has been totally healed. A person has read the bible and has had the revelation that physical healing is in the atonement and has been healed of migraines. Someone else might get healed without anybody praying for them in the presence of God. Sometimes a single word- migraine be gone. You are healed, and the person is healed. Many get healed by praise and worship. Hallelujah. God heals in many different ways. It is Him that heals, so we look at Him. Now when you are healed of migraines they might want to come back. You have to find your way of stopping it, preventive medicine! I used to go through the whole mechanisms of disease like healing any conflict, forgiving, declaring my brain vessels, neurons, and neurotransmitters healed. No vasoconstriction or vasodilatation, normal levels of serotonin, normal electrical activity, casting out the demon of migraine, praising, worshiping, speaking in tongues.

That sounds extensive but it is only a few minutes and it stops it completely. Full blown aggressive migraines can be disabling and can last for days. There are many patients that have become addicted to opiates and sedatives because of pain syndromes and that creates another major problem with many ramifications. What I believe might be controversial, but we have to ask ourselves if most chemical dependencies have a powerful spiritual component and the need for deliverance.

I once had a patient with severe low back pain that we could not control with any methods of pain control. We decided to anesthetize the lower part of her body to the degree that she could not feel anything whatsoever. I wanted to be sure that she did not feel anything so I pinched her with progressive force and she was totally unaware of it. When I asked her if she had any back pain she said "oh yes, the pain is killing me". So even with our science we could see that her pain somehow was embedded in her mind and brain and that no matter what we did to her back it would not go away.

When she became addicted, now we not only had her back problem, but the addiction, the craving, the withdrawal, the mental and mood changes, and the progressive deterioration. This is an area in which we need a powerful intervention of our Lord. We would pray for healing of her back and healing of her brain, neuroreceptors and neurotransmitters, moods, emotions, craving, withdrawal syndrome, addictive spirits, naming all the drugs the person is addicted to as spirits, for example: spirit of oxycodone come out, spirit of valium come out in the name of Jesus etc.

We pray with the anointing, revelation and knowledge that God gives us. If I pray specifically because I know a bit of medicine it is probably because God wants me to. You can do the same healing or a better healing with whatever He has given you. It is Him!

A week after I received the Holy Ghost still being pretty shaken and not knowing any scriptures or really nothing at all I laid my hands on a woman with a pancreatic mass and I said my Lord would you heal her, and He healed her. In the day of her surgery the mass was totally gone.

73

God is good. We have a good God. We probably should not get too complicated.

This week I prayed with two patients that had strokes, cerebral vascular accidents, with right sided weakness. I prayed the same way for both: first the prayer of salvation; then I prayed for the restoration of the brain, that where there was neuron death, life would come, that new neurons will start to grow, that the whole brain would be healed, that the vessels would be healed, that the right arm would regain total strength, in the name of Jesus.

The first patient regained much function of the right arm. She could not raise it at all and she easily raised it after the prayer. The second patient showed no significant physical improvement of her function, but she was shinning, as hope and joy fell on her, and she said, doctor please, can I come for prayer often. God touches everybody we pray for.

Rotator cuff tears are a gold mind. Patients have pain on the shoulder and they cant raise the arm. They have seen the orthopedist, received injections and rehab, they might need surgery; they have a hopelessness with their wounded shoulder. Jesus has already healed our wounds, sickness, and infirmities. 1 Peter 2:24.

Our God is a God of miracles, He thinks different than we do. His ways are different than ours. Isaiah 55:8.

His word is truth.

Attend to His words, and keep them in the midst of your heart, for they are life unto those who find them, and health to all their flesh Proverbs 4:20-22.

I place my hand on their shoulder and declare it healed in the name of Jesus. Or call upon the presence of God and pray- let the kingdom come and His will to be done on earth and it is in heaven. There are no illnesses in heaven. The God that heals is upon you, be healed.

Or declare a normal joint, capsule, tendon, ligaments, articulation vessels and nerves healed in the name of Jesus, or pray a combination of these prayers. At times I cast out the spirit of pain and infirmity in the name of Jesus.

In my experience most musculoskeletal conditions are totally healed or there is a definite improvement, and forget the MRI's. I pray that we all receive increments in faith and call those things which be not as though they were. Romans 4:17. I pray that we receive the spirit of wisdom and revelation in the knowledge of Him and that the eyes of our understanding be enlightened. Ephesians 1:17-18.

As a physician many times I use a prayer that involves what I know medically, for example: a patient with coronary heart disease. I declare the coronary arteries to be cleansed and opened by the mighty hand of God. I declare the inflammation of the vessel wall to be gone, and the fat to be gone in the name of Jesus.

If there has been a myocardial infarction (a heart attack) I declare that dead muscle to be healed and to function normally, and declare that in the next echocardiogram we will see a great increase in the ejection fraction. The ejection fraction is an indicator of the function of the heart, normal being 55-60%. In people with severe heart attacks and significant muscle damage the ejection fraction can be low, less that 30%. Less than 10 % is incompatible with life. In general when the ejection fraction is low people can have symptoms of heart failure: tiredness, weakness, shortness of breath, edema-fluid in the legs, fluid in the lungs, etc. We pray for improvement of the heart and the disappearance of the heart failure.

There are many other causes of heart disease, for example: hypertension- we pray for the normalization of the blood pressure and of the heart muscle, the normalization of the vessel wall, and of the kidneys. Valvular heart disease- we pray for the healing of the valves. Just pray with faith for healing and God will respond.

In diabetes mellitus there is a failure of the pancreas and lack of insulin and other substances. There is also insulin resistance, the body not responding well to the effects of insulin which is to bring the sugar into the cell. The whole body can be affected in diabetes: eyes, heart, nerves, circulation etc. Why does the pancreas fail? We pray for healing of the pancreas. We pray life to the pancreas, brake old curses that have attacked the pancreas. We declare the pancreatic cells to be healed in the name of Jesus. We declare a normal production of insulin in the name of Jesus and a good response of the body to the secreted insulin and normalization of the blood sugar. We declare healing to whatever area of the body that has been affected by diabetes, restoration of the retina in the eyes (diabetic retinopathy), restoration of the heart, restoration of the kidneys (diabetic nephropathy), and restoration of the circulation in every part of the body for example: legs (peripheral vascular disease), etc. Renal disease has many etiologies (causes). When the kidneys severely fail there's the need for dialysis. We follow a blood test- the creatinine in the blood- to asses' renal function, normal levels are usually 1mg or less. We attack the cause of the kidney disease; we break the power of diabetes, hypertension, or whatever is causing renal failure, and declare the creatinine to be normal in the name of Jesus. We cast out the demon of kidney failure.

At times we have prayed for new kidneys. We have access to heavenly realms. Ephesians 2:6. We call upon a creative miracle and bring kidneys from heaven into the patient here in earth. Let His will be done on earth as it is done in heaven. His will is that we be healed; He has already done it in the cross. Jesus did what the Father wanted. He healed all that came to him. He is still doing it. Amen.

There are many immunological illnesses. The most classic is systemic lupus erythematosus (S.L.E.). This is a disease with varying degrees of severity. The severe variant will affect the brain, the kidneys, the blood vessels (vasculitis), the heart, the skin, the bowel, the lungs etc, and it can be fatal. There are auto antibodies in this illness that causes the damage (antinuclear antibodies, anti-dna antibodies etc). You are attacking yourself. There is something in you that turns against you.

Many years ago I attempted to help a young woman with SLE (systemic lupus erythematosus). She shared that as a child she was constantly attacked by different members of her family. We realized that the systematic attack was now inside of her. An attack that had come from the outside was now attacking from the inside. Something that originally had been in the soul: mental and emotional, had transferred into the body. The hate from the outside became self hate inside; somehow that transferred into the body and immunological system. The body began to attack itself. Auto-antibodies began to destroy the body. A spiritual immune failure became a physical immune failure. I believe that this is one of the mechanisms of disease.

Recently I prayed for a Christian woman with SLE and painful joints, her erythrocyte sedimentation rate that indicates inflammation was 120 (very high). I just commanded the spirit of SLE and pain to leave her in the name of Jesus. She became pain free immediately and the sed rate in the blood came down to 10 (normal). Hallelujah.

If I think of the woman that the family attacked, I would probably:
-do healing of the generations and breaking of curses.
-healing of ungodly believes and inner vows.
-prayer of repentance and renunciation of sin.
-prayer of inner healing and forgiveness.
-prayer of physical healing- restoration of the immune system to its normal function and the casting out of the spirit of SLE, spirit of the attacking family, spirit of self hate, self attack, etc.

Rheumatoid arthritis is another common autoimmune disease with evidence of circulatory anti-globulin antibodies called rheumatoid factors. It is a progressive destructive and deforming poly-arthritis. Different areas of the body can also be affected. Not uncommonly we can see bitterness and unforgiveness, self pity and self hate, control, manipulation and domination issues. I would pray for rheumatoid arthritis in a similar way than SLE. I would command the spirit of rheumatoid arthritis to leave in the name of Jesus. I would decree healing of the immune system. I would deal with the root of bitterness, the judgment, the unforgiveness, etc. with inner healing and deliverance. At times there are bitter demons, unforgiving demons etc. that need to be cast out. I would pray for the healing of the hand, joints, bones, cartilage, and restoration to normalcy.

Marietta was an elderly evangelist and psalmist. I met her at our extensive care center for the terminally ill. She was in a wheelchair due to massive damage and deformity of her knees due to rheumatoid arthritis. She was on constant oxygen therapy as the rheumatoid arthritis had destroyed most of her lungs. We prayed intensely for Marietta in the office. Even three times per week for six months. I prayed all the possible prayers that I knew and that the Holy Ghost guided me to. We went through the 33 blocks to healing from Henry Wright's book "A more excellent way" be in health. We spent a long time in the unforgiveness area.

One day while doing a deliverance prayer over her lungs she began to manifest with an uncontrollable cough and foaming at the mouth. At that time the oxygen saturation went very low. Many times when we do deliverance there is coughing as the spirits come out, but I commanded the cough to stop and it immediately stopped. It seemed that the evil spirits were making her cough into asphyxiation and at the same time they broke the oxygen equipment. There was significant restoration of her lungs that day and she did not need constant oxygen therapy anymore. She would come to the office without the oxygen tank, feeling well. Unfortunately I had a nonbelieving nurse at that time that totally freaked out watching the whole event. She wanted to call 911, but I prohibited her from doing it. She talked to the director of our program and I had a lot of trouble attempting to explain what had happened.

Another head of one of our departments said sarcastically, "I heard that you almost did her in with one of your prayers."

Bless you Jesus Lord and savior. Your love is everlasting.

Marietta did not improve too much more in spite of constant praying. I wondered if she was getting some benefits from her illness. She was very demanding and was able to obtain many things because of her sickness. Maybe that created a block to healing.

One day I shared my frustration with her, already a year of persistent prayer. She told me, "Doctor, have faith. God will heal me completely. I am singing again in church!" Oh, that really touched my heart. I was frustrated, confused, complaining, and she was able to sing again in church.

I moved to a new office in Miami Beach, and rarely saw Marietta after that. One day I received a call that she had died. I know that she is in glory, but when Randy Clark, at his school of healing and impartation taught us about the agony of defeat, I placed Marietta under that category.

Yesterday, it was a tough day at the office. A cloud of unbelief and death surrounded us. It was very hard to pray. It's like nobody believed and I was dragged down. A woman that really likes me as a doctor, and who comes from very far away to see me, had pain in a toe! She wanted an MRI, referrals, etc. She knows that I pray for healing and she has been healed of other things before. I could not take it any longer. I banged my desk and said forcefully, "we have the spirit of resurrection and creation inside of us, how can God not heal a toe! Please! I had a very hard day today; are we denying the cross of Jesus; you are not going to leave this office without being healed", so I laid hands on her toe and God totally healed her. This was really a violent taking of the kingdom by force. Rarely do I do this but the healing of the little toe saved some of the day. Pain was defeated again. Thank you Jesus.

In the evening I saw prophet Kobus Van Rensburg from South Africa, and received a mighty refreshing zap from him. In the morning I became a joyous grandfather for the first time. My daughter gave birth to Luke in St. Luke the apostle day. God is Good. The office work was great: preaching, exhortation, prophesying, ministering salvation, healing and deliverance. A regular Christian doctor's day at the office.

A couple received the baptism of the Holy Ghost; they were filled with the Holy Ghost and spoke fluidly in tongues. Many were healed of different pains. I prayed for a woman's back pain and at the same time that the pain was totally gone, her hands that had been restricted and constricted became loosed and normal. I liked that. Thank you Lord.

I saw my grandson at the hospital and upon my return home I saw my neighbor with a very stiff neck. He is very stoic and noncomplaining, but he was in severe pain. I asked him if I could pray for him and he said yes. So I laid my hands on his neck and declared the healing already done at the cross of Jesus and the pain was gone. He was very surprised, could move the neck well and praised Jesus.

There are many conditions that are considered by many physicians to have a psychosomatic component: migraines, irritable bowel syndrome, asthma, back pain, chest discomfort, palpitations, inflammatory bowel disease, etc. Many times we see large charts filled with all kinds of tests without a clear diagnosis. At times we deal with a new symptom at each visit. At other times patients come with a large list of symptoms. Occasionally we see a new series of tests and specialists referrals every month. We really don't want to miss anything, but that's another story. Whatever the patient has if he or she is willing we can pray for healing.

Now days we are seeing a lot of cases of fibromyalgia. We have seen complete healings of fibromyalgia with prayers for healing and with deliverance prayers. It is just possible that in some cases, when we physicians create a certain diagnosis, it can open the way for an epidemic. Remember, our words give life or death, blessings or curses. We could participate in the diseases process in a negative way. Don't get me wrong, medical science has been doing wonders for many years, but we need to also look at the whole picture. Specifically, there are certain cases of fibromyalgia and many other illnesses in which we can do extensive workups and all kinds of special therapies, but all that will not cast out the demon that is the disease itself. I know that I could get in some trouble discussing this issues spiritually, but my God is the true God, my protector, the rock of my salvation in whom I trust and the truth shall set us free. We need to discern the wiles of the devil.

At times I have participated in the devil's opinion regarding a patient. If I say you have such illness and there is no cure and you will die I might just be cursing the patient. I know what the medical book says, but I also know what the Truth Book says. He took our infirmities and carried our sorrows. By His stripes we are healed. I had to transform my mind and learn a new language. The language of life instead of the language of death. The language of blessings instead of the language of curses.

I have to be very honest and tell the patient what the medical sciences suggest but I have to tell them also what God says. I tell my patients that I will fight with them for a healing and a miracle; that with God I fight for life. I believe that God is giving us more power, authority, and keys for healing and to defeat illnesses.

Some healers have a grip on certain diseases; it is like they have taken dominion and heal specific illnesses.

In David Hogan's ministry there have been near five hundred people raised from the dead! In prophet Kobus ministry there have been near 10,000 cripples healed. In Bill Johnson's church dozens of people with manic depression have been totally healed. This and more is happening in many ministries all over the world. AIDS is being totally healed, hepatitis is being totally healed. Right now I am pushing for healing of metastatic colon, breast, lung, other cancers, multiple myeloma, Alzheimer disease, Parkinson's disease, really any disease. Peter, explaining Cornelius about Jesus in Acts 10:38 said, how God anointed Jesus of Nazareth with the Holy Ghost and with power: who went about doing good, and healing all that were oppressed of the devil; for God was with him.

This is our commission, cancer must generally be demonic. Whatever prayer I do like closing all entrance doors (we will discuss this further in the deliverance session) I always cast out the demon of the specific cancer. For example: In the name of Jesus, spirit of breast cancer come out now. I command you to leave this person now. We have been given power and authority over all evil and we must enforce it.

There are many lung disorders. I find that in asthma there is an underlying emotional condition that needs to be healed. I declare healing of the bronchi with relief of the bronchospasm and the inflammation and cast out the spirit of asthma in the name of Jesus. In chronic obstructive lung disease (COPD) I declare healing of all the structures of the lung, bronchi, alveoli, interstitium, vessels. Sometimes we can call for new lungs. The oxygenation always goes up with prayer.

The threat of MRSA is now coming in the newspaper daily. This is a methicillin resistant staphylococcus aureus, a bacteria not responding to antibiotics. It can be a lethal nosocomial infection acquired in the hospital, infecting already sick people, but has been found outside the hospital in healthy people, in schools, even children have died from it. We bind, brake, and cast out the spirit of MRSA. We sever any curses in the name of Jesus. We command the bacteria and their toxins to leave the body in the name of Jesus. We declare the blood stream and all organs and tissues to be healed in the name of Jesus. We call upon the spirit of revelation to fall on scientists to bring a new weapon from heaven to destroy MRSA when necessary and I believe that this is here now.

Luke 4:18, 21
This day is this scripture fulfilled in your ears.

Sirach 38
2- The physician's gift of healing comes from the Most High.
4- The Lord created medicines out of the earth...
6- He gave skills to human beings that he might be glorified in his marvelous works.
7- By them the physician heals.
13- There may come a time when recovery lies in the hands of physicians.

MRSA was already defeated at the cross by our Lord.

I have given here an overview of prayer for physical healing and have mentioned a few diseases and different ways that people get healed. Whatever sickness you have just declare the healing that has already been done at the cross of Jesus; you might also do a prayer of deliverance for the spirit of the illness in the name of Jesus.

Conclusion-Prayer for Physical Healing

Approaching the patient:
Step one- what does the patient want prayer for?
Randy Clark is aware that we need to ask when the condition started. What is the cause? Is it known? If there was any significant event occurring at the time the condition started.

Last night we had a guest prophet in my house that ministered to about 30 people. There was a blind lady and people spontaneously prayed for her after the meeting. I usually do the same wherever I find sickness, just pray, but this time I just sat with her and asked her when did she become blind? What happened? She said, "I have familiar retinoblastoma and I became blind when I was 1 year of age; this illness has affected my three children and my nine grandchildren. My son just died from a sarcoma and two of my grandchildren have died from the disease; many are blind." I found out that literally hundreds of people had prayed for her, and that included many anointed healers. It made me think about cancer, genetics, and inheritance. It made me think about generational curses, illness, and the demonic. Cancer arises through changes in the DNA that result in cells growing out of control. There are two major classes of cancer genes. The first class are:

The oncogenes that affect cell growth positively.
Tumor suppressor genes that affect cell growth negatively.
The second class of cancer genes are:
The caretakers that maintain the integrity of the genome.
These genes can be altered in cancer causing, a.) Unregulated cell growth, b.) Inability to regulate cell growth, c.) Inability to maintain integrity.

This is a very preliminary simplistic and limited overview of cancer, but I was led by the spirit to also look in that direction. At times we declare be healed in the name of Jesus and whatever cancer is healed. At other times we might need to do a prolonged healing that would include generational curses, sins, traumas, inner vows, soul ties, demonization, etc. and it might be that at other times scientists oncologists would pray with an incredible precision knowing the intimate and deep mechanisms of diseases and would destroy evil that way. All good things come from above!

We were on step one: what does the patient want prayer for. I diverge a bit at times as I have daily experiences in healing and I believe that the Holy Spirit wants me to share some of them. In the office we know the diagnosis; we would ask- would you like prayer, can we pray together, can I pray for your pain or illness. Remember to investigate gently if the person has accepted Jesus as Lord and savior and to lead them in the prayer of salvation that includes repentance of sin and forgiving of someone if they need to. We want to always be guided by the Holy Spirit. We need to be open to receive the different gifts whenever we need them to minister most effectively.

We use our regular senses and our spiritual senses. I have seen many medallions, rings, bracelets, and chains that I have strongly recommended my patients to destroy. Most do. I have discerned all kinds of issues and oppressions, have given many words of knowledge and prophetic words. There is a lot of unforgiveness in people and we need to lead them in forgiveness prayers.

The fruits of the spirit have also manifested. A full blown manic-depressive patient, one that was very hard to deal with, was healed when the love of God filled me and fell on her. I told her from the heart of God and from my heart- God loves you so much and I love you so much. You are so special. The love of God filled her. She wept and was healed. I love it when she comes now for her appointments. So we are open to what the Holy Spirit wants us to do.

Step two- we have the request. We know the problem. Be ready to receive more input from the Holy Ghost. We pray- we need to train and equip- there are different types of prayer.

A. Prayer of petition- asking God to heal. For example: Father in the name of Jesus I ask you to heal this ankle sprain. We don't say if it is your will. We know the will of the Father and we know about the cross. We don't want doubt.

B. Prayer of command- declaring healing. For example: thank you Lord that you have already healed the ankle sprain. Thank you Jesus that the swelling, pain, and tenderness is gone. I command all pain and swelling to leave the ankle in the name of Jesus. Thank you Lord. All prayers of deliverance are prayers of command. For example: I command you, demon of lung cancer to leave right now in the name of Jesus.

C. The Lord's prayer- I call it Bill Johnson's prayer because the revelation of the power of that prayer came to me when a group from Bethel Church came to teach at PPMI (prophetic people ministry international), prophet Norman Spencer's ministry here in Miami. I declare let the kingdom come, let his will be done on earth as it is in heaven. There are no illnesses in heaven. With the kingdom comes the King. There are no illnesses in the presence of the King: be healed.

D. Most of the times I lay hands when I pray. At Christian healing ministries there is a certain ministry time when we lay hands on the sick in the presence of the Lord in silence and there is healing. Luke 8:43-46. When the woman with the issue of blood touched Jesus, Jesus said somebody hath touched me: for I perceive that virtue-power- is gone out of me. That power that came out of Jesus into that woman healed her immediately. We do have the same Holy Spirit and the same power! We all need to absolutely be baptized by Jesus with the Holy Ghost and fire.

E. Sometimes we lay hands and pray in tongues (we always ask the person if we can pray with our prayer language)

Romans 8:26-27. The spirit maketh intercession for us according to the will of God.

F. Soaking prayer- in the context of healing prayer it really refers about   spending time, even lots of time praying for a sick person. It could be in silence, with words, with tongues, and or a combination of these. At Christian Healing Ministries there is the four day intense prayer week.

I have prayed for people weekly for a year. It requires endurance, persistence, pressing power, compassion, the breaking of hopelessness and other hindrances when they surface.

Remember to explain to the patient the need to keep their healing. I already explained what I would do with migraines. The enemy always wants to retaliate, and he is the deceiver and the father of lies, so we stand firm on the rock which is Jesus Christ and his word, and declare what he says.

I pray to you Psalm 103:1-5

1-Bless the LORD, O my soul: and all that is within me, *bless* his holy name.

2- Bless the LORD, O my soul, and forget not all his benefits:

3-Who forgiveth all thine iniquities; who healeth all thy diseases;

4- Who reedemeth thy life from destruction; who crowneth thee with loving kindness and tender mercies;

5- Who satisfieth thy mouth with good things; so that thy youth is renewed like the eagle's. Amen.

Chapter Four

"INNER HEALING-FORGIVENESS"

There is no forgiveness without the shedding of blood. There is no healing without forgiveness. The blood of the lamb is the unique ingredient necessary for forgiveness and healing.

A year ago a 40 year-old married woman came to see me in distress as she had trouble getting an appointment for a fertilization specialist. She was childless and had been unsuccessfully attempting to get pregnant following all kinds of instructions and guidelines. She was a churchgoing woman and supplicated God for a child. I found that her insurance would not cover such specialist. I asked her if she wanted to pray. She had done the prayer of salvation previously and Jesus was her Lord and savior. I sensed in the spirit that there was an important issue that needed healing. It was a controlling mother issue. She felt the pain, the rejection, the criticism, the resentment that plagued her throughout her life. She repented from judging her mother. We removed the root of bitterness. She forgave her mother and felt love and forgiveness. The presence of God fell on her and on her womb. All fears left her. I felt God in her womb and prophesied that she would certainly conceive a child.

We decided to do the routine medical center tests and then attempted to obtain the referrals that she wanted. I went to lunch at our kitchen in the medical center and suddenly I knew that she was pregnant. I ran out of the kitchen and stopped her before she would have the routine x-rays. I told her that she needed a pregnancy test. She said that she had been doing them daily. She complied and the pregnancy test was positive. The whole center rejoiced because they knew her plight.

Isn't God awesome? Isn't God fun? Hallelujah. She has already given birth to a wonderful miracle child. Thank you Jesus.

Judith MacNutt in the school of healing prayer level one[17] emphasizes that memories can wound, cripple, and bind people, often keeping them in bondage and preventing God's healing power from working in them, God's love however, can transform even our memories to set us free from them. We call this transformation inner or emotional

healing. Agnes Sandford called it healing of memories. At CHM
(Christian healing ministry) the term inner healing is used. Inner healing
refers to the healing of the inner person, who carries all that we are and all
our experiences, our memories, life experiences, damaged emotions,
distorted self image, personality and temperament etc.

Jesus is the one who heals, not any psychological mechanism. There
is no true healing without the cross. Jesus came to heal the brokenhearted
and set the captives free. He has opened all prison doors. He can reach into
any stage of one's life including the womb and set us free. Jesus was
overwhelmed at the Mount of Olives knowing that He would carry all of
our sins, all of our hurts, and all of our diseases. He was in agony and
sweated blood. He accepted such cup for us. An angel came from heaven
to strengthen Him. It is all about His love for us.

John 3:16
For God so loved the world, that he gave his only begotten Son,
that whosoever believeth in him should not perish, but have
everlasting life.
17- For God sent not his only Son into the world to condemn the
world; but that the world through him might be saved.

Romans 5:8
But God commendeth his love toward us, in that, while we were
yet sinners, Christ died for us.

1 Peter 2:24
Who his own self bare our sins in his own body on the tree…
By whose stripes ye were healed.

Hebrews 12:2
Looking unto Jesus the author and finisher of our faith, who for the
joy that was set before him endured the cross, despising the
shame, and is set down at the right hand of the throne of God.

1 Corinthians 13:8 A
Love never fails.

In the biblical basis for ministry John Sandford from Elijah House Ministries[18] discusses how the gospel and the ministry of the inner man is the word of God.

> Hebrews 4
> 12- For the word of God is quick, and powerful, and sharper than any two edged sword, piercing even to the dividing asunder of soul and spirit, and of the joints and marrow, and is a discerner of the thoughts and intents of the heart.
> 13- Neither is there any creature that is not manifest in his sight: but all things are naked and opened unto the eyes of him with whom we have to do.
> 2 Timothy 3
> 16- All scripture is given by inspiration of God, and is profitable for doctrine, for reproof, for correction, for instruction in righteousness:
> 17- That the man of God may be perfect, thoroughly furnished unto all good works.

God says in Isaiah 55:8 that his thoughts are not our thoughts neither are our ways his ways.

We absolutely need to ground ourselves in the word of God.

We must keep the words of God in the midst of our hearts because they are life and health.

Matthew 3:10 tells us that we need to find the roots and lay the ax to the roots. Lay the ax to the cause, the source, the beginning, the root. We need to go there for healing.

> Deuteronomy 5:16
> Honour thy father and thy mother, as the Lord thy God has commanded thee, that thy days may be prolonged, and that it may go well with thee, in the land which the Lord thy God giveth thee. This is the only commandment with a promise.

In the area that you have not honored your father or mother, in that area, life will not go well with you.

I definitely had a problem there- I felt humiliation, shame, rejection, being unloved, unrecognized etc. I believed the kingdom of darkness amplified those feelings tremendously. I judged my parents and had resentments and bitterness throughout most of my life: most of my life was affected adversely mainly in the area of personal fulfillment and relationships. No psychological therapy changed my inner man or my inner child.

It was only the cross of my Christ that opened the way of healing. I was forgiven, my sins were forgiven. The love of God came into my life. I could then repent and renounce judgments, resentments, bitterness and unforgiveness, and was healed.

My parents are in the glory. I love them dearly. They were so good. The Lord changes all- we need to become available. He changes the way we see things, the way we feel, the way we believe. He destroys the lies of the devil. He transfers us from the kingdom of darkness to the kingdom of light. We do become new creatures.

Matthew 7
Judge not, that ye be not judged
1- Judge not, that ye be not judged.
2- For with what judgment ye judge, ye shall be judged: and with what measure ye mete, it shall be measured to you again.
3- And why beholdest thou the mote that is in thy brother's eye, but considerest not the beam that is in thine own eye?
4- Or how wilt thou say to thy brother, Let me pull out the mote out of thine eye; and, behold, a beam is in thine own eye?
5- Thou hypocrite, first cast out the beam out of thine own eye; and then shalt thou see clearly to cast out the mote out of thy brother's eye.

Galatians 6:7
Be not deceived; God is not mocked: for whatsoever a man soweth, that shall he also reap.

Romans 2:1
Therefore thou art inexcusable, O man, whosoever thou art that judgest: for wherein thou judgest another, thou condemnest thyself; for thou that judgest doest the same things.

Proverbs 18:21
Death and life are in the power of the tongue.

James 3
6- And the tongue is a fire, a world of iniquity: so is the tongue among our members, that it defileth the whole body, and setteth on fire the course of nature; and it is set on fire of hell.
8- But the tongue can no man tame; it is an unruly evil, full of deadly poison.
10- Out of the same mouth proceedeth blessing and cursing. My brethren, these things ought not so to be.

We can clearly see God's word for us. These are powerful life directions that we must fully understand and appropriate for the healing of the inner man. Let us closely watch for double mindedness. For let not that man think that he shall receive anything of the Lord. A double minded man is unstable in all his ways James 1:7-8.

We must learn to observe our fruits and follow the roots and what is not of the Kingdom of God we axe out. My spirit rejoices with the following teaching from John Sandford.[19]

At the moment that we invite Jesus into our lives we are born anew. Sins are washed away in the blood. Sin nature has been dealt a death blow; but we are not perfected all at once. Inner healing is the process of sanctification and transformation. It is the gospel of prayer ministry to the inner man. It is the process of bringing to death the old nature with the old patterns. When we received Jesus, our old self died. We need to make it effective.

In Luke 6, we have lots of direction. We will focus now on verses 42-49 and later on earlier verses.

V- 42b: Thou hypocrite, cast out first the beam out of thine own eye, and then shalt thou see clearly…

V-44: look at the fruit, every tree is known by his own fruit
V-45: inspect the treasure of your heart, listen to what you say for
 of the abundance of the heart the mouth speaketh.
V-46: don't keep calling Him Lord when you do whatever you
want.
V-47,48:when you do as He says you dig deep and lay the
foundations on the rock, otherwise,
V-49: a great ruin will fall on the house

In summary-
Clear your eyes.
Look at fruits-roots.
Inspect the treasure of your heart
Obey God.
Dig deep.
Lay the foundations on Christ.

Through the history of Christianity I have read and heard and seen great men of God falling in shocking ways. This is not to judge them but I have wondered: did they have hidden unhealed issues that the devil took a hold of.

I know that I have lots of stuff. As part of my Christian life I set up daily time when I invite, submit and yield to the Holy Ghost for a deep inspection of the inner man and the heart.

We have hidden dimensions in our lives that affect us in dramatic ways. We know what God wants from us; that we love Him above all things, with all our heart, with all our soul, with all our strength, with our entire mind, and our neighbor as our selves, Luke 10:27.

It is easier said than done.

Scripture says that the heart is deceitful above all things, and desperately wicked: who can know it? Jeremiah 17:9.

The pride of the heart can deceive us... Obadiah 1:3.

Out of the heart proceed evil thoughts... Matthew 15:19.

Our hearts could be uncircumcised, at least in some areas and we could resist the Holy Ghost, Acts 7:51. We can have idols in our hearts. Ezekiel 14:3 and our hearts can go after our idols, Ezekiel 20:16.

In Luke 12:34, we see that for where our treasure is, there will be our hearts also.

The Lord looketh on the heart, 1 Samuel 16:7.

The Lord triest the reins and the heart, Jeremiah 11:20.

We must purify our hearts, James 4:8.

We must keep our heart with all diligence for out of it are the issues of live, Proverbs 4:23.

We ask God to search us and to know our hearts, Psalm 139:23.

We hide the word of God in our hearts, Psalms 119:11.

We get a new heart and a new spirit, Ezekiel 36:25-30.

We have Christ dwelling in our hearts, Ephesians 3:17.

We do the will of God from the heart, Ephesians 6:6.

We sanctify the Lord God in our hearts, 1 Peter 3:15.

Forgiveness is absolute necessary and it is a heart issue. When we first come to Christ we must repent of our sins, believe in our hearts, confess Jesus as Lord and Savior and receive forgiveness, salvation and relationship with God. This is the new creation. There is no salvation without forgiveness. There is no healing without forgiveness.

Unforgiveness is a major block to healing.

In Matthew 18:22 Jesus said to forgive 70X7.

In the parable of the King which would take account of his servants. Jesus showed us what would happen to the unforgiving servant.

Matthew 18
32- Then His Lord, after that He had called Him, said unto him, O thou wicked servant, I forgave thee all that debt, because thou desiredst mc:
33- Shouldest not thou also have had compassion on thy fellow servant, even as I had pity on thee?
34- And his Lord was wroth, and delivered him to the tormentors till he should pay all that was due to unto Him.
35- So likewise shall my heavenly Father do also unto you, if ye from your heart forgive not every one of his brothers their trespasses.

There is something about the heart and honesty. I believe the Spirit is bringing me to memory my early years in recovery from alcoholism and drug addiction. Such as struggle! After seven weeks in the hospital's addiction treatment program I thought that I was cured; while still in the hospital I had a dream where I was using cocaine; when I woke up I knew that I had to use again. So I ran away and relapsed. It was awful; I hated it, but could not stop. That day I did the first step of alcoholics anonymous from the heart. I am powerless and my life is unmanageable. I became convinced of my powerlessness over the drug. I got in my car and left for a long term treatment center in Mississippi. There; as I mentioned earlier, the Lord healed me sovereignly at "God's Pond." I do believe that my reaching bottom, surrendering, and becoming willing to do whatever it took was orchestrated by the Lord.

Bill W. the founder of AA, while in the hospital, had a dramatic spiritual experience in which he was totally healed of alcoholism. Bill wanted for all the alcoholics to have the same miraculous instantaneous divine healing but it just did not happen that way, so he created the twelve steps of AA- steps that would lead to a spiritual awakening and recovery for most people. I struggled many years after the Lord healed my drug-alcohol addiction until I found the true higher power- Jesus Christ and after his Holy Spirit came to abide in me, giving me the power to obtain

93

victory on all fronts. While in the treatment center in Mississippi I became very interested in denial as denial was related to relapse. Bill W. in the AA book mentioned those unfortunates who could not recover because they could not be honest.

There was a mystery in denial. People made rational sense, they would explain their plan to remain sober, an intellectually sound plan that they believed but there was a vital ingredient missing. They would repeatedly relapse. I became involved in a chronic relapser professional group made mostly by physicians and attorneys-what a mixture, right? We did psychological testing that involved the right and left brain. We can give information to the right brain in several ways: visually, spatial arrangements, block designs.

The left brain is the verbal brain, the logical, rational, and intellectual brain. We do need both brains for wholeness and balance. The testing showed a dramatic discrepancy between the right and left brains: very high scores on the left brain and very low scores on the right brain. I related the right brain dysfunction to denial, to an inability to connect to feelings, emotions, and spirituality, to an inability to be honest and a propensity to relapse.

Later I found studies from the noble laureate Dr. Sperry in people with intractable epilepsy. He had to cut the corpus callosum, the connection between the two brains to help stop the progression of the abnormal electrical waves. He then did further studies in these patients. He gave specific nonverbal information to the right brain and when he asked the patient about it, the left brain, the verbal brain, answered incorrectly and the patient believed the lie! There was an identification with a limited part of us related to the intellect, rationality, and speech. A part of us that did not know the truth. In the case of the addicted population an error that could prove fatal. While in Miami working on an addiction treatment center in a hospital, I treated a physician that showed extreme denial and was placing his life and the life of others in danger. The psychological testing showed a dramatic difference between the two brains and the PET scan showed almost no function on the right brain, a finding of which I never got a good explanation for, but he needed to be institutionalized permanently because he could not recover.

I guess I was lead to write about mechanisms of denial because this also applies to us Christians. We can have hidden issues, hidden agendas, hurts, emotional traumas, etc still lingering in our depths and affecting our lives, relationships, and ministries. We could have developed defenses and survival mechanisms and reactive ways and patterns that could still be active in us blocking us from wholeness. Just today a good friend called me to share an experience that she had at 2 am in the morning. She had been suffering from migraines for many years and took medicines to control the symptoms. There was a family history of freemasonry and her mother had been extremely controlling. She had three marriages and three divorces. So her life had not gone well. She suffered significantly but when Christ came into her life and she was born again fifteen years previously, things began to gradually improve. She had been involved in serious bible studies, studied the bible daily, was baptized with the Holy Spirit, spoke in tongues daily, and was involved in worship, prophetic, healing and deliverance ministries.

A migraine came upon her and God lead her to take a stand. She did not take any medicines, invited the Holy Spirit to take over, and continuously spoke in tongues; an activity of surrendering prevailed. Somehow a part of her that had been in control that she called the head, submitted. The Lord removed a mind that was blocking the revelation of her wounded self. The beam out of her eye was removed and she was able to see clearly. She digged deep, saw the fruit and the root and inspected the treasure of her heart. The Holy Spirit took her to the area of the emotions. She experienced all the deep recurrent hurts that began in early childhood. She understood strongholds. There was a core of rejection and shame covered by fear, self hate, bitterness, unforgiveness, and resentments. She had developed unhealthy ways of judging out of the bitterness deep within.

A facade of pride and control covered it all. She repented and renounced such ways. There was deep hurt and great rage. The Lord began to show her the people in her life that had hurt her and that she hated and she was lead to express all her hidden feelings and was then able to forgive from her heart one by one. She then said a demon of migraine was exposed and with a new power and strength she commanded it to leave in the name of Jesus but behind that demon was who she called the strongman, the demon of rage; he was commanded to leave and had to leave in Jesus most holy name. There were no unhealed wounds for the demonic to attach. Evil lost its legal rights. My friend says that throughout the whole process she kept surrendering her mind and a new mind, the mind of Christ began to make inroads in her being. We must place in our hearts the key of forgiveness and live in the ways of forgiveness.

In Mark 11:24-26 Jesus tells us,
24- Therefore I say unto you, What things soever ye desire, when ye pray, believe that ye receive them, and ye shall have them.
25- And when you stand praying, forgive, if you have aught against any: that your Father also which is in heaven may forgive you your trespasses
26- But if you do not forgive, neither will your Father which is in heaven forgive tour trespasses.

Back in Luke 6 we read
27- But I say unto you which hear, Love your enemies, and do good to them which hate you
28- Bless them that curse you, and pray for them which despitefully use you
35- But love ye your enemies, and do good and lend, hoping for nothing again; and your reward shall be great, and ye shall be the children of the Highest: for he is kind unto the unthankful and to the evil
36- Be ye therefore merciful, as your Father also is merciful.
37- Judge not, and you shall not be judged: condemned not and you shall not be condemned: forgive, and ye shall be forgiven.
38- Give, and it shall be given unto you; good measure, pressed down, and shaken together, and running over, shall men give into your bosom. For with the same measure that ye mete withal it shall be measured to you again.

It is absolutely clear what God wants to do, the way He wants us to be and He will absolutely help us each step of the way. He obtained all the victory at the cross for us and he gave us the Holy Ghost! Today I had a wonderful experience at the office. A very tall, big, and strong patient came in. He was kind of quiet and had a large tattoo of a totally naked woman filling his arm. I knew something was going to happen in the office. As I took the medical history I asked him if he was going to church and he just said no. I waited a while and then asked him if he was saved; again, he just said no; now the excitement of the presence of God began to infill me and I asked God what's next: I heard the still small voice that said ask him if he has a bible and who gave it to him. So I asked him: do you have a bible and who gave it to you. Immediately tears began to come out of the big man's eyes. He then said before my mother died she gave me her bible and told me that one day I would be saved. Hallelujah; then I told him this is the day. We held hands and prayed. He repented of longstanding sin patterns, renounced evil, felt the forgiveness of God, and accepted Jesus as Lord and Savior. We then talked about the next steps in his new life.

I remembered Francis MacNutt's teachings. It is in his book "Healing" in the chapter of forgiveness of sins. He begins by saying that the first and deepest kind of healing that Christ brings is the forgiveness of our sins. Our repentance and God's forgiveness. This is salvation and healing at the deepest level.

Later on in the chapter he mentions that the first condition for seeking healing is to cast out sin, especially the root of bitterness and that the church generally seems to be insensitive to our worst sins: those of bitterness and resentment. After I finished the previous page I went to the market to get pens and while in the line to pay I conversed with two wonderful ladies. An 80 year-old mother and a 60 year-old daughter. We talked about the great church they were members of and I shared that I was writing a book on healing and that right this day I was writing about woundings and forgiveness. The daughter looked at me with a questioning face and said what does healing has to do with forgiveness? I just said the scriptures say that we need to forgive as we have been forgiven; it also says that we can be thrown into the tormentors if we don't forgive. I want to forgive just because God wants me to forgive.

In my way home I cried. I felt a deep sadness from the question: what does healing has to do with forgiveness. Maybe I felt hopelessness and despair but also humility and compassion and later strength and joy, even joy that I am writing this book. Thank you Lord.

Romans 6:23
For the wages of sin is death; but the gift of God is eternal life through Jesus Christ our Lord.

Salvation is healing.

Our spirit is dead in sin, is doomed for eternal damnation, and is separated from God.

Ephesians 1:7
In Jesus we have redemption through his blood, the forgiveness of sin, according to the riches of his grace.

Salvation is the biggest healing. It is the miracle of the healing of our spirit. When we repent and accept Jesus in our heart, we receive forgiveness of sin, our spirit becomes alive. The Spirit of God unites with our spirit. We move from death to life. Our repentance and His forgiveness opens the way.

It is the new birth. It is the spiritual birth.

Romans 8
1- There is therefore now no condemnation to them which are in Christ Jesus, who walk not after the flesh, but after the spirit.
2- For the law of the spirit of life in Christ Jesus hath made me free from the law of sin and death.
14- For as many as are lead by the Spirit of God, they are the sons of God,
35-39 who shall separate us from the love of Christ.... Nothing shall be able to separate us from the love of God, which is in Christ Jesus our Lord.

Hallelujah, what healing!

Colossians 1

19- For it pleased the Father that in him should all fullness dwell.
20- And having made peace through the blood of his cross, by
him to reconcile all things unto himself; by him, I say, whether
they be things in earth, or things in heaven.
21- And you, that were sometimes alienated and enemies in your
mind by wicked works, yet now hath he reconciled.
22- In the body of his flesh through death, to present you holy and
unblameable and unreproveable in his sight.

Don't you feel good?

I am looking for the ladies to proclaim: Forgiveness has everything
to do with healing.
Forgiveness and salvation also include our souls and our bodies.
Sozo, as we explained previously- is to be saved completely. If we don't
forgive someone who has hurt us, our soul remains poisoned with
bitterness, judgments, resentments etc. and that emotional poison can
affect our bodies with diverse illnesses. Unforgiveness is an open door to
the demonic. Emotional illnesses can be transmitted through the
generations. Bitterness can defile many around us.
Several times I have seen arthritis ravished hands opening up after
a forgiveness prayer. If God forgave us at the cross we need to forgive
others. I know that we have been hurt, some severely, but we must
forgive. The Holy Spirit will help us and it is a process.
It took me 56 years to repent and receive God's forgiveness and
forgive myself and forgive others. Now I have eternity in the glory. The
cross is about forgiveness. We must go through the cross to the new life.
Carrying the cross means going through the cross. It is doing the will of
God and the will of God is that we forgive. There are wonderful teachings
on forgiveness and forgiveness prayers. Four references. [20] [21] [22] [23]
A key bible verse related to inner healing is Hebrews 12:15-
Looking diligently least any man fail of the grace of God; lest any root of
bitterness springing up trouble you, and thereby many be defiled.
I received the teachings about bitter roots from Dr. Tom
Wilkerson[24] at CHM (Christian Healing Ministries). He gave credit to

John and Paula Sandford.[25] Bitter roots refer to how we have sinned as a result of what has been done to us by others. If we make a judgment it is sin. It is our sinful reaction and our condemning judgments of people and our refusal or inability to forgive. It is our reaction, our response. Most of the time bitter root judgments have to do with our parents. Many times we have forgotten and the judgments have taken a life of their own. Bitter roots are hidden. It springs up, jumps on you, takes over, defile.

A pattern could be developed: judging, blaming, accusing, condemning, gossiping, resenting. What is lodged in our hearts, hidden, repressed, unknown, unexpressed, once formed, judgments must bring results. Unhealed bitter roots must defile. Bitter roots are perhaps the most negative forces in our lives, bringing destruction not only to us but to all around us. You really have to want to change. At times, resistant strongholds are created- we will discuss those later. We first need to recognize the patterns; the recognition of the bitter root judgments and how they defile many. Then we have to confess those sinful reactions: the judgments and the wounding it caused others; then we repent and declare the desire to change: the desire to stop the negative patterns: we renounce all things not of God.

1 John 1:9
If we confess our sins, he is faithful and just to forgive us our sins, and to cleanse us from all unrighteousness
10- If we say that we have not sinned, we make him a liar, and his word is not in us.

We must also learn to reckon the old man dead with his practices, habits, and ways of being.

See Romans 6
Romans 6:6
Knowing this, that our old man is crucified with him, that the body of sin might be destroyed, that henceforth we should not serve sin.
2 Corinthians 5:17
Therefore if any man be in Christ, he is a new creature: old things

have passed away; behold, all things are become new.

We always forgive, and ask God to forgive us. It's done. Thank you Lord.

Only today a patient with multiple advanced illnesses came for a pre-operative clearance. She had already entered the final stages of kidney failure and needed a fistulae for dialysis. I had known this patient for several years. She went regularly to church and was saved. I had given her healing scriptures and had prayed with her regularly. She said, there are many people older than me in the church and they have so much better health., my husband says that I am ill because of my sins. What do you think. He is an unbeliever and never goes to church. Well, I said, that sounds like accusation so lets put that aside. I said, you know that we have talked about the cross, the blood, the body of the Lord, that one of the reasons He died was so you would be healed, but it is also true that there might be blockages to healing. Would you like us to explore that? She agreed.

The first thing I asked her is have you forgiven your father? She said, no, and I won't forgive him. I said, God loves you and He forgave you and He wants you to forgive him. What did he do to you. She said, really nothing but I never liked him. He was a minister but I saw him hit my mother a couple of times. I will not forgive him. We talked more about it, even that her illness could well be related to an open demonic door of unforgiveness. I told her that I would continue to pray with her, but that she needed to ask the Lord to help her forgive her father. One of the illnesses that she had was multiple myeloma which is a malignant proliferation of plasma cells derived from a single clone of B lymphocytes.

There is a loss of control of the production of a specific line of antibody secreting plasma cells. You can get bone involvement, pain, fractures, increased calcium, renal failure, anemia, infections, bleeding, neuralgic symptoms, mass lesions etc.

Today I saw another patient with very advanced and disseminated multiple myeloma. He had intractable unforgiveness issues from way back in the Second World War. It was very hard to pray due to other religion issues, unbelief, unforgiveness, etc.

I began to remember other patients with multiple myeloma and unforgiveness. As a physician I want to understand the mechanisms of disease and also as a prayer minister. There might be a very important relationship between multiple myeloma and unforgiveness. Sometimes we receive keys to healing and we have to follow through.

Today a man was rapidly healed from a painful mass in his neck, and a catholic charismatic lady got rid of her walker when her end stage knees were totally healed. The charismatic lady rested in the spirit while sitting in my office and eventually I had to get her out of her deep Holy Spirit bliss. I thought, wouldn't it be wonderful to have a room filled with holy stretchers full of patients slained in the spirit and saints just soaking them in silent prayers. This is the new office coming soon. Get ready for exponential increases in healings. Thank you Lord.

Shame: A painful emotion, sense of guilt, embarrassment, unworthiness, disgrace, condemnation, dishonor, disappointment, deep seeded hurt, heaviness in the heart.

Core: Deformed, flawed, something wrong with me, unlovable, unworthy, ugly, deficient, inferior, fear of self exposure, a core identity.

All evil began when we rebelled, disobeyed, and fell. We had everything going for us.

Genesis 1
27- God created us in his own image.
28- God blessed us and said be fruitful, and multiply, and replenish the earth, and subdue it, and have dominion.
31- And God saw everything that he had made, and behold, it was very good.

Genesis 2
15- And the Lord God took the man and put him into the Garden of Eden to dress it and to keep it.
16- And the Lord God commanded the man saying, Of every tree of the garden thou mayest freely eat
17- But of the tree of the knowledge of good and evil thou shall not eat of it: for in the day that thou eatest thereof thou shalt

surely die.

25- And they were both naked, the man and his wife, and were not ashamed.

Genesis 3 :(The Temptation And The Fall)
Ye shall be as Gods, knowing good and evil.
They ate of what was forbidden.

When the Lord came calling for his children Adam said
10- I heard the voice in the garden, and I was afraid, because I was naked; and I hid myself.

So we see the birth of shame right at the beginning.

Out of pride, arrogance, disobedience, rebellion, stubbornness, idolatry, lust, deception, temptation won. Sin was born. What were our parents feeling when they were naked and hiding: shame!

Soon came everything else.

Death: the wages of sin is death, a death which is a separation from God. Sorrows, pains, curses, rejection, abandonment, self pity, self hate, bitterness. Maybe anger towards God. Cain the first offspring, had probably all the above plus envy, jealousy, rage… he killed his brother Abel.

There is nothing that we can do to heal ourselves.

Acts 4:12
Neither is there salvation in any other: for there is none other name under heaven given among men whereby we must be saved-healed.

Ephesians 2:8
For by grace are you saved through faith; and that not of yourselves: it is the gift of God.
Sozo Salvation- complete salvation and healing has been accomplished at the cross.

Matthew 18:11
The son of man is come to save that which was lost.

1 John 3:8
For this reason was the Son of God manifested, that he might destroy the works of the devil.
We have to appropriate the healing done at the cross.

Philippians 2:12b
Work out your own salvation with fear and trembling.

Matthew 11:12
The violent take the kingdom by force.

All has been done at the cross, learn Isaiah 53:4-5.

The deceiver has planted seeds in us, seeds that threaten our identity, purpose, destiny and blessings. Seeds of deception.

Revelations 12:9
The great dragon, the old serpent, called the devil, and Satan, which deceiveth the whole world.

John 10:10
The thief cometh not, but for to steal, and to kill, and to destroy.
He wants to take away our inheritance.

John 8:44b: the devil is a liar and the father of lies.

The devil wants to stop the manifest presence of God in us, the power of the Holy Ghost. Antichrist means anti-anointing. He wants to steal our anointing. We have to go deep within us into the place of the stranglehold. The place of the deepest hurt, the place of the deepest shame. We have to recognize the false self-the old man-the false identity. It thrives in ungodly beliefs. Through lies it has formed alliances with evil.

through:
generational curses
sins
emotional wounding
inner vows
ungodly beliefs
demonization
soul ties
A stronghold can be created.

Strongholds:
The American heritage dictionary defines strongholds as:
a fortified place or fortress
a place of survival or refuge
a hiding place
An area dominated or occupied by a special group or
distinguished by a special quality.

We will now look at some scriptures that relate to strongholds.

Proverbs 21:22 (A.B)
A wise man scales the city walls of the mighty and brings down
the stronghold in which they trust.

Amos 5:9 (A.B)
The Lord is His name who causes sudden destruction to flash
forth upon the strong so that destruction comes upon the fortress.

Jeremiah 1:10 (A.B)
See, I have this day appointed you to the oversight of the nations
and of the kingdoms to root out and pull down, to destroy and to
overthrow, to build and to plant.

Jeremiah 23:29 (A.B)
Is not My word like fire [that consumes all that cannot endure the
test]? Says the Lord, and like a hammer that breaks in pieces the

rock [of most stubborn resistance]?

Jeremiah 51:51
We are confounded, because we have heard reproach: shame hath covered our faces: for strangers are come into the sanctuaries of the Lord's house.

Jeremiah 51:53 (A.B)
Though Babylon should mount up to heaven, and though she should fortify her strong height (her lofty stronghold), yet destroyers would come upon her from Me, says the Lord.

Isaiah 25:12 (A.B)
And the high fortification of your walls [the Lord] will bring down, lay low, and bring to the ground, even to the dust.

In restoring the foundations the Kylstras describe in detail the control, rebellion, rejection stronghold, and the shame, fear, control stronghold. I can definitely identify with a rejection, shame, rebellion stronghold. A stronghold is created surrounding the deepest wounds. I use the onion design of different layers.

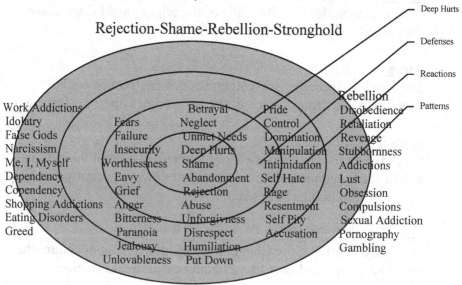

Rejection-Shame-Rebellion-Stronghold

Deep Hurts

Defenses

Reactions

Patterns

Work Addictions		Betrayal	Pride	Rebellion
Idolatry	Fears	Neglect	Control	Disobedience
False Gods	Failure	Unmet Needs	Domination	Retaliation
Narcissism	Insecurity	Deep Hurts	Manipulation	Revenge
Me, I, Myself	Worthlessness	Shame	Intimidation	Stubbornness
Dependency	Envy	Abandonment	Self Hate	Addictions
Codependency	Grief	Rejection	Rage	Lust
Shopping Addictions	Anger	Abuse	Resentment	Obsession
Eating Disorders	Bitterness	Unforgivness	Self Pity	Compulsions
Greed	Paranoia	Disrespect	Accusation	Sexual Addiction
	Jealousy	Humiliation		Pornography
	Unlovableness	Put Down		Gambling

Remember the two thieves at the cross. How much pain, shame, and abuse they must have suffered throughout their lives. There were probable generational curses, issues of hurt and abuse; they became criminals, were severely punished, and were crucified! It was a life of shame, humiliation, rebellion, pain. One said, Lord, remember me, and our crucified savior in the midst of terrible sufferings told him verily I say unto thee. Today shalt thou be with me in paradise.

Joel 2:32
Whosoever shall call on the name of the Lord shall be delivered.

Inner Healing Activation Soaking Prayer:
The following section of shame was part of a healing though the word meeting that we do at St. Louis Catholic Church in Miami. So you can use it for healing:
Today we are going to call upon the name of the Lord and we shall be delivered.
We are going to cry out to our King in repentance, humility and forgiveness.
Deliverance is now.
The knowledge of God is healing.
The revelation of God is healing.
I am the God that healeth thee Exodus 15:26.
It is finished, Jesus said at the cross.
On the cross He bore our shame.
By His wounds we were healed.

Today with fear, humility, trembling, and violence we are going to appropriate our total salvation; what our Lord Jesus accomplished at the cross.
Jesus invites us into the depth of the spirit.

2 Chronicles 16:9
For the eyes of the LORD run to and fro throughout the whole Earth, to shew himself strong in the behalf of *them* whose heart *is* perfect toward him.

Move into the Presence of the Lord

Here we began inner healing activation with soaking music while I slowly prayed the following:

Expose your wounds to the Lord.
Uncover yourselves.
Be open, naked, vulnerable, broken, and frail, Psalm 39.
Do not hide.
Move into the deep.
Psalm 42:7 Deep calleth unto deep.
Let the love of the Father do a mighty cleansing.
Let the old heart be gone.
Receive the heart that the Lord has prepared for you since the beginning of times.
Receive the love of the Father.
Receive the Holy Ghost.
Let the Lord give you a new garment.
Come and drink you who are thirsty.
Receive sustenance from above.
Set your affections above.
Have a deep encounter with your mighty Lord.
In the presence of God you know who you are.
Your identity has been fully restored.
Your destiny and blessings are at hand-grab on, do not let go.
Receive the spirit of wisdom and revelation.
Open the eyes of the heart.
Seeds of deception be gone.
We are born again in a deeper way.
I have an encounter with my Savior.
Reality has manifested in me.
I have a new heart; new life.
I turn my life over to Him again and again.
The strangleholds have been chocked out of me.
Captivity has been taken captive, Psalm 68:18.
Freedom is in this house.

All fear is gone.
I don't need to control.
His majesty is in control.
No shame can separate us from the love of God in Christ Jesus,
Romans 8:39.

The stronghold of shame has been rooted out, Jeremiah 1:10 &
Isaiah 61:7. We have been given all power and authority over all
the power of the enemy and nothing shall hurt us, Luke 10:19.

We have now boldness to enter into the holiest by the blood of
Jesus, Hebrews 10:19.
Dance and rejoice as royal priesthood and exalt our Lord. Amen.
Inner healing prayer can be performed individually on in groups.
It is a prayer that focuses on healing of the deep wound, emotions,
and memories.
God can act anywhere, in the couch in my house, in a conference,
in my office, in the streets.
In schedule appointments for inner healing prayer we close our
eyes and ask the Lord to be with us all the way.
We ask our Father to release the Holy Spirit who knows where we
need to go. We submit, yield, and trust.
There are hidden places of wounds, abuse, hurt.
The places that need healing.
We allow the Holy Spirit to direct the process.
Many times we need to repent, forgive, and forgive ourselves.
We direct the prayee to Jesus.
He is the healer.
There can be powerful healings of old conditions and also
wonderful experiences of the glory of God, heavens, the throne,
the river of life, the lover of our soul.
I believe everybody needs this intimate relation with Jesus and the
healing that He can only bring.
I love to keep giving actual reports and testimonies.
The testimony of Jesus is the spirit prophecy.

I went in a pilgrimage to Abbotsford, Canada, to see Todd Bentley from FFM (Fresh Fire Ministries) for the power of impartation conference on November 2007. He laid hands on me and I received more power from God. I came back to Miami on Sunday evening and Tuesday at the office I saw 40 patients, more than I have ever seen in my whole life in one day. It was awesome. I fasted and the power of the Holy Ghost was unquenchable throughout the whole day. There was persistent preaching of the good news and many salvations and healings.

The office is a mission field. The Lord is pouring out His spirit over many physicians. Millions will be saved and healed at the doctor's office!

A new patient with classical **fibromyalgia** came: generalized muscle skeletal aching, stiffness and fatigue. She had pain in the neck, pain in her back, pain in her arms, and pain in her knees. She had the American college of rheumatology criteria for fibromyalgia and the 18 tender points.

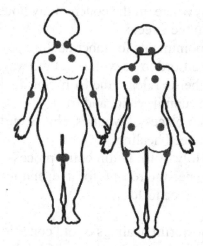

A word of knowledge came about her woundings, hurt, depression, unforgiveness and bitterness. She accepted Jesus as Lord and savior, repented from her judgments and sins. Forgave and received forgiveness. We cast out the whole spirit of fibromyalgia. She was pain free, loosed, and full of joy. The Lord has given us the key to fibromyalgia. People are getting instantly healed, delivered, free. Amen. Thank you Lord.

Pain is usually not just pain. The spirit of fibromyalgia is a spirit of pain with rigidity, stiffness, tiredness, hurt, depression, unforgiveness, constriction, self pity, bitterness. This woman received Sozo salvation in a few minutes at the office!

New birth

Emotional healing and inner healing

Physical healing

Deliverance

That Tuesday many were healed of the abortion trauma. There was repentance, forgiveness, healing, naming the babies, and seeing them with our savior. This is major inner healing! Thank you Jesus.

Going back now to inner healing and the circle representing the stronghold of shame on page 106.

After the teaching and the prayer for inner healing where we invite Jesus to heal our deepest wounds, where we use soaking prayer, and still times; if guided by the Holy Ghost we do group deliverance. We tell the prayee to declare the following commandments:

In the name of Jesus I command out of me… here, we name several spirits at a time. For example, spirit of shame, spirit of fear, control, humiliation, anger, resentment, bitterness, etc.

Next we declare:

I command them to leave me now in Jesus name.

I guide the group into taking a deep breath and cough them out in Jesus name and I keep commanding those spirits to come out.

We repeat these steps several times with groupings of spirits.

At the end we could do one on one deliverance if needed.

We command the spirits never to return and invite a complete infilling of the Holy Ghost. We train the saints to do self deliverance when necessary. I believe it is very effective.

For several years we have a regular once a month ministry in my house with Pastor Frank Marzullo Jr. in which we receive a spiritual warfare teaching and group deliverance. I believe it is wonderful. It's like getting a powerful Holy Spirit shower and major cleansing.

Many of us feel lighter, clearer, and full of joy and freedom after the meeting. We can all get contaminated and need to establish discernment and a rapid cleansing practice, Amen.

Most early mornings as part of my prayer time I lie down and seek Jesus. I have had many supernatural blessed encounters; what I rather have above all is to be able to love Him more and be able to receive more of His love, but sometimes I get a teaching and a healing and a deliverance that is not only for me but for many. The following experience I named the **Workshop of the Broken Heart** 11/25/07. The day before I had received a notice that my mortgage payments would be increased by $1,300.00 per month. Of course I freaked out but I prayed very hard and stood in peace, but as I woke up the next morning this statement spontaneously came out of me:

Lord help me search my heart.

My soul is downcast.

I then invited the Holy Spirit to guide me fully into the process; we first expose the negative and then brake it. So hang in there and there will be healings.

Psalm 3

3- But thou, O Lord, art a shield for me; my glory, and the lifter up of mine head.

4- I cried unto the Lord with my voice, and he heard me out of his holy hill.

Lord, everything is between you and me. Downcast, eyes looking down, limited eyes, eyes of the past, generational eyes, wounded eyes, grieving eyes, eyes looking back. Experiences of the past, woundings and mood disorders, the mood is held down, captive mood, mood in prison, defeat, failure, grief, despair, hopelessness.

A Spirit of Depression.

A familiar spirit of depression.

Attacks lead to depression.

The ostrich places its head in the sand: sandstorms.

All I see is sand.

Life gets colored by the color of the storm.

Ways of reacting, tendencies.

Habits of the mind, soul, emotions.

Disconnection from the truth.
Captivity, isolation, splits.
When did I learn how to split, going inside the conch?
Loneliness and depression, oppression.
Lies of the devil, failure and defeat.
Self pity, anger turned inwards.
Introversion, hostile introversion.
Open doors.
The negative comes in.
<u>Proverbs 26:28</u>
Spirit out of control- broken down walls.

The doors are broken down from the inside. Hooks from outside
now rip my heart apart.

Wounded heart from the past.
Vulnerable place. Wrong defenses.
Old ways of coping.
Old negative ways of coping.
Self defeating ways of coping.
The affected mood from the past.
What did I receive in the womb?
What did I receive later on?
Roots of despair.
Roots of existential despair.
No way out, stuck in the womb.
Negative intellect.
Negative emotions.
Walls of blindness and hopelessness.
Captivity, negativity, self hate.
Desperation, anger, resentment.
Bitterness.
Stronghold of self pity and self hate.
Pride, narcissism, issue of needs.
Self righteousness, self seeking.
Me, me, me.

I was hurt: I demand,
Sociopathic trait of drug addiction.
Self destruction.
Spirit of self destruction.
Disconnection from God. Split.
Self will run riot. Wrong will.
Soul out of control.
The spirit beckons me, the small voice.
Heartache, broken heart of life.
Life gives you a broken heart.
The legacy of life.
The legacy of the world.
The legacy of the flesh: the broken heart.
Grief, sadness, captivity.
Heart imprisoned, heart of unbelief.
Stronghold of the broken heart.
Heart of stone, heart of unbelief.
Waxed heart, blind heart and captive heart.
Split heart, wounded heart.
Undeserving heart.
Heart of shame, rejection, abandonment.
Worthlessness, rage, hate.
Heart of self destruction.
The heart of heart attack.
Anguish, depression, despair, giving up.
Heart of suicide.
A deep hopelessness in the heart.

It is in the womb that we receive such heart. It is a fetal wounding of the heart. These are old memories hidden deeply within the heart. All issues of life come from the heart. What is in the heart creates us, molds us, imprint us, and influence us throughout our lives.

Have to dig deep.
Generational healing.
Womb healing- traumas, patterns.

Who am I?
Ungodly beliefs.
Strongholds.
Insecurity, security depending on money?
I am a giver.
There is a heart of giving.
Somewhere within there is a speck from my Father.
I AM BORN AGAIN, YOU KNOW?
I have something from God.
The still small voice says you have it all my son.
All things come from the heart and you have all blessings in
  heavenly places in Christ.
HEART TRANSPLANT
Be cleansed. Be washed.
Go under the waters.
Old self dies again and again.
Hold on to the cross.
Receive the cross.
Receive the blood and the body of Jesus.
Eat the word.
He is the giver of life.
Everlasting Life, True Life, Real Life.
Not the life of the world.
The giver lives in me.
He has taken over my heart.
Old heart of unbelief.
Now new heart of giving.
Giving to me, nourishing me.
Loving me.

I have the heart of God in me. The Holy Ghost heart. There has
been an exchange. The old sickened heart went to the cross of my King. I
received the heart of God. The heart of giving. It is better to give than to
receive. He gives me first. He loved me first. I have to learn how to
receive. He made me worthy. He took away all shame. He destroyed all
strongholds. He made me new. He opened me up. He raised my head so I

could look at Him. He is my all. He is my Jesus. I cannot live one second without you Lord. He gives me, heals me, and makes me new and whole. It is all by grace. JUST SAY THE WORD AND I WILL BE HEALED. He blows healing upon me.

There is still a place in the belly. I want to hang on to old life. There is still something there for me, prestige, money, fame, recognition, women, power. I need to succeed in the world. Wrong submission of the world. The world subduing the world, cars, issues, houses, money, security, worth.

If I go, who would you be? Identity to issues of the world: recognition, pride, prestige.

Jesus you are my all. Not this thing in my belly. The last stronghold holding on. Survival mechanisms. Holding on to the reality of the world. Seeking more of the world, hands trying to grab, hold on, wont let go. My security does not come from the world. MY ROCK IS JESUS UNDER ANY CIRCUMSTANCE. I cannot use my reality to go beyond the word of God.

He who lives in me is more powerful than the one in the world. Issues of the world: money, recognition, prestige, security, peace from the world. His peace is beyond understanding. His love is everlasting. His blessings are assured. HE IS GOD. His word never fails. Love never fails. This last giant in my belly needs to go.

Fear, insecurity, grabbing on to the old.

Relationship to the world.

Dependency on the things of the world.

We live in the world but we are not of the world. I depend on you to the uttermost. I am saved to the uttermost. The flesh is always insecure. The flesh depends on old structures of the flesh. Deeply embedded in us are things that need sanctification and death on the cross. Deliverance too. A change of mind. A change of heart. Old structures in the belly go! Flesh feeding itself things of the flesh go!

Philippians 3
Philippians 4
Colossians 3

Death is receding
God is doing a deep cleansing of the belly
A change of heart brings new territories to our Lord
He is the Lord of the land
He rules in my land
I give it all to you
Take over, Lord
I yield and submit to the Holy Spirit
A mantle of His presence falls on me.
Oh Jesus I don't want to go through such wilderness.

It is a matter of idolatry, iniquity, rebellion, disobedience, stubbornness that is the inheritance of the flesh. I release the revelation that you are an heir to the throne. That you are a son of God, that you are part of Christ, that you are bringing the Kingdom on. Kingdom on! That the old has passed away, that you carry the name above all names, that all bows to the name of Jesus. That evil has no power over you, that you are blessed, that your family is blessed; that you can give. All shame is gone. Have a double portion anointing. There is a war. Kingdom of God vs. kingdom of hell, but we have already won. I have the keys from heaven, binding and loosing, opening and closing. I want the heart of giving, Lord. The heart of love and compassion.

Come, Lord Jesus. Finish the good thing that you began in me. Angels come and bring gold. I am a treasure in an earthen vessel. I have gold inside of me. I have a lot of you Lord, but I want more of you, more of you inside of me. Lord also brake all deceptions and lies of the devil. Make me really new for you. Let your kingdom come. Let your will be done on earth as it is in heaven. Let it all be new for you Lord, Amen.

Chapter Five

"Curses"

Curse:
The American heritage dictionary definition:
> a.) An appeal or prayer for evil or misfortune to befall someone or something.
> b.) The evil or misfortune that comes in or as if in response to such an appeal.
> 2. One that is accursed.
> 3. A source or cause of evil.

Curses have spiritual demonic power to damage every area of our lives. I find that many Christians are totally unaware of the curse issue.

Proverbs 29:18
Where there is no vision, the people perish.

Isaiah 5:13
Therefore my people are gone into captivity, because they have no knowledge.

Proverbs 10:21
Fools die for want of wisdom.

Hosea 4:6
My people are destroyed for lack of knowledge.

I believe that most patients I see are under generational curses, self imposed curses, and curses imposed by others.

Remember and watch carefully the tongue.

Proverbs 18:21
Death and life are in the power of the tongue.

Please, read my sister Maria Vadia's first book, "There Is Power in Your Tongue"[26].

A lot of my practice of medicine includes breaking curses and giving instruction to the patients so they stop cursing themselves; at times we have to break doctor's curses! See James 3: the tongue is a fire, a world of iniquity... it defileth the whole body, and setteth on fire the course of nature; and it is set on fire of hell..... It is an unruly evil, full of deadly poison...

I find many people that can't stop judging, gossiping, and condemning others. There is a huge area of curses in the church. This cursing can affect others but if you curse others by judging them you condemn yourself, Romans 2:1. These people need repentance, renunciation, forgiveness, inner healing, and deliverance. Satan is a legalist. I can see his huge legal department in the second heavens ready to invade our cursed areas. Unbroken curses give him rights to steal, kill, and destroy ourselves, our families, our generations, our soul, body, and spirit, our finances and properties, our churches, our ministry and anointing, our cities and nations. Unbroken curses are a persistent open door to the demonic and it creates a wall that prevents salvation, healing, deliverance, and all the blessings and provisions of the kingdom of God.

Curses began at the beginning by disobedience- the fall of man.

Genesis 2:17
But of the tree of knowledge of good and evil, thou shall not eat of it: for in the day that thou eatest thereof, thou shalt surely die.

In Genesis 3 we see the Lord cursing the serpent, the woman, man, and the ground. Sorrow began.

Genesis 3:19
In the sweat of thy face shalt thou eat bread, till thou return unto the ground; for out of it was thou taken: for dust thou art, and into dust shalt thou return.

Death began.

Genesis 3:24
Man was driven out of the garden, away from the tree of life.

Romans 6:23a
For the wages of sin is death.

Romans 5:12
Wherefore, as by one man sin entered into the world, and death
  by sin; and so death passed upon all men, for that all have sinned.

Romans 8:2
There is a law of sin and death.

Psalm 51:5
Behold I was shapen in iniquity; and in sin did my mother
conceived me.

Probably the worst effect of curses is unbelief.

John 12
39a- Therefore they could not believe.
40- He has blinded their eyes, and hardened their hearts; that they
  should not see with their eyes, not understand with their heart,
  and be converted, and I should heal them.

Matthew 13:15
For this people's heart is waxed gross, and their ears are dull of
hearing, and their eyes they have closed; lest at any time they
should see with their eyes, and hear with their ears, and should
understand with their heart, and should be converted, and I should
heal them.

My family has been intensely praying for certain persons for many years and it just seem not to touch them.

Matthew 13:4
It's like the seeds falling on the wayside and the fowls coming
and devouring them immediately.

Such unbelief is a result of curses and is a sin.

John 16
8- When the Holy Spirit comes, he will reprove the world of sin,
and of righteousness, and of judgment,
9- Of sin, because they believe not on me.

There is a leaven of hell with barriers, walls, hindrances and
blockages. We have an infestation with evil spirits of unbelief, deaf,
dumb, blind, waxed heart spirits. These are generational curses of unbelief
and fruits of unbelief.

My family in Cuba looked away from God and worshipped false
gods: science, medicine, politics, business, prestige, power, properties,
university, money. We sought God in the world. Where your heart is there
your treasure lies. All issues come from the heart. I rebelled beyond the
norm and ended addicted to drugs and sex; but even the apostles in the
boat at Mark 8 while being with Jesus seemed to have been moved to the
arena of blindness and unbelief.

Mark 8
14- Now the disciples had forgotten to take bread, neither had
they in the ship with them more than one loaf.
15- And he charged them, saying, Take heed, beware of the
leaven of the Pharisees, and of the leaven of Herod.
16- And they reasoned among themselves, saying, It is because
we have no bread.
17- And when Jesus knew it, he saith unto them, Why reason ye,
because ye have no bread? Perceive ye not yet, neither
understand? Have ye your heart yet hardened?
18- Having eyes, see ye not? And having ears, hear ye not? And

do ye not remember?

19- When I brake the five loaves among five thousand, how many baskets full of fragments took ye up? They say unto him, Twelve.

20- And when the seven among four thousand, how many baskets full of fragments took ye up? And they said, Seven.

21- And he said unto them, how is it that ye do not understand?

The father of the boy with the mute and epileptic spirit in Mark 9:24 cried out and said with tears, "Lord, I believe; help thou mine unbelief".

Mark 9:23
IF THOU CANST BELIEVE, ALL THINGS ARE POSSIBLE TO HIM THAT BELIEVETH.

The cross came. Jesus came. Holy Ghost dunamis explosive power came. We have won. Hell is a defeated foe. We have risen higher than hell and the issues of hell. The devil and the demons are under our feet. No weapon of evil can harm us. Let's practice freedom before we continue. Lets repent of unbelief in ourselves and in our generations. Lets renounce unbelief. We have been forgiven, cleansed, delivered, redeemed, justified, and sanctified. Lets command the spirits to leave us now.

In the name of Jesus I command out of me spirits of unbelief, anti-Christ, defeat, despair, deception, lies, failure, shame, weakness, self pity, python, leviathan, abbadon, jezebel, deaf, dumb, blind, waxed heart, iniquity, perversion, sewer rats, familiar spirits, poverty, sadness, passivity, sloth, disobedience, false gods, the world, reason, flesh, carnal mind. I command them to leave me now in the name of Jesus. Take a deep breath and cough them out. Command them never to return. Fill your house with the Holy Spirit and the faith of God. Now we can continue.

Curses are extremely common. Today in the office I saw many patients that were clearly affected by curses. I saw an individual with persistent pains in an area of his body. He said that he prayed but felt totally blocked and distanced from God. I asked him, who in your family followed things not of Christ Jesus. He immediately remembered that his mother was involved in spiritism (seeking knowledge from spirits and the spirits of the dead) for many years.

My patient again accepted Jesus as Lord and savior, repented and renounced all things of satan, repented for his family, and we cast out a multitude of spirits: divination spirits, necromancy spirits, blocking spirits, heaviness, black clouds, depression, infirmity, etc. He coughed for a long time. We commanded these spirits never to return and filled him with the Holy Spirit. Of course he felt better!

Another patient suffered from chronic syncopal episodes (fainting spells); this ran in his family! This is clearly strange and weird. There were no medical causes of this condition like epilepsy or arrhythmia so as far as I was concerned it was clearly spiritual. So again, there was history of worship to San Lazaro (we do not worship anybody but God-Father, Son and the Holy Ghost) and there was also history of freemasonry. Two clear causes of generational curses and demonization. He accepted Jesus as Lord and savior and repented and renounced such Santeria witchcraft and freemasonry. We declared healing of such fainting spells and commanded the spirit of syncope to leave him in the name of Jesus.

I saw an old lady with advanced dementia: significant loss of judgment, intellect, affect, orientation, and memory. She had a history of heart disease and head trauma. She seemed old, tired and depressed. She accepted Jesus as Lord and savior and suddenly she cried out: would He forgive my abortions. We did a prayer of forgiveness and handed the babies to Jesus and the Lord's forgiveness invaded her. Her whole complexion changed and we prayed for healing of dementia and of heart disease. We always have follow up appointments so we keep pushing for healing breakthroughs.

A new patient came and he was an active freemason. We had a lively discussion and planted seeds. Another one came with a San Lazaro chain, a Virgen de la Caridad del Cobre medallion, and the ring of the Indian. All symbols of Santeria witchcraft. He was also involved in The Caballeros De La Luz secret society- a derivative of freemasonry. We had a lively confrontation and he said I had been wondering why I wanted to get rid of all this stuff and now I am going to. He had a follow up appointment with me and I know that he will accept Jesus as Lord and savior. So again, the office is a mission field and most people I see are under curses, generational and otherwise.

In Genesis we see curses and blessings. In Genesis 6 God cursed and destroyed wickedness and violence. In Genesis 7 He blessed righteousness. In Genesis 9 God blessed Noah and his sons and again He said,

Be fruitful and multiply and
Replenish the earth.

He made an everlasting covenant that the rainbow reminds us of. In Genesis 12:2-3 we see blessings and curses. We have a major problem if we curse Israel! We receive God's blessings if we bless Israel.

Genesis 13:2
Abraham was very rich.

Genesis 14
18- And Melchizedek King of Salem brought forth bread and wine: and he was the priest of the most high God.
19- And he blessed him, and said, Blessed be Abram of the most high God, possessor of heaven and earth.

Genesis 15
1- After these things the word of the Lord came unto Abram in a vision, saying, Fear not, Abram: I am thy shield, and thy exceeding great reward.
6- And he believed in the Lord; and he counted it to him for righteousness.
18- In the same day the Lord made a covenant with Abram, saying, unto thy seed have I given this land, from the river of Egypt unto the great river, the river Euphrates.

Genesis 17:7
And I will establish my covenant between me and thee and thy seed after thee in their generations for an everlasting covenant, to be a God unto thee, and to thy seed after thee.

Genesis 20:17
So Abraham prayed unto God: and God healed Abimelech, and
his wife, and his maidservants; and they bare children.

Genesis 22
14- And Abraham called the name of that place Jehovahjireh: as it
is said to this day, In the mount of the Lord it shall be seen.
(Provided)
15- And the angel of the Lord called unto Abraham out of heaven
the second time.
16- And said, By myself I have sworn, saith the Lord, for because
 thou hast done this thing, and hast not withheld thy son, thine
only son:
17- That in blessing I will bless thee, and in multiplying I will
 multiply thy seed, as the stars of heaven, and as the sand which is
upon the sea shore; and thy seed shall possess the gate of his
enemies;
18- And in thy seed shall all the nations of the Earth be blessed;
because thou hast obeyed my voice.

Genesis 24:1
And Abraham was old, and well stricken in age: and the Lord had
blessed Abraham in all things.

Genesis 26:
1- And there was a famine in the land, beside the first famine that
was in the days of Abraham. And Isaac went unto Abimelech
 king of the Philistines unto Gerar.
2- And the Lord appeared unto him, and said, Go not down into
 Egypt; dwell in the land which I shall tell thee of:
3- Sojourn in this land, and I will be with thee, and will bless
thee; for unto thee, and unto thy seed, I will give all these
countries, and I will perform the oath which I sware unto
Abraham thy father;
4- And I will make thy seed to multiply as the stars of heaven,
 and I will give unto thy seed all these countries; and in thy seed

shall all the nations of the earth be blessed;

5- Because that Abraham obeyed my voice, and kept my charge, my commandments, my statutes, and my laws.

12- Then Isaac sowed in that land, and received in the same year an hundredfold: and the Lord blessed him.

18- And Isaac digged again the wells...

24- And the Lord appeared unto him the same night, and said, I am the God of Abraham thy father; fear not, for I am with thee, and will bless thee, and multiply thy seed for my servant Abraham's sake.

In Exodus 15 God manifests one of His names and character-Jehova Rapha.

V26- The Lord that healeth thee.

We are saved by grace through faith... The gift of God, but there are conditions even repentance, the prayer of salvation, the changing of directions, sanctification etc.

The Christian life is by grace but we have to fight for salvation with fear and trembling. We cannot be ignorant of the wiles and legalities of Satan. It is a progressive conquering of inner and outer lands. Here we are investigating curses, so we can break them and move into our inheritance- The blessings of God. 3 John 1:2.

Galatians 3:14
We have now the blessing of Abraham through our Lord Jesus Christ.

Through the cross we are into the new covenant. Hebrews 9:15.

He has redeemed us from the curse of the law, being made a curse for us; for it is written, cursed is everyone that hangeth on a tree Galatians 3:13.

We who have accepted Jesus as Lord and savior are under the law of the Spirit of life. Romans 8:2.

We have to totally close the door of curses and in victory declare Proverbs 26:2:

The curse causeless shall not come.

Deuteronomy clearly discurses blessings, curses, obedience and disobedience.

Deuteronomy 1 (N.I.V)

8- See, I have given you this land. Go in and take possession of the land that the Lord swore he would give to your fathers- to Abraham, Isaac and Jacob- and to their descendants after them.

30- (N.I.V) - The Lord your God, who is going before you, will fight for you...

See Deuteronomy 5 (N.I.V): The Ten Commandments.

7- You shall have no other God before me.

16- honor you father and mother.

18- you shall not commit adultery.

See all the commandments.

29- Oh, that their hearts should be inclined to fear me and keep all my commandments always, so that it might go well with them and their children forever!

Deuteronomy 7 (N.I.V)

1- When the Lord your God brings you into the land you are entering to possess and drives out before you many nations-the Hittites, Girgashites, Amorites, Canaanites, Perizzites, Hivites, and Jebusites, seven nations larger and stronger than you-

2- And when the Lord your God has delivered them over to you and you have defeated them, then you must destroy them totally. Make no treaty with them, and show them no mercy...

There are demonic strategies or hindrances that keep us from walking into the promised land, schemes and tactics of the devil that oppose and hinder us, that will rob us of our destiny.

Numbers 14:9 (N.I.V)

Only do not rebel against the Lord. And do not be afraid of the people of the land, because we will swallow them up. Their protection is gone, but the Lord is with us. Do not be afraid of them.

A.) The Hittites: Fear, insecurity, rejection, unworthiness. Emotional strongholds that bind us.

B.) Girgashites: Compromise, alliances with the enemy, the gray, lukewarm, no fire or passion for Christ.

C.) Amorites: Pride, disobedience, rebellion, haughtiness, exaltation, self righteousness, accusation, judgment, bitterness, and stubborn self will.

D.) Canaanites: Covetousness, materialism, sinful attachment to money, one leg in the world.

E.) Perizittes: Spirit of Babylon, immorality, lust, seduction, pride, power, greed, condemnation.

F.) Hivites: Humanism, self exaltation, kingdom of this world, narcissism.

G.) Jebuzites: Defeat, discouragement, overwhelmed, downtrodden, failure, depression, weakness, heaviness, anger, frustration, bitterness, I cant, I don't see how, it is not for me, I'll never be able to, etc.[27]

These are mind sets, wrong perspectives, ungodly believes, inner vows, unholy alliances.

Proverbs 13:12
Hope deferred makes the heart sick.

Deuteronomy 7 (N.I.V)
6- For you are a people holy to the Lord your God. The Lord your God has chosen you…, His treasured possession!
7- The Lord set his affection on you…
8- Because the Lord loved you and kept the oath he swore to your forefathers…
9- Know therefore that the Lord your God; He is the faithful God, keeping His covenant of love to a thousand generations of those who love Him and keep His commands.

Deuteronomy 11 (N.I.V)
18- Fix these words of mine in your hearts and mind; tie them as symbols on your hands and bind them on your foreheads.
19- Teach them to your children...
26- See, I am setting before you today a blessing and a curse-
27- The blessing if you obey the commands of the Lord your God that I am giving you today;
28- The curse if you disobey the commands of the Lord your God and turn from the way that I command you today by following other gods, which you have not known.

Jesus relates love to obedience.

John 14
21- He that hath my commandments, and keepeth them, he it is that loveth me...
23- If a man loves me, he will keep my words...

John 15
10- If you keep my commandments, ye shall abide in my love...
14- Ye are my friends, if ye do whatsoever I command you.

This is not a dictator. Our Lord knows what is best for us. He wants us to be under the blessings and promises of God.

Deuteronomy 13:17
God promised on an oath!

I believe that God is eager for His promises to be fulfilled. He is pushing us so we can get all of our inheritance in Christ Jesus.

Deuteronomy 20:4 (N.I.V)
For the Lord your God is the one who goes with you to fight for you against your enemies to give you victory.
But we have a problem, a key verse of what our problem is
1 Samuel 15:22-23.

And Samuel said, Hath the Lord as great delight in burnt offerings and sacrifices, as in obeying the voice of the Lord? Behold, to obey is better than sacrifice, and to hearken than the fat of rams.

23- For rebellion is as the sin of witchcraft, and stubbornness is as iniquity and idolatry. Because thou hast rejected the word of the Lord, he hath also rejected thee from being king.

1 Samuel 15 (N.I.V)

22- But Samuel replied: "Does the Lord delight in burnt offerings and sacrifices as much as in obeying the voice of the Lord? To obey is better than sacrifice, and to heed is better than the fat of rams.

23- For rebellion is like the sin of divination, and arrogance like the evil of idolatry. Because you have rejected the word of the Lord, he has rejected you as king".

Look at Deuteronomy 9 (N.I.V):

23- And when the Lord sent you out from Kadesh Barnea, he said, "Go up and take possession of the land I have given you". But you rebelled against the command of the Lord your God. You did not trust him or obey him.

24- You have been rebellious against the Lord ever since I have known you.

In Exodus 20:2 the Lord tells us that he has brought us out of the house of bondage. In the old testament that referred to Egypt, captivity, slavery. In the new testament Jesus' atonement did it for us. We have to appropriate Sozo Salvation; this includes the braking of curses and generational curses.

Galatians 3

13- Christ hath redeemed us from the curse of the law, being made a curse for us: for it is written, Cursed is every one that hangeth on a tree:

14- That the blessing of Abraham might come on the Gentiles through Jesus Christ; that we might receive the promise of the

Spirit through faith.

1 Peter 1
18- Forasmuch as ye know that ye were not redeemed with corruptible things, as silver and gold, from your vain conversation received by tradition from your fathers;
19- but with the precious blood of Christ, as of a lamb without blemish and without spot:

We cannot be ignorant of the wiles of the devil. We cannot befriend Jezebel. Many generations can be affected and curses and demoniztion can be transmitted for lack of knowledge.

Hosea 4:6
My people are destroyed for lack of knowledge: because thou hast rejected knowledge, I will also reject thee, that thou shalt be no priest to me: seeing thou hast forgotten the law of thy God, I will also forget thy children.

Exodus 20
1- And God spake all these words, saying.
2- I am the Lord thy God, which have brought thee out of the land of Egypt, out of the house of bondage.
3- Thou shalt have no other gods before me.
4- Thou shalt not make unto thee any graven image, or any likeness of any thing that is in heaven above, or that is in the earth beneath, or that is in the water under the earth:
5- Thou shalt not bow down thyself to them, nor serve them: for I the Lord thy God am a jealous God, visiting the iniquity of the fathers upon the children unto the third and fourth generation of them that hate me.
6- And showing mercy unto thousands of them that love me, and keep my commandments.

See Leviticus 26 and always remember that in breaking

generational curses we must confess and repent of our iniquity and the iniquity of our fathers! Levit 26:40. And to have a circumcised humble heart.

At the end of this study we will do a powerful prayer to break the curses of Deuteronomy 27 and 28 and claim the blessings. Always choose blessings and life Deuteronomy 30:19.

The word absolutely tells us in Exodus 20:3 you shall have no other Gods before me.

Isaiah 45:5
I am the Lord, and there is none else, there is no God beside me.

Mark 12
29- And Jesus answered him, the first of all commandments is, Hear, O Israel; The Lord our God is one Lord:
30- and thou shalt love the Lord thy God with all thy heart, and with all thy soul, and with all thy mind, and with all thy strength: this is the first commandment.
31- And the second commandment is like, namely this, thou shalt love thy neighbor as thy self. There is none other commandment greater than these.

The scriptures are absolutely clear that:
There is one God.
That all parts of the trinity are God.
God the Father.
Jesus, The Word, The Son.
The spirit of God… The Holy Ghost.
That there is only one way to God: through Jesus Christ.

Since the beginning of Christianity there have been many movements attempting to change this reality. For example Arius denied that Jesus was God or coeternal with the Father. Today, the Jehova's witnesses believe that there is a one person God called Jehova. No trinity. Jesus is the first thing Jehova created.

The New Age movement is a demonically contaminated mixed

system of believes and practices that deny Jesus as the one True God. It is a spiritual smorgasbord where you choose whatsoever you like and may do whatsoever you like. One leader I met said that it believed in serial monogamy. This person was going through its six marriage; another leader I met related to sex as organic, giving him permission to get involved with whomever felt right; of course there were many hurt feelings and problems.

My own inner guides encouraged adultery! Only Jesus and the Holy Spirit took me out and away from such deception and bondage. Other religions have their own concepts of God. The Buddha himself did not believe in the existence of God. Islam believes that Jesus was another teacher. Mormonism even believes that God the Father was once a man. Scientology rarely mentions Jesus. In Christian Science Jesus was no the Christ. In Unity, Jesus was, but a man etc, etc, etc.

These are all antichrist systems and causes of curses, generational curses and demonization, and blockages to healing. So we have to be very clear, be filled with the Holy Spirit and know our scriptures because part of our ministry is bringing the lost into salvation.

Acts 4:12
Neither is there salvation in any other: for there is none other name under heaven given among men, whereby we must be saved.

John 3
16- For God so loved the world, that he gave his only begotten Son, that whosoever believeth in him should not perish, but have everlasting life
17- For God sent not his Son into the world to condemn the world; but that the world through him might be saved.

John 1
1- In the beginning was the Word, and the Word was with God, and the Word was God.
2- The same was in the beginning with God.
3- All things were made by him; and without him was not

anything made that was made.

4- In him was life; and the life was the light of men.

5- And the light shineth in darkness; and the darkness comprehended it not.

6- There was a man sent from God, whose name was John.

7- The same came for a witness, to bear witness of the Light, that all men through him might believe.

8- He was not that Light, but was sent to bear witness of that Light.

9- That was the true Light, which lighteth every man that cometh into the world.

10- He was in the world, and the world was made by him, and the world knew him not.

11- He came unto his own, and his own received him not.

12- But as many as received him, to them gave he power to become the sons of God, even to them that believe on his name.

13- Which were born, not of blood, nor of the will of the flesh, nor of the will of man, but of God.

14- And the Word was made flesh, and dwelt among us, (and we beheld his glory, the glory as of the only begotten of the Father,) full of grace and truth.

John 14:6

Jesus saith unto him, I am the way, the truth, and the life: no man cometh unto the Father, but by me.

Colossians 2:9

For in him dwelleth all the fulness of the Godhead bodily.

Everything that is not the gospel of Christ-Romans 1:16 the power of God unto salvation- is false and counterfeit. It can never lead to salvation, true healing, deliverance, eternal life. It always leads to deception, bondage, captivity, sin and death, and it is transmitted to your children.

Right at the beginning our forefathers sought knowledge and power from the wrong source: this is the occult. We know the consequences. We have been in war since then.

Ephesians 6:12
For we wrestle not against flesh and blood, but against
principalities, against powers, against the rulers of the darkness of
this world, against spiritual wickedness in high places.

A synonym for the kingdom of darkness is the kingdom of
deception.

2 Corinthians 4
3- But if our gospel be hid, it is hid to them that are lost
4- In whom the god of this world hath blinded the minds of them
which believe not, lest the light of the glorious gospel of Christ,
who is the image of God, should shine unto them.

John 8:44
Ye are of your father the devil, and the lusts of your father ye will
do. He was a murderer from the beginning, and abode not in the truth,
because there is no truth in him. When he speaketh a lie, he speaketh of
his own: for he is a liar, and the father of it.

Satan can even manifest as an angel of light 2 Corinthians 11:14.

Millions are sucked into the beautiful side of evil. In my search for
God I was sucked into the beautiful side of evil. I lived in bondage, sin,
and captivity for dozens of years searching for God. We do have the
victory in Jesus Christ our savior. All occult activities are sin and bring
curses, demonization, and blockages to salvation and healing to ourselves
and our families for many generations. The list of occultic things is
overwhelming. We will discuss a few areas.
I know that some readers will be surprised and might even get
angry and reject this teaching especially if you are involved in such
activities. One reason that we don't run to Jesus and abandon our old life
is that we want to remain in sin and often it is sexual sin.
There is a relationship between the occult and sexual sin. We will

later briefly touch on that area. What we will be discussing now are **causes of curses**, causes of generational curses, open doors to the demonic, and blockages to healing.

The Occult[28]

A. Divination:

The knowledge from forbidden sources, foretelling, fortunetelling, revealing occult knowledge.
Deuteronomy 18:9-14.
Isaiah 47:9-15.
Acts 16:16.

Clearly detestable, forbidden, demonic practices: an abomination to the Lord: fortunetelling, psychics, palm reading, crystal ball, tea leaves, tarot cards, Ouija board, mediums, numerology, channeling, automatic writing, water witching, astrology, clairaudience, clairvoyance, pendulum, iridology, kabala, mind reading, omens, séances, telepathy, the 1 ching, tunes, trance, spirit guides, crystal gazing, horoscope, zodiac, books about it, objects, etc.

B. Spiritism:

Seeking knowledge through communication with the dead (necromancy) or other spirit beings, familiar spirits.
1 Samuel 28:7, 2 Kings 21:6, Isaiah 8:19, Leviticus 20:27, Leviticus 19:31, Leviticus 20:6.

Séances in which a demon, a familiar spirit, mimics a deceased family member and speaks through the psychic.
Communication with "ascended masters".
Communication with spirits through drugs.

Many of the systems of the occult, cults, secret societies, and other religions as we will see include elaborate and vast ways of obtaining knowledge from forbidden sources, seeking contact with forbidden spiritual realms, seeking power from forbidden spiritual sources.

C. Witchcraft, Magic, Sorcery:

The power branch of the occult. We see here evil ungodly agendas of power, control, domination, manipulation, intimidation. A familiar spirit of witchcraft can be transferred through the generations and a member of the family who never practiced any occultic ways can be affected by severe issues of control, power, manipulation, domination, intimidation, bitterness, judgementalism, etc. At times we can even see a prophet or prophetess in the church affected by a familiar jezebellic spirit causing trouble everywhere, 1 Samuel 15:23, 2Kings 9:22, 1 Chronicles 10:13, Micah 5:12, 2 Chronicles 33:6.

Casting spells, dungeons and dragons, black magic, white magic, psychic healings, new age healings, charms, amulets, talisman, fetishes, chakras, kundalini. All these practices are related to the kingdom of darkness-Satan's kingdom- and the activities of demons.

There are obvious levels of demonization for example: someone who once unknowingly played the Ouija board and has been mildly to moderately affected needs to receive Christ, repent, renounce, and break any curse and cast out any afflicting demon, this can be relatively easy.

The other extreme would be a Satanist, one who has made a blood pact and offered his life to Satan and has been involved in abominable practices including murder etc; that, we rarely see but the deliverance can be a prolonged and even violent process. Satanic ritual abuse victims with multiple personality disorder usually require long term healing and deliverance with trained and experienced practitioners.

Here in Miami we often see witchcraft Santeria cults relatively common in the Cuban population. Santeria is a religion from Africa brought to the new world with the slaves. There is a relation, communication, and worship of deities. In an effort to hide their practices from the Spaniards there was an identification of their deities with the saints of the Catholic Church. This is called syncretism. The deities worshiped in Santeria have been identified with the catholic saints. Santeria is a primitive religion with magic, rituals and ceremonies. There is idolatry, there are deities or orishas, there is idol worship, there are priests of Santeria, there are supernatural forces, there are curses, hexes, spells, influence, domination of others, there are all kinds of offerings to the deities and animal sacrifices, there are sacred herbs, stones, seashells, water, coconuts, there are systems of divination, spiritism, magic, sorcery, witchcraft, necromancy, counterfeit healings, solutions of problems, (obtaining ones desire by selling your soul to the devil), initiations, drums, spirit possession which is demon possession, counterfeit prophetic words: words from demons.

An extreme in Santeria is certain paleros that consciously work with the devil and multiple evil spirits of the dead etc. This is the extreme of the occult in Santeria and can progress to devil worship, Satanism, satanic ritual abuse, human sacrifices, eating and drinking human flesh, curses, sexual orgies, murder, etc. This is beyond the scope of this book.

The major orisha- Catholic syncretisms are:
    Eleggua- Saint Anthony
    Orunmila- Saint Francis of Assisi
    Obatala- Our Lady of Mercy
    Chango- Santa Barbara
    Oggun- Saint Peter
    Ochosi- Saint Norbert
    Aganyu- Saint Christopher
    Babalu Aye- Saint Lazarus
    Yemaya- Our Lady of Regla
    Oshun- Our Lady of Charity
    Oya- Our Lady of Candelaria

A few times a week I see a patient that is involved in Santeria, has been involved in Santeria, or someone in prior generations has been involved in Santeria. Invariably there are curses, generational curses, and demonization producing all kinds of afflictions in the body, soul, mind, emotions, finances, physical and mental disorders, immorality, abortions, barrenness, suicide, divorces, accidents, untimely deaths etc.

A new patient was brought to me in a stretcher. He had been listless and bedridden for months. I felt a lot of oppression and bound all blocking demons. He then shared his story. Major involvement in Santeria witchcraft, ceremonies, reading the shells, animal sacrifice, spirit possession, prophetic utterances (this is counterfeit prophesying through a familiar spirit or other spirit), casting spells, witchcraft practices to obtain women, make money, curse others, etc.

He eventually attempted suicide and suffered brain damage. He carried a diagnosis of schizophrenia and manic depressive disorder. He had multiple illnesses including heart disease, diabetes, etc. His wife had a terminal illness and his only son died a terrible untimely death.

The grace and mercy of Jesus was there in our meeting. He repented of his sins and accepted Jesus as Lord and savior. Whatever was holding him down in bed was cast out and he got out of bed and walked normally. His mind and thinking processes began to improve dramatically. The Lord delivered him of major witchcraft demons. We called upon the infilling of the Holy Spirit. He felt the presence of God and turned his life around.

I gave him a bible and trained him in spiritual warfare. He memorized several vital verses and came twice a week to the office for prayer and to continue in his Christian development. He became very clear about the demonic voices "that want to return". He was also clear about his power and authority in Christ Jesus. He learned to pray and decree and "the demons always have to go". Thank you, Lord.

Even today a Jewish man came to see me with many severe medical problems. I felt, discerned that he had been in occult activities in the past. He admitted that when he was in Brazil he had been involved in Condomble. This is a spiritual tradition similar to Cuban's Santeria. They worship saints that hide the African deities (syncretism). They have initiations, rituals, animal sacrifices, drinking of blood, spirit possession, etc. Other occultic primitive religions in the Brazilian area are Macumba, Umbanda, and Quimbanda that has black magic components.

All of these practices are all in the realm of darkness and major causes of demonizations, curses, generational curses, and blockages to salvation and healing. My patient dates the beginnings of his progressive illness to the time when he became involved in Condomble. I proclaimed the messiah, showed him Isaiah 53, discussed curses, blessing and demonization, salvation, healing and deliverance, but he said that he was not ready yet to accept Jesus as his savior.

My experience is that many of the seeds that we plant give good fruit. I expect this man to return, receive Jesus, and be healed, Amen.

Voodoo is also very common in Miami due to the Haitian

population. This is another African religion coming to the Caribbean. Some of the Haitian population that I see have been affected by generational curses from the practice of Voodoo by a previous family member. We always need to investigate the generational lines to brake and stop the curse line.

There is an epidemic with demonic infestations related to the occult, other religions, secret societies, spirits of unbelief, and the spirit of the world. My first patient today had chronic abdominal pain that I sensed was occultic abdominal pain; of course as a physician I must rule out every cause of abdominal pain. The patient had a complete work-up of her abdominal pain, including physical exam, blood test, x-rays, cat scans, endoscopies, etc. It is hard to explain how I perceive occultic abdominal pain; it is nonspecific, noncharacterizable, intermittent, chronic.

The patient has an affect that is captive and tied to the pain and the Holy Ghost sounds the alarm! It is discernment of spirits, one of the gifts of the Holy Ghost.

I have to emphasize that I have a good relationship with most of my patient and I ask them with respect and boundaries if they would like to investigate spiritual issues related to their illnesses. Don't just barge in and invade their integrity. This is the doctor's office and we are under the established medical authorities. The office is not a church. Maybe my office is now half church. The thing is that my patients know that I want the best for them and we have achieved a place of trust. Thank you, Holy Ghost. So with my patient with "occultic abdominal pain" we drew a family tree.

1.) Grandfather:freemason- Secret society
2.) Mother- Involved in spiritism, seeking knowledge from forbidden spiritual realms.
3.) Patient had cards read- Divination

We discovered causes of curses and demonization that I believe were causing her abdominal pains. ALWAYS DO A FAMILY TREE.

Plan:

Accept Jesus as Lord and savior

Repent and renounce your sin and the sin of the antecessors.

Cast out the evil spirits involved; freemason, spiritism, divination, cards, abdominal pains.

Fill the patient up with the presence of God.

Command those spirits never to return.

Train in keeping healing, freedom, deliverance.

Learn the word, etc.

The second patient today came because of bleeding in the urine. This had been a recurrent problem since he had radiation therapy for the treatment of prostate cancer. He was a free of cancer but his bladder had been hurt from the radiation and he bled at times. There seemed to be a major spiritual block in understanding salvation, like the preaching could not reach him .I asked him if there was a history of freemasonry in his family. He had been a freemason himself. I saw the hoodwink and bound the spirit of hoodwink that was keeping him blind, deaf, and unable to receive the word of God. We both had been feeling blocked and hopeless but after binding the demon a spiritual avenue opened. He became eager in accepting Jesus as Lord and savior and he did and we commanded total healing of his bladder. I had run out of bibles and promised him a bible. He eagerly said, "When, when, can I pick it up". There were other female patients in the nurse's station that were exalting the word of God. Jesus in the office! Thank you, Lord.

A third patient today suffered from chronic depression. He is a very nice man that everybody likes. He felt good about himself as "I never harm anybody and I do good to people". I preached salvation to him and again there was something blocking the word. He denied any history of occultism, occult societies, etc. He said that his antecessors had been good churchgoers, but that he was not too involved. I asked him that if he would die where would he go. He said I have my coffin and my lot in the cemetery all paid for. He had no vision of a spiritual world. There was something dead in him. Somehow he became willing to accept Jesus as Lord and savior, and receive eternal life, but lo and behold he could not say the word Jesus; his tongue became totally blocked.

I had a word of knowledge: Spirit of the world. I bound the spirit of the world in the name of Jesus and it was a struggle. I kept binding and loosing his tongue. We had to fight for each word in the sinner's prayer. Eventually we could go through the whole salvation prayer and there was an obvious change in him. He was now alive, born again, depression was gone. Thank you, Lord.

Today there were also regular physical healings of knee pain, back pains, sciatic pains, but the last patient of the day was a young woman with an apparently advanced incurable immunologic illness; when I mentioned that there could be healing, there was an immediate reaction from a defiant, rebellious, hostile spirit.

The patient declared that she did not believe in any biblical God but that she had her own believes in energetically and cosmic forces, mental powers, etc. So I said, ok, and I took her history that included involvement in primitive spiritual practices of the Santeria witchcraft kind. I knew then the spirits that were causing her illness, but there was a major demonic wall to even listen about Jesus. I gave her my story of searching everywhere for God until He rescued me and she showed a bit of interest in that. I referred her to a specialist and gave her my card with my number. I told her to call me if she needed help and also if she would become interested in the healing Jesus does. We parted friends. Thank you Lord, that was the best I could do with that patient.

D. Secret Societies:

Freemasonry- also very common in my office. It seems that in Cuba the patriots who fought against the Spaniards turned to freemasonry as the church sided with the Spanish army. I also believe that it is common in Europe, and in North and South America. I don't believe freemasons accept Jesus as Lord and savior, God Himself, the Word and the Word made flesh and that only through the cross, death and resurrection of our Lord, salvation can be achieved by grace through faith. Freemasons refer to God as the Great Architect of the Universe. Freemasons in their private devotions can pray to whomever they want to. What is taught in higher degrees of masonry has little to do with the God of the Bible.

The freemason's name of God is Jah-bul-on. It seems this refers to Yahweh, Baal-On. Remember Baal, the demonic deity of the Old Testament! This is all already demonic and Anti-Christ, but then there are also major and extensive vows and oaths: CURSES! involving the freemasons and their families; and remember, the scriptures clearly state that this unbelief in the True God and idolatry to anything else brings curses and demonization for several generations.

In my experience an area affected by the freemason's curses is the head: pride, self righteousness, rigidity, inflation, control, domination, power, manipulation, intimidation, anger, bitterness, rage, mood disorders, head trauma, strokes, brain tumors, brain hemorrhages, spiritual blindness due to initiations into darkness and the spirit of the hoodwink. It is reported that as a consequence of the freemason demonization through the generations there is spiritual blindness and searching through false pathways: cults, other religions, new age, psycho spiritual psychologies, etc.

My grandfather was a major freemason and hell was released into our whole family. I did not learn about freemasonry, but I did go in a major search for God in many wrong places, and when I obtained an extensive prayer of renunciation from Selwyn Stevens (http://www.jubilee.org.nz - you can download the prayer[29]), I found that deep spiritual forces related to freemasonry were active in me when I wrote a book by the title "Seeds of Enlightenment- Death, Rebirth, and Transformation through Imagery". I believe the curses of freemasonry can affect the spirit, soul and body: divorces and addictions are common as well as many other illnesses and infirmities.

> Repent for yourselves and for the previous generations.
> Renounce freemasonry: all vows and initiations curses.
> Declare the forgiveness of the cross.
> Break the freemasonry curse over all the family.
> Cast out freemason demons.
> Declare healing of whatever area of your life has been affected.
> Command those demons never to return.
> Be infilled by the Holy Ghost and begin living the true Christian way.

Here we are giving you examples of common practices under each heading. There are whole books and extensive literature on each subject.

E. Other Religions

You can only receive salvation and relationship to the True God through Jesus Christ our Lord and savior. Any involvement with another religion is sin and brings curses and demonization to the person and its family for many generations. This is not about how good anyone can be, or how well a teacher speaks of God, or how gentle someone appears, etc. the kingdom of darkness is the kingdom of deception.

A case in point is Tibetan Buddhism. The Dali Lama "a reincarnation" of another lama, which constantly teaches about compassion and many good things. About twenty years ago, I participated in the Kalachakra Tantra initiation in Los Angeles. We were supposed to merge with 720 deities! As I was actively involved in the practice with other participants, a beautiful woman and me became suddenly caught in obsessive lust and loss of control, and ended up having sexual intercourse. I believe that we were very influenced by these so called deities. These so called deities are evil spirits bent on deception, sin, destruction and death.

A few months ago I read in the newspaper about the Oracle of the Dali Lama; a seer involved in divination and other practices. The newspaper mentioned that the oracle (the monk) gets possessed by a spirit and can see and predict things and can even communicate with the dead. These are the old practices that were an abomination to God: divination, familiar spirits, necromancy, obtaining knowledge and power from forbidden sources, and spirit possession. It is witchcraft, divination, sorcery, etc.

I needed repentance, renunciation, forgiveness and deliverance. Recently I read about a group of Christian warriors that fight the release of the 720 deities of the Kalachakra Tantra over territories whenever that practice is performed. Any other religion, alternate spirituality, cult is not of the kingdom of the True God. This includes the Jehovah's witness, Mormonism, Christian science, unity, scientology, Wicca, new age, Islam, Hinduism, Buddhism, transcendental meditation, anthroposophical society, Edgar Cayce, Carlos Castaneda, a course in miracles, Gurdjieff, kabbalah, guruship, rebirthing, reiki, reincarnation, Silva mind control, meditation, yoga, martial arts, (when the wrong spirits and religions get involved,) chakras and kundalini practices, taoism, taichi and qigong, theosophy, transpersonal and psychospiritual psychologies, psychologies with idolatries to persons or teachings, etc.

Other causes of curses, generational curses, and blockages to healings are contact with cursed objects, intimate relationship with a demonized person, protracted sinful activities, drug and alcohol addictions, satanic music, the tongue out of control, hurt, abuse, rejection, unforgivness, bitterness, persistent anger, pride, greed, fear, unbelief, control, ignorance, idolatry, rebellion, disobedience, robbing God of tithes, (Malachi 3:8-11,) traumas and illnesses, curses, ungodly believes, inner vows, etc.

It is very beneficial to do a family tree[30] as far back as we can, to diagram the problems affecting each person so we can pray, break the curses, and heal the sins of the generations.
Problem Areas:

Suicide, murder, accidents, abortions, miscarriages, mental illness, traumas, the occult, fornication, adultery, prostitution, homosexuality, incest, pornography, lust, addictions, soul ties, violence, abuse, prejudice, pride, greed, materialism, arrogance, hatred, unforgiveness, selfishness, judgments, control, manipulation, rebellion, idolatry, divorce, hostility, revenge, anger, depression, other religions, atheism, new age, cults, the occult, secret societies, psycho spiritual psychologies, any in utero wounding of any kind, disease, illness, infirmities.
At Christian Healing Ministries we celebrate the Holy Eucharist for the healing of the generations. It is taken from the Book of Common Prayer which is used by the Episcopal Church. As part of this celebration we renounce all occult sinful involvement and reaffirm the baptismal covenant. We receive the blood and body of Jesus and burn the generational tree declaring the healing of the generations. If you do the healing of the generation on your own or a group, fill up the form and repent for your sins and the sins of each person and renounce it, forgive each person, and call upon God's forgiveness and break each curse and sin, remember Galatians 3:13 and Romans 8:1,2.

Cast out demons if necessary by commanding them to leave in the name of Jesus and call upon blessings to the whole tree, to yourself, your partner, your family and offspring. The King did it all at the cross. This is appropriation, total salvation.

I saw a picture of the city of Havana in 1959 and it was a very beautiful city, and I thought wow, how would it had been now in 2007 if things had gone well, but things were never well. Curses progressed since the beginning. The eradication of the natives, slavery, the freemasonry of the patriots and subsequent generations, the Santeria witchcraft, the spiritism, the sexual immorality, the abortions, the prostitution, the ungodliness, the greed and materialism, the idolatry to the world. When we did not accept a boat full of Jewish people in World War 2 and sent them back to their deaths.

Curses overwhelmed my country. We were all cursed. I am in exile. I lost my land and wealth. Cuba is a devastated poor country now. What was on the way of becoming a jewel is now a landscape from hell. There is massive witchcraft; people even go from other countries to get initiated in Santeria witchcraft. There is sexual immorality and prostitution; even young adolescent girls are getting involved in prostitution.

There is massive ungodliness, and most of us just blame Fidel. Fidel is a manifestation of the generational curse from which all the Cubans need to repent, renounce, circumcise our hearts, forgive, even Fidel! Start breaking the bronze demonical geographical heavens upon the island.

It's like we think that if Fidel goes, all will be well. We are the problem that brought the curses that placed Fidel in leadership and we have not changed. So hell will continue with Fidel or without Fidel. WE NEED TO CHANGE: this is all about two kingdoms and spiritual warfare, which most people do not know anything about.

So we pray today reaffirming that Jesus is our Lord and savior and that His spirit is fully in us. We repent of massacring the natives and stealing their land. We repent of freemasonry, Santeria witchcraft and spiritism. We repent of slavery. We repent of sexual immortality, fornication, adultery, pornography, abortions, addictions, rebellion, disobedience, idolatry to the world, greed, materialism, pride, narcissism, machismo, control, manipulation, domination, fear, bitterness, resentment, revenge, conflict, strife, divisions, politics, self centeredness, self righteousness, ungodliness, unbelief.

Lord forgive all the sins and iniquity of us Cubans. Destroy all demonic strongholds over us and our island. Thank you Lord that in Leviticus 26:40-42 says, If they shall confess their iniquity, and the iniquity of their fathers, with their trespass which they trespassed against me, and that also they have walked contrary unto me;

41- And that I also have walked contrary unto them, and have brought them into the land of their enemies; if then their uncircumcised hearts be humbled, and they then accept of the punishment of their iniquity.

42- Then will I remember my covenant with Jacob, and also my covenant with Isaac, and also my covenant with Abraham will I remember; and I will remember the land.

Thank you Jesus that through the atonement you forgave us, delivered us, cleansed us, justified us, redeemed us, and sanctified us.

We break the power of the spirit of death that has taken over our island. Anti-Christ spirits, accusation spirits, communism spirits, leviathan, jezebel, abaddon, deaf, dumb, blind, waxed heart, python spirits. Cleanse our inner lands, oh Lord, cleanse our Cuba, Jesus. We break down strongholds and destroy the giants that have taken our land. We believe Lord, you walk with us. Victory is on our side, amen.

To end this chapter we will break the curses of Deuteronomy 27 and 28. My dear friend Frank Marzullo Jr, of Christian Covenant Fellowship, Inc. graciously allowed me to use the following excellent material created by his late father Frank Marzullo[31].

Breaking the Curses

I see many of God's people suffering because of curses directed against them or in their blood line. They do not know how to fight the power of these curses, or how these curses invaded their lives.

As Christians, we are in a covenant relationship with God through our covenant head, the Lord Jesus Christ. Unfortunately, most Christians don't understand what it means to be in a covenant. While we can't take the time in this short booklet to fully cover this, you should understand the basic fact that a covenant is an agreement between two parties. Your bible is the story of two covenants: the Old Covenant (or Testament) and the New Covenant (or Testament).

Marriage is a type of covenant between two equals. Two people are joined and everything each has belongs to the other. But our covenant with God is an unequal covenant, where one party- God-does it all. Even so, as in all covenants entered into around the world from the beginning of time, there are blessings decreed for observing the covenant, and curses for not doing so.

We see the Old Covenant being promised and then entered into between God and Abram in Genesis chapters 12 and 15. And in Deuteronomy we read about the blessings and curses of this Old Covenant. I believe that the curses mentioned in Deuteronomy chapters 27 and 28 cover just about all the curses that can afflict God's people and I've written this book to help you to understand more fully the source of these curses and to help in setting the captive free.

HOW DO CURSES COME UPON A PERSON?

Curses and the demons that Satan sends to implement them come into a person through the sin gate. Anytime a person does not obey the word of God, there is a curse connected to that act of rebellion. As Deuteronomy 27:26 puts it, "Cursed is the one who does not confirm all the words of this law. And all the people shall say, 'Amen.'"

Then there are sins that some do not consider to be sin. For example, anger. Some would say that anger is an emotion. Yes it is, but if a person disobeys the Word concerning anger then the sin gate is open to a curse. Ephesians 4:26-27 says, "Be angry, and do not sin. Do not let the sun go down on your wrath nor give place to the devil."

If I were to be angry with my wife over something and I go to sleep with my anger still in me, I could give a place to the devil because I disobeyed the word of God.

Another sin that is common among God's people is unforgiveness. We have been commanded to forgive even our enemies. When we do not choose to forgive, Father God will send us the tormentors. (Matt. 18:34-

35). Often, because of resentment and unforgiveness in our hearts, many of us are cursed with various infirmities.

The wearing of amulets or good-luck charms on you body, or having them in your home, also opens the door to curses:

You shall burn the carved images of their gods with fire; you shall not covet the silver or gold that is on them, nor take it for yourselves, lest you be snared by it; for it is an abomination to the Lord your God. Nor shall you bring an abomination into your house, lest you be doomed to destruction like it; but you shall utterly detest it and utterly abhor it, for it is an accursed thing. (Deuteronomy 7:25-26).

Involvement in any form of occultism is an abomination to the Lord our God. Among the dozens of practices in the occultism are:

Divination
ESP
Hypnotism
Horoscope
Levitation
Water witching
Black magic
White magic
Charms
Devil worship
Soul travel
Necromancy

Deuteronomy 18:10-13 states it very clearly:

There shall not be found among you anyone who makes his son or his daughter pass trough the fire, or one who practices witchcraft, or a soothsayer, or one who interprets omens, or a sorcerer, or one who conjures spells, or a medium, or a spiritist, or one who calls up the dead. For all who do these things are an abomination to the Lord, and because of these abominations the Lord your God drives them out from before you. You shall be blameless before the Lord your God.

We can also inherit curses in our blood line from our ancestors.

We were in our father's loins, in our grandmother's loins, in our great grandfather's loins, etc. A curse can come in as far back as ten generations: "One of illegitimate birth shall not enter the congregation of the Lord; even to the tenth generation none of his descendants shall enter the congregation of the Lord." (Deuteronomy 23:20).

We also see from Exodus 20:5 that curses can come onto the blood line because of what our forefathers did: "For I. the Lord your God, am a jealous God, visiting the iniquity of the fathers on the children to the third and fourth generations of those who hate Me."

Now we are going to cancel these curses and command the demons that operate in us because of them to leave in the name of Jesus.

HOW DO DEMONS SPIRITS COME OUT?

As always, we get the answers to our questions from the Word of God. In Mark 1:23-26, we read how Jesus cast out demons:

Now there was a man in their synagogue with an unclean spirit. And he cried out, saying, "Let us alone! What have we to do with You, Jesus of Nazareth? Did You come to destroy us? I know who You are-the Holy One of God!" But Jesus rebuked him, saying, "Be quiet, and come out of him!" And when the unclean spirit had convulsed him and cried out with a loud voice, he came out of him.

The bible says that the demons came out "with a loud voice." When you cry out with a loud voice, you expel a lot of breath. You cannot utter a loud voice without letting a lot of breath out of you. Try screaming without letting a lot of breath out-it is impossible.

When you command demons to come out in the name of Jesus, evil spirits often leave by you expelling your breath. In the Greek, the word for spirit and the word for breath is the same, *pneuma.* So, spirits are cast out in the name of Jesus through any means of expelling the breath, such as coughing, burping, sneezing, yawning, crying, or sighing.

We do not tolerate loud voices or screaming, however, we will command demons to come out quietly in the name of Jesus, because we have been given the authority over all the power of the enemy in Jesus' name, and nothing shall by any means hurt us. (Luke 10:19).

STEPS TO DELIVERANCE

The first step in a deliverance session, are to cover yourself and those to whom you're ministering from head to toe with the precious Blood of Jesus and to put on the full armor of God. (Eph 6:14-17).

After getting ready to do battle with the enemy, I make sure that the person or persons I am dealing with are saved, because an unsaved person will not be able to keep their deliverance. The Stronger Man, Jesus, is needed to keep the demons from coming back in even greater number. (Matt 12:43-45). So I ask everyone to repeat this prayer:

Lord Jesus Christ, I believe that You are the Son of God. You are the Messiah come in the flesh to destroy the works of the devil. You died on the cross for my sins and the third day rose again from the dead. I now confess all my sins and repent. Please forgive me and cleanse me in Your precious Blood. I believe that Your Blood cleanses me from all sins. Come into my heart, Lord Jesus, for I want to follow You from this day on.

Now we are ready to break the power of all curses, especially those mentioned in Deuteronomy 27-28, and command the demons that came into us through curses to leave in the name of Jesus.

PRAYER FOR BREAKING INHERITANCE CURSES

To begin breaking these curses, I have everyone repeat this prayer:

Thank You Jesus for dying that I might be set free. I invite You, Jesus, to be Lord of my family and especially Lord of my children. I confess that my ancestors and I have sinned and I agree that our sin is rebellion against the Living God. Forgive me for my personal sins that have influenced my children. I ask You to set my children free from any curse on their lives as a result of my sins, especially sins of sexual nature. I now bring my children to You, Lord Jesus, and I renounce the claim that Satan has put upon them whatever it is in the name of Jesus.

In the name of Jesus and by the Blood of Jesus Christ, I now nullify every curse of Deuteronomy 27 and 28 and every evil word spoken against me and my blood-line by any person living or dead. I ask You, heavenly Father, to forgive the iniquities that have been passed down from generation to generation, as far back as ten generations. I command the release of every spirit from their assignment against me and my blood-line and to leave me and my blood-line, now, in the name of Jesus.

Now I tell everyone to take a deep breath and let it out. Then I begin going through each of the curses found in these two chapters in the same manner. You, too, can use the following prayers to break the curses in your life and the lives of those in your family. However, make sure you go through all the prayers of preparation we've just given before proceeding in either self or group deliverance.

Deuteronomy 27:15
Father, I break every curse of idle words that cause generations to go after the gods of this world. I command the curse of idolatry and paganistic practices in me and my blood-line to leave in Jesus name. (Take a deep breath and let it out.)

I also command out of me and my blood-line the spirits of witchcraft, warlock, Jezebel, Ahab, domination, control and manipulation in the name of Jesus. (Take a deep breath and let it out.)

Deuteronomy 27:18
I command out of me and my blood-line the spirits of physical abuse, verbal abuse, and sexual abuse, and also the spirit that would cause me to abuse others, in the name of Jesus. (Take a

deep breath and let it out.)

Deuteronomy 27:20-25
I break the curse of lust, fantasy lust, perversion, fornication, adultery, masturbation, oral sex, sex with animals, bestiality, incest, rape, sodomy, sex with spirits, incubus, succubus, pornography, lust of the eyes, pride of life, lust of the world, abortion, prostitution, and whoredom, as far back as ten generations, and I command out all these spirits in the name of Jesus. (Take a deep breath and let it out.)

Deuteronomy 28:13
I command out of me every spirit that would make me the tail and not the head, also spirits of depression, despair, retardation, and insanity in Jesus' name. (Take a deep breath and let it out.)

Deuteronomy 28:15-17
In the name of Jesus, I break the curse of rebellion and disobedience, selfishness and greed in my blood-line. I break the curse on my possessions, my lands, and my inheritance. I break the curse of the fruit of my body, my children, my descendants, my food and storehouse. I command all these spirits and poverty to leave me in the name of Jesus. (Take a deep breath and let it out.)

Deuteronomy 28:19
I break the power of every curse put upon my traveling, my going out and my coming in, by any mode of travel and I command every spirit of accident and injury to leave in Jesus' name. (Take a deep breath and let it out.)

I claim Psalm 121:8 for my protection: "The Lord shall preserve your going out and coming in from this time forth, and even forevermore."

Deuteronomy 28:20-22
I command the spirit of confusion, the spirit of Babylon, the spirit of occultism, lusting after other gods, to leave me and my blood-

line as far back as ten generations, in Jesus' name. (Take a deep breath and let it out.)

I come against every spirit of pestilence, epidemic, infirmities, cancer, diseases, consumption, fever, inflammation, fiery heat, sword, and drought. I command them to leave me and any blood-line in Jesus' name. (Take a deep breath and let it out.)

I break the curse of the thief and liar in me and my blood-line, also the spirit of pride, haughtiness, contention, perfection, self righteousness, and all religious spirits. I command them all to leave me and my blood-line in Jesus name. (Take deep breath and let it out.)

Deuteronomy 28:23
I break the power of the spirits that cause the heavens to be bronze and the earth to be iron, that does not cause my prayers to be answered. I break the power of the spirits that do not let me hear the Word of God nor do they let me prophesy or have visions to leave me in Jesus name. (Take a deep breath and let it out.

Deuteronomy 28:25
I break the curse that causes me to be stuck down before my enemies, the spirit of failure, self-hate, death, death wish, premature death, and suicide, and command these spirits out in Jesus' name. (Take a deep breath and let it out.)

Deuteronomy 28:27
I break the curse of scurvy, itch, all skin diseases, and things that will not heal, herpes, psoriasis, shingles, madness, AIDS, sexually transmitted diseases, HPV, and I command these spirits to leave me and my blood-line in the name of Jesus. (Take a deep breath and let it go.)

Deuteronomy 28:28
I break the curse of discouragement, dismay, dismay of mind and heart, mental anguish, mental torment, and every spirit under the control of Apollyon, the destroyer, and command these spirits to

leave me and my blood-line in Jesus' name. (Take a deep breath and let it go.)

Deuteronomy 28:29
I break the curse of failure, laziness, passivity, apathy, lethargy, and poverty, and command these spirits to leave me and my blood-line in Jesus' name. (Take a deep breath and let it out.)

Deuteronomy 28:30
I command the curse of divorce, division, separation in me and my blood-line to leave in Jesus name. (Take a deep breath and let it out.)

OTHER CURSES

Leviticus 20:18 says, "If a man lies with a woman during her sickness and uncovers her nakedness, he has discovered her flow, and she has uncovered the flow of her blood. Both of them shall be cut off from their people." If you have committed this sin then say, "Lord Jesus, forgive me, and I command any curse that came into me and my blood-line because of this sin to leave me now in the name of Jesus. (Take a deep breath and let it out.)

While we are commanding all these spirits out, let us add a few more. Say, "I command out of me all spirits of fear, anger, anti-Christ, addiction, tobacco, alcohol, drugs, gluttony, insecurity, rejection, doubt, and unforgiveness. I command them all out in Jesus' name." (Take a deep breath and let it out.)

BREAKING EVERY COVENANT MADE WITH SATAN

Now say, "I break every covenant and agreement that I ever made with Satan and his demons, or that was made by any of my ancestors as far back as ten generations on behalf of my blood-line. I now command the assignments put upon me and my blood-line to be canceled and all the spirits pertaining to these assignments to be out of me and my blood-line in the name of Jesus." (Take a deep breath and let it out.)

Claiming the blessings of Deuteronomy

Now we confess who we are and what we have because of our covenant relationship with God the Father through our Covenant Head, our Lord, Jesus Christ. For our obedience, these are the promises God makes to us in verses 1-13 of chapter 28:

In the name of Jesus Christ, I declare upon me the following blessings which shall overtake me because I obey the voice of the Lord, my God:

Vs. 1-2- I will diligently harken to the voice of the Lord my God to keep all His commandments so that His blessings will overtake me wherever I will be:

Vs. 4-5- That the fruit of my body, my children, and the works of my hand will be blessed. That I will always be able to afford my groceries.

Vs. 6-7- That I will be blessed in my travels. That my enemies, spiritual or physical, will flee before my face.

Vs. 10- That I will be blessed wherever I live. That I will always have His anointing upon me as I keep His commandments. That people will see God's anointing upon me and know that I am a son of God.

Vs. 12- That I will be prosperous and be able to lend to many and not be a borrower. That I will be the head and not the tail, a leader among men, acceptable to God and approved by men.

I again declare all these blessings to come upon me and overtake me because I obey the voice of the Lord, my God, in the precious name of Jesus Christ, the Son of the Living God.

Now, Father God, Lord Jesus, and Holy Spirit, I worship you. I give all that I am to You and I surrender all my life to You. Cause me to be filled with all the fruit of the Holy Spirit. Direct my pathway so that I will reach my potential and fulfill Your plan for my life. I ask this in the name of Jesus.

Holy Spirit, please come into me and take the place of all the evil spirits of curses that have been commanded out me and my blood-line, in Jesus' name.

You have now been set free from the curses and have called upon yourself the blessings of the Covenant. Remember, to keep your deliverance, there are many steps you must follow. We will discuss this in the next chapter.

Chapter Six

"DELIVERANCE"

A daily occurrence at the medical office. Jesus cast out demons mostly at the marketplace. Normal Christianity: The children's bread.

Mark 7:25-30
Mark 7:29 and he said unto her, For this saying go thy way, the devil is gone out of thy daughter.

Wow, He sends the word and the evil spirit left the Syrophenician woman's daughter.

Now days we have developed a good system of deliverance. We usually want the person to be saved: born again. We want the person to be in a Christian fellowship, to be filled with the Holy Ghost, to know the scriptures, to renounce curses, to be healed of emotions, inner vows, ungodly believes, sin life, soul ties, to close all demonic doors, to have a prayer life, and the bigger you ministry the bigger the need for intercessors.

Deliverance is really a routine regular life long Christian process. One of the definitions of the word deliver in the American heritage dictionary is: TO SET FREE FROM EVIL: deliver a captive from slavery.

Deliverance: rescue from bondage. .

The process of freeing a person from evil spirits is called deliverance.

In "primitive" Christianity: Real Christianity: (the first few hundred years), it seems everybody would go through deliverance. That routine normal practice stopped long ago, but the demons are still here with us. We all need deliverance, need to learn to keep our deliverance, and be ready to fight evil at any time.

1 Peter 5:8
Be sober, be vigilant; because your adversary the devil, as a roaring lion, walketh about, seeking whom he may devour.

<u>6 Ephesians 6:13</u>
Wherefore take unto you the whole armour of God, that ye may
be able to withstand in the evil day, and having done all, to stand.

We absolutely need the Holy Spirit and to be very comfortable in
cleansing ourselves of any contamination.

The ministry of deliverance at the medical office is most of the
time relatively easy and simple. We do not do intense prolonged warfare
there. If I discern that there would be violent, foul, nasty, defiant, resistant
spirits, I would set up appointments for the prayer room in my house or
other experienced mature ministries in Miami.

I love it when people also go to Christian Healing Ministries and
receive the four day intense healing prayer week and even better if they
continue training at levels 1, 2, and 3.

Probably some of the toughest strongholds I see are in Holy Spirit
filled, word filled, long standing Christians, that have gone through
conferences, trainings, healing ministries, etc. but there is clear double
mindedness. It is very confusing, it's like there is a place inside not ruled
by the Holy Spirit. The saint could know and decree the word of God
perfectly well and soon declare something that is not in agreement at all
with the Spirit. There could be fear, confusion, obsessions, unbelief,
shame, bitterness, and control issues. This double minded state keeps
reappearing and these are anointed people! It is baffling.

I think that there might have been an infestation by evil spirits very
early on, for example: in the womb; when the psychospiritual immune
system was not developed and this other foreign part just stuck to the
developing personality and now there is a total blindness about it-that it is
not you! There is a false identity attached to the identity, like a double,
that at times just expresses itself. Spiritually it sounds wrong and feels
wrong and the person does not seem to be able to recognize it or do
anything about it.

Another characteristic is that it does defile others. It's like I could
feel that other wrong spirit in my gut. I call these spirits, personality
demons, mimicking demons, even familiar demons. The first time I saw

this spirit was in me. I had a vision of me in relation to an emotional agenda so I asked the Lord to heal me, but the Lord said that's not you, cast him out and I said but it looks just like me, how can I cast myself out, and the Lord said it is a spirit that looks just like you, cast him out. So I did cast him out in the name of Jesus and the spirit and the agenda disappeared from my life.

In Isaiah 29:4, we read that our voice can be as one that has a familiar spirit. In Jeremiah 51:51 we are confounded, because we have heard reproach: shame hath covered our faces: for strangers are come into the sanctuaries of the Lord's house.

Proverbs 25:28
He that hath no rule over his own spirit is like a city that is broken down, and without walls.

A simple but dramatic practice is to learn how to use Romans 6 to reckon the flesh dead, and to cast the spirits out.

Get it deep inside: Jesus already defeated Satan and his army.

Luke 10:19
Behold, I give unto you power to tread on serpents and scorpions, and over all the power of the enemy, and nothing shall by any means hurt you.

We need to place several deliverance scriptures deep in our heart and Luke 10:19 is one of them.

When Jesus in Luke 4, was tempted three times in the dessert by the devil, each time he quoted scriptures: the devil had to go.

Job 22:28
Thou shall decree a thing and it shall be established unto thee.

Hebrews 4
12- For the word of God is quick, and powerful, and sharper than any two edged sword, piercing even to the dividing asunder of

soul and spirit, and of the joints and marrow, and is a discerner of the thoughts and intents of the heart.
13- Neither is there any creature that is not manifest in his sight: but all things are naked and opened unto the eyes of Him with whom we have to do.

Are demons real? Is the Bible real? Jesus and the apostles cast out many evil spirits. For this purpose the Son of God was manifested, that he might destroy the works of the devil, 1 John 3:8.

Even the demons complained that He had arrived, Matthew 8:29.

And, behold, they cried out, saying, What have we to do with thee, Jesus, thou Son of God? art thou come hither to torment us before the time?

Demons are earthbound spirit beings with all the characteristics of a person: will, intellect, emotions, speech, etc... Fallen angels seem to inhabit heavenly realms.
Matthew 12:43 refers to the earthbound demons that can inhabit people. When the unclean spirit is gone out of a man, he walketh through dry places, seeking rest, and findeth none.
In Daniel 10 we see another kind of supernatural- spiritual beings: angels fighting in the heavens: the second heaven.
In Daniel 10 as Daniel fasted and prayed an angel came and spoke to him. In Daniel 10:13 we learn about angels fighting in the heavenlies (spiritual warfare in the second heavens).

Daniel 10:13
But the prince of the kingdom of Persia withstood me one and twenty days: but, lo, Michael, one of the chief princes came to help me; and I remained there with the kings of Persia.

Ephesians 6:12 points to different kinds of evil beings.
12- For we wrestle not against flesh and blood, but against principalities, against powers, against the rulers of the darkness of

this world, against spiritual wickedness in high places (heavenly places).

In 2 Corinthians 12, Paul speaks about the third heaven: paradise, where God abides. This is different from the second heaven where Satan directs his warfare against nations, regions, cities, institutions, households, and individuals. We need to learn, train, and equip ourselves corporately to wage warfare against the territorial spirits in the second heaven. The first heaven is the sky we see.

There is always the question can a Christian be demonized, can a Christian have a demon, can a Christian be possessed. I believe all of the above are possible. We have seen anointed powerful generals, captains, soldiers, saints of God, that have fallen in dramatic fashions: with megalomania, delusions, mental disorders, deception, obsessions, greed, lust, addictions, fornication, adultery, homosexuality, pornography, stealing, abuses, fraud, pride, strife, control, manipulation, bitterness. What about many of our illnesses like schizophrenia? The Hammonds in their book pigs in the parlor believe that schizophrenia can be demonically induced. What about cancer. Many Christian healers believe cancer is a demonically induced illness.

I have seen Christians with every possible mental, emotional, physical disorders including pain syndromes and addictions to opiates and sedatives. The truth is that there are many mysteries in these areas of healing and deliverance. We don't have the revelation control and power that we would like to have.

As a physician in the office I ponder what is the cause of this infirmity; where are illnesses coming from? In a general way illnesses come from Satan. Illnesses, disease, infirmities, appeared after the fall of man. They are consequences of disobedience, rebellion, sin, idolatry, iniquity. The wages of sin is death, Romans 6:23.

Satan comes to steal, kill, and destroy. Right away at the beginning of this book we began to weave and explore all the areas of our humanity where evil could have a hold in us and to repeat and reinforce that Jesus came to absolutely defeat all evil hold on us and that as far as the word of God goes He has already done so, 1 Peter 2:24.

We need the Holy Ghost but don't just say I have the Holy Ghost. Do you speak in tongues? Do you have the gifts of the spirit? We need to cast out devils and we need power and discernment. We need faith but not our faith, BUT THE FAITH OF GOD. This is about supernatural living and about really knowing Jesus and our identity in Christ.

In covenant ministries- at the school of the prophets directed by prophet Randy Lechner[32] we always decree the profession and confession of the saints: We say the same thing as the Lord says about me.

It is written in Psalm. 107:2, "Let the redeemed of the Lord SAY SO, Whom He has redeemed (delivered) out of the hand of the enemy."

It is written in Revelations 12:11, "I overcome by testifying to what the word of God says the Blood of the Covenant of the Lord Jesus Christ does for me. I don't care if I die in the process."

It is written in Ephesians 1:7, By the Blood of the Covenant of the Lord Jesus Christ, "I have been redeemed out of the hand of the wicked one."

It is also written in Ephesians 1:7, "By the Blood of the Covenant of the Lord Jesus Christ I have the forgiveness of all my SINS."

It is written in 1 John 1:7, "By the Blood of the Covenant of the Lord Jesus Christ I have been cleansed of all my SIN; i.e. I am continuously cleansed continually from the root of all my sin by the Blood of the Covenant of the Lord Jesus Christ."

It is written in Romans 5:9, "By the Blood of the Covenant of the Lord Jesus Christ, I have been justified. I have been made "just as if I'd" never sinned, by the blood of His everlasting Covenant."

It is written in Hebrews 13:12, "By the Blood of the Covenant of the Lord Jesus Christ, I have been "set apart" by God, for God, to God, trough God, by the blood of His everlasting Covenant."

It is written in 1 Corinthians 6:13,19,20, "By the blood of the Covenant of the Lord Jesus Christ, my body is for the Lord, and the Lord is for my body, I don't belong to myself, I belong to Almighty God. He bought me with the Blood of the Covenant of the Lord Jesus Christ."

"Now, because I have been REDEEMED, DELIVERED, FORGIVEN, CLEANSED, JUSTIFIED, SANCTIFIED, and because God is for my body and I don't belong to myself, I therefore declare to all principalities and powers; you have no power or authority over me, in me, around me, because of the power of the blood of the everlasting Covenant of the Lord Jesus Christ, my Savior."

We don't want to be like the sons of Sceva that did not know Jesus and the devil kicked their butt. We don't want to be like the Pharisees, very religious but did not know Jesus, or political like Pilate who had the truth in front of him and said to Jesus, but what is truth.

The true knowledge of Jesus is a heart thing that we need to cultivate.

In the last chapter dreaming of God we will go deeper into knowing Jesus.

We cannot cast out devils with the power of the flesh. We need real power that only comes through the Holy Ghost, Act 1:8. Some people tell me I have the Holy Ghost, I was saved or I had confirmation, whatever. It is true but the Holy Ghost can be hidden in a casket. People, you need the resurrection of the Holy Ghost in you. The spirit that resurrected Jesus from the dead is the Holy Ghost. When Jesus says all power I am giving unto you, He is talking about an alive and active Holy Ghost in us.

In Acts we see that the first manifestation of the baptism and activation of the Holy Ghost is speaking in tongues. Cessasionism is a demon! There are cessasionistic religious, political, and antichrist demons totally opposed to the power of God (the Holy Ghost). Some even say that there are no demons and that demons cannot touch Christians-that's a demon speaking!

In 1 Corinthians 12: Paul says don't be ignorant of the gifts. Let the Holy Spirit manifest. I have talked about these things in previous chapters but I really want you to get it. THAT IF YOU BELIEVE IN JESUS you first cast out devils in His name, Mark 16:17. Of course we have to train, Hebrews 5:13, 14.

Jesus trained the apostles and gave them power and authority to

heal the sick and cast out demons. After the heavens opened and the Holy
Spirit descended upon Jesus at the river Jordan (Luke 3:22), he became
full of the Holy Spirit and was lead by the spirit into the wilderness (Luke
4) where He fasted and was tempted by the devil. Jesus resisted the devil
using scriptures.

Luke 4:4
It is written, That man shall not live by bread alone, but by every
word of God.

Luke 4:8
It is written, Thou shalt worship the Lord thy God, and Him only
shalt thou serve.

Luke 4:12
It is said, Thou shall not tempt the Lord thy God.

Luke 4:14
And Jesus returned in the power of the Spirit into Galilee and like
Francis MacNutt says, that in Jesus' state of the union first speech
at Nazareth He declares the plan of his government: Luke 4:18,
19, 21.

Of course, the religious people were filled with wrath and wanted
to kill Him.
And He came down to Capernaum and at a synagogue He
commanded a demon out of a man, and he came out of him, and the
people were amazed at his authority and power over demons. He then laid
hands and healed every sick person and demons also came out of many.
He then said I must preach the kingdom of God to other cities also.
Luke 4 is a capsule of Jesus' ministry of teaching, healing and
deliverance. Jesus received the anointing of God. The fullness and power
of the Holy Ghost, and in Luke 4:18 declared what He was going to do
and began doing it right away-bringing on the kingdom of God.
We will review episodes of deliverance throughout the gospels and
Acts of the Apostles and His anointing and commission for us. The

demons have not gone away. We must do what Jesus did and commissioned us to do.

Matthew 28:16-20, Mark 16:15-20.

In Mark 16:17 Jesus said that the first sign that shall follow them that believe is: IN MY NAME SHALL THEY CAST OUT DEMONS. Sometimes I want to ask Christians how many demons have they cast out this week, or this month, or this year, or ever. It seems judgmental and I rarely do it, but please believe the word of God and activate your commission.

Today a middle aged patient came with a chronic crippling pain on her feet and trouble walking. The medical work-up had been negative: x-rays, MRI's, etc. The diagnosis we could give her was idiopathic peripheral neuropathy, an affliction of the nerves of the feet causing unbearable pain. She showed signs and symptoms of a demonically induced illness.

Idiopathic- we don't know where is coming from.

She seemed to have an obsession with the pain. A constant thinking and mentioning of the pain. Her affect was immersed in the pain.

Spiritual discernment indicated a barrier, an oppression, a hopelessness.

I knew in the Spirit that there was occultism in the generational lines manifesting as the illness now. I asked the patient if anybody in her family had been involved in occultic non-Christian activities. She mentioned that her mother had been intensively involved with spiritists and that she would go with her as a child to such sessions. She mentioned that the "spirits of the dead" possessed some participants and that they would speak to them. Her mother eventually began seeing these "dead spirits" in her own house.

My patient states that her mother developed severe dementia, became bedridden, and died a horrible death. I discussed with my patient allopathic medicine and divine healing. She also understood the two kingdoms, curses, demonization and illnesses. She repented of her sins, her mother sins, renounced spiritism, accepted Jesus as Lord and savior and received forgiveness.

We did a deliverance prayer casting out all the spirits that entered her as a child and that were causing her the pain now. She was delivered and walked normally without pain. We commanded the spirits not to return and prayed for an infilling of the Holy Ghost.

This woman had never been involved in Christianity. I gave her a Bible and several references. I recommended her to find a church so she would congregate, gave her several alternatives, also told her that these spirits would want to come back, and that she needed to retain her freedom. To establish a relationship with the Holy Ghost, Jesus, and Father God, and that whenever the spirits, and the spirit of pain would want to return, to command them to go, and not to enter her again in the name of Jesus.

An elderly patient came with a classical spirit of infirmity. He had been afflicted with a severe pain that traveled throughout his body. It was first in his lower back, and then moved up into his mid back, and it was now lodged in his left arm. He had not been able to sleep because of the pain. Pain meds and massages had not helped. At times when pain comes it seems to overwhelm the belief system. All the attention is focused on the pain. He did not want prayer but his wife who is a Catholic charismatic believer did believe in healing, and urged him to allow prayer. I commanded the spirit of infirmity and pain to leave him in the name of Jesus. After the first prayer there was a mild decrease of the pain. I prayed two more times and the pain went from a ten to a five.

I always do what I am supposed to do as an allopathic M.D. I did an EKG as angina and a myocardial infarction can manifest as left arm pain. I also did cervical spine x-rays as an affected nerve in the neck can also manifest as left arm pain. One hour later, after he had the tests done he came back to my office to review the EKG and x-rays, and the pain was totally gone. I love God in medicine. I love that we can integrate both approaches. Whenever you really get God in the picture He rules. Thank you Lord.

A patient of mine complained that his wife had totally changed after intensively taking care of her sick father, staying in the hospital and nursing home with him until the end when he died of terminal Alzheimer's disease. He said that his wife's personality was totally changed; she seemed very far away and was a stranger to him. She did not want to go to church or get help. Their daughter was very worried. I sensed spiritual oppression beyond any grief reaction that entered her at the hospital-nursing home-sickness-death of her father. We prayed at a distance binding any spirits that could have entered her during the process of sickness and death of her father.

The husband said that after our prayer he saw a significant change in his wife, and she became willing to come and see me at the office. So they both came to the office. She accepted Jesus as Lord and savior and we cast out multiple oppressive illness-hospital-nursing home- death spirits. We prayed for an infilling of the Holy Spirit and a change of garments. She became filled with the oil of gladness. She was totally changed, joyful, and reacting appropriately to her husband. Thank you Lord.

We absolutely need protection. I pray Francis MacNutt's prayer of protection and prayer to be set free everyday. It's about consciously declaring and taking authority over the enemy. Most of my patients have no idea about protecting themselves. Also spirits of illness and infirmity can be transferred and especially at the moment of death. I have often seen someone dying and his or her partner or sibling getting ill even with the same illness. For example: lupus, cancer, or anything else. There was a spiritual transference of illness.

Numbers 19:11 states that he that toucheth the dead body of any man shall be unclean seven days. Verse 14: also, whomever is in the tent where the man died is unclean. Numbers 19 is about purification. We have the Holy Spirit within us, but we need to be consciously aware of such transferences and protect ourselves and cast out any invading spirit in the name of Jesus.

Let's get the word deep inside of us, what Jesus did and what we are supposed to do: the will of God:

Matthew 4:24
And his fame went throughout all Syria: and they brought unto him all sick people that were taken with divers diseases and torments, and those which were possessed with devils, and those which were lunatick, and those that had the palsy; and he healed them.

Matthew 8

16- When the even was come, they brought unto him many that were possessed with devils: and he cast out the spirits with his word, and healed all that were sick:

17- That it might be fulfilled which was spoken by Esaias the prophet, saying, Himself took our infirmities, and bare our sicknesses.

Matthew 10:1

And when he had called unto him his twelve disciples, he gave them power against unclean spirits, to cast them out, and to heal all manner of sickness and all manner of disease.

Matthew 10

7- And as ye go, preach, saying, The kingdom of heaven is at hand.

8- Heal the sick, cleanse the lepers, raise the dead, cast out devils: freely ye have received, freely give.

Mark 3

11- And unclean spirits, when they saw him, fell down before him, and cried, saying, Thou art the Son of God.

14- And he ordained twelve, that they should be with him, and that he might send them forth to preach.

15-And to have power to heal sicknesses, and to cast out devils:

Mark 5:1-19

The gaderene demoniac. The legion.

Mark 6:7

And he called unto him the twelve, and began to send them forth by two and two; and gave them power over unclean spirits;

Mark 6:13

And they cast out many devils, and anointed with oil many that were sick, and healed them.

Luke 6:18

And they that were vexed with unclean spirits: and they were healed.

Luke 7:21

And in that same hour he cured many of their infirmities and plagues, and of evil spirits; and unto many that were blind he gave sight.

Luke 10:1

After these things the Lord appointed other seventy also, and sent them two and two before his face into every city and place, whither he himself would come.

Luke 10

17- And the seventy returned again with joy, saying, Lord, even the devils are subject unto us through thy name.

18- And he said unto them, I beheld Satan as lightning fall from heaven.

19- Behold, I give unto you power to tread on serpents and scorpions, and over all the power of the enemy: and nothing shall by any means hurt you.

20- Notwithstanding in this rejoice not, that the spirits are subject unto you; but rather rejoice, because your names are written in heaven.

Luke 11

20- But if I with the finger of God cast out devils, no doubt the kingdom of God is come upon you.

21- When a strong man armed keepeth his palace, his goods are in peace:

22- But when a stronger than he shall come upon him, and overcome him, he taketh from him all his armour wherein he trusted, and divideth his spoils.

Acts 5:16
There came also a multitude out of the cities round about unto
Jerusalem, bringing sick folks, and them which were vexed with
unclean spirits: and they were healed every one.

Acts 8:7
For unclean spirits, crying with loud voice came out of many that
were possessed with them: and many taken with palsies, and that
were lame, were healed.

Acts 16
16- And it came to pass, as we went to prayer, a certain damsel
possessed with a spirit of divination met us, which brought her
masters much gain by soothsaying:
17- The same followed Paul and us, and cried, saying, These men
are the servants of the most high God, which show unto us the way
of salvation.
18- And this did she many days. But, Paul, being grieved, turned
and said to the spirit, I command thee in the name of Jesus Christ
to come out of her. And he came out the same hour.

Acts 19
13- Then certain of the vagabond Jews, exorcists, took upon them
to call over them which had evil spirits the name of the Lord Jesus,
saying, We adjure you by Jesus whom Paul preacheth.
14- And there were seven sons of one Sceva, a Jew, and chief of
the priests, which did so.
15- And the evil spirits answered and said, Jesus I know, and Paul
I know; but who are ye?
16- And the man in whom the evil spirit was leaped on them, and
overcame them, and prevailed against them, so that they fled out of
that house naked and wounded.

Demonic entrance doors, open avenues, entry points[33] [34] [35] [36] [37] [38]

I- Curses and demonization

1.) Sins of the generations, generational curses, generational demonization transference. (See chapter on curses).
Exodus 20:3-5
Exodus 34:6-7

The occult, freemasons, other religions, new age, abuse, sexual sins, abortions, addictions, pride, unforgiveness, rejection, witchcraft, etc.

Demons can come down the family line, demons of disease, infirmities, illnesses, demons of mental illness, demons of suicide, demons of addiction, fornication, adultery, demons of emotional conditions, bitterness, control, fear, rage, shame, rejection, pride, depression, demons of divorce, demons of specific sins, any kind of demon can come through the family line. Demons of spiritual blindness and ungodliness.

2.) Your tongue.
a.) Self inflicted curses.
For example: I curse the hour of my birth, I want to die, I don't want to live like this, I'll probably die young, etc, etc.
b.) Judging, blaming, accusing, attacking, condemning, gossip: one can curse others but it brings curses upon one's self, Romans 2:1.

3.) Being cursed by others.
a.) Careless statements from others especially parents.
For example: you don't know how to do anything.
b.) Christian witchcraft- very common- talking bad about each other
c.) Curses from Satanists, witch doctors etc. the most dangerous.
We must pray daily for protection and more intensely if we discern that we are being attacked.

4.) Every disobedience, ignorance, sin, wrong theology can bring a curse.
-We must be living the Christian life filled with the Holy Ghost.

- Living the word.
- Doing the things of Jesus.
A curse causeless shall not come, Proverbs 26:2.
Galatians 3:13
Romans 8:1, 2

II- Personal sin

Genesis 4:7, Isaiah 64:6, Ezekiel 18:4, Psalm 19:13, Isaiah 1:16-20, Romans 6:23, John 3:16, 1 John 1:9, 10.

We know the Ten Commandments. We have discussed curses; curses come from sin. Gross obvious sins are the occult, addictions, sexual sins, new age, dishonoring father and mother, etc. but there are subtler sins related to the flesh and the world that can become entry points for the demonic.

Fear: 2 Timothy 1:7, Romans 8:15.
Anger: Ephesians 4:26, 27.
Judgment: Romans 2:1, Matthew 7:1, 2.
Bitterness: Hebrews 12:15.
Unforgivness: Matthew 18:33-35.
Faith: Romans 14:23.
The Tongue: James 3:10.
Pride: James 4:6.
Lusts: James 4:1-3.
Righteousness: 1 John 5:17.

The World:
James 4:4
Ye adulterers and adulteresses, know ye not that the friendship of the world is enmity with God? Whosoever therefore will be a friend of the world is the enemy of God.

Romans 12:2
And be not conformed to this world: but be ye transformed by the renewing of your mind, that ye may prove what is that good, and acceptable, and perfect, will of God.

2 Corinthians 4:4
In whom the god of this world hath blinded the minds of them which believe not, lest the light of the glorious gospel of Christ, who is the image of God, should shine unto them.

Galatians 1:4
Who gave himself for our sins, that he might deliver us from this present evil world, according to the will of God and our Father:

Ephesians 2:2
Wherein in time past ye walked according to the course of this world, according to the prince of the power of the air, the spirit that now worketh in the children of disobedience:

1 John 2
15- Love not the world, neither the things that are in the world. If any man love the world, the love of the Father is not in him.
16- For all that is in the world, the lust of the flesh, and the lust of the eyes, and the pride of the life, is not of the Father, but is of the world.

1 John 5:19
And we know that we are of God, and the whole world lieth in wickedness.

1 John 3:1
Behold, what manner of love the Father hath bestowed upon us, that we should be called the sons of God: therefore the world knoweth us not, because it knew him not.

Mark 4:19
And the cares of this world, and the deceitfulness of riches, and the lusts of other things entering in, choke the word, and it becometh unfruitful.

2 Timothy 2
3- Thou therefore endure hardness, as a good soldier of Jesus
Christ.
4- No man that warreth entangleth himself with the affairs of this
life; that he may please him who hath chosen him to be a soldier.

1 Timothy 6

1 Timothy 6:10
For the love of money is the root of all evil: which while some
coveted after, they have erred from the faith, and pierced
themselves through with many sorrows.

2 Timothy 3

2 Timothy 3:5
Having a form of godliness, but denying the power thereof: from
such turn away.

The flesh:
Galatians 5:16-21, James 3:14-16

We must live in the ongoing process of sanctification, renewal of
the mind, transformation, becoming more and more like Jesus, carrying
our cross: becoming obedient, dying daily, hearing more and more of Him
within, bringing both feet into the kingdom, walking in the Spirit.

III- Traumas-Hurts-Abuse-Woundings
Things done to us:
For example: abandonment, rejection, abuses, humiliation, sexual
abuse, rape, sexual soul ties and bondages, demonic transfers, etc.
Rejection- It is very prevalent and it brings with it other companions:
shame, unlovableness, unworthiness, weakness, inferiority, self pity. It can
be transferred through the generations. It can begin in the womb, at birth,
childhood, or at any time. Then, things get much worse when defenses and
walls are erected to hide the wounded self. (See onion diagram on Inner

Healing, Chapter 4.)

Probably a major focus of Satan's kingdom is to hurt you very early on, making it impossible to change. But to God everything is possible, and He did it all at the cross. We can absolutely and totally change. We have the mightiest deliverer living with us.

I saw a woman today who I had seen before but rejected my approaches to help her, and had been with another physician. My nurse said that she wanted prayer. I was very surprised. She had a diagnosis of paranoid personality disorder, schizoid, borderline, anxious and depressed personality disorder. I asked the Lord how to pray, and the Lord reminded me of the Leper who asked Jesus, Do you want to heal me and JESUS SAID YES I WANT TO HEAL YOU. BE HEALED. The Lord said to me, use my mighty right hand. That meant to me go for it.

So she came in and I saw the spirits in her eyes. I told her, stand firm with me, the Lord will make you free today. I commanded the spirits of abuse, rejection, humiliation, shame, unforgiveness, anger, hate, insanity, all the psychiatric diagnosis to come out in the name of Jesus. She coughed them out for a long time as I kept commanding them out. I called upon the Holy Ghost to establish the peace of Jesus and the love of God in her; to fill every crevice in her. She wept as she was being freed. She had not been able to hug, but she hugged me and felt the love of God. I gave her a Bible and homework; taught her to prevent the spirits from returning. Told her of a Church were she could congregate and a return consult in three days.

This is the normal Christian medical office. The emotional trauma chapter is enormous. Search inside and see where your wounding lies.

Divorces, separations, abandonments, any kind of abuse, even if your parents were rigid and did not express their love for you; control, domination, intimidation, manipulation, death, accidents, illnesses, poverty. The core is usually rejection, fear and shame. Layers begin to cover the core with self pity, bitterness… Outside we usually have witchcraft, control, manipulation, intimidation, domination, any addiction, greed, lusts, idolatry, etc.

These inner woundings and the next area of infestation: ungodly beliefs are for some the hardest places to conquer. We could be anointed and minister powerfully, but if there remains an unhealed, unredeemed

area, there is a danger that it could erupt, and we could be taken captives at any time.
See chapter on Inner Healing.

IV- Ungodly beliefs-Inner Vows (alliances with Satan)

We can be infected with ungodly beliefs. We can be full of inner vows. These are allegiances with evil. We have to confess, repent, renounce, forgive, be forgiven, be healed, be delivered, and believe the truth. What God says we are. Who God says we are. It is a change of garments. A change of identity. We have to live in Godly beliefs.

I lived most of my life in anger against my parents. I did judge them, and by judging them dishonored them. I broke God's law and sin took hold of me, bitter roots that are our sinful reactions and our condemning judgments of people, and our refusal and inability to forgive took deep roots in me.

In my case my response was much greater than anything they could have unconsciously done to me. Actually they were good parents. Due to generational traumata such as rejection, abandonment and shame I was infected with demons of rejection and shame.

I lived with these poisons in me that then applied to all my relationships. I broke many spiritual laws out of such woundings and demonizations, and my responses and reactions to the woundings and further sins and demonization.

A.) Dishonor father and mother.
B.) Roots of bitterness and unforgiveness.
C.) Rebellion, stubbornness, disobedience, idolatry,
D.) Addictions.
E.) Occultism.

Born of deception regarding childhood woundings a demonic snowball was created that almost killed me. We can observe that we have multidimensional areas of sin and entry points for the demonic. I am overstressing these points all throughout the book. This is an instruction, training, integrating, teaching, equipping, activating, anointing manual to release the saint for the ministry of Jesus.

Ungodly beliefs-Inner Vows-Heart of stone can be very hard to eradicate. These conditions have their roots very early in our lives. They are most commonly created out of our dysfunctional relationship with our parents.

Roots, Wound, Rejection, Shame,	⟹	Intense Emotions and Feelings, Unlovableness, Unworthiness,	⟹	Defenses, Ungodly Beliefs, Inner Vows, Heart of Stone, Demonic Expectations.	⟹	Rebellion, Cravings, Obsessions, Compulsion, Depression, Illnesses Mental and Physical

Most of these phenomena are partially unconscious. They can become strongholds in Christians- unredeemed places in the heart- places that block the healing and transforming love of God.

Examples of ungodly beliefs, Inner vows, heart of stone (mostly hidden, what's underneath the tip of the iceberg):

There is something basically wrong with me.

I am wrong.

If my parents did not love me, who can love me.

I am unlovable.

I'll always be rejected so I reject.

I'll never open to anybody.

I reject love.

I am unworthy.

I'll always get hurt.

I'll always be abandoned.

If they knew me they'll hate me.

I have to be closed up with rigid boundaries.

No one will ever really know me.

I have to hide who I really am.

No one will ever tell me what to do.

No one will ever control me.

I have to be in control.

I have to find "love" wherever I can etc.

Evil can infect any area of trauma, and a deception stronghold can be created in which the whole area of the wounding gets defiled, augmented, and increased. It is true that we have been hurt, but the hurt can become an oozing unhealed abscess permeating unforgiveness, bitterness, resentment, blame, accusation, attack, strife, control, manipulation, etc.

I just finished praying for Max at the prayer room in my house. Throughout most of this book the individual's histories are real, but are made in such a way that it would be impossible for the prayee to recognize himself/herself in the stories.

Max is a 36 year old businessman from Atlanta, Georgia, who while visiting relatives in Miami was referred to me because of infidelity.

He had been married for nine years and for the past four years had multiple sexual encounters with many different women. He said that his life was miserable because he found himself in these situations and he could not take it any longer. The disgust, nausea, guilt, shame, aversion, self hate, fear, depression were overwhelming him. He vowed many times never to do it again, but "ended up in bed with women that he did not love at all".

In my house I can take all the time I want to, so we make a family tree for the sins of the generations as far back as possible and take a complete history of their lives and their family's life. The history includes: relationships to parents, siblings, significant others, children, relatives, partners, womb time, birth, childhood, schooling, teachers, peers, friends, first sexual encounter, any abuse: physical, mental, emotional, sexual, of any kind, all significant and intimate relationships, illnesses, divorces, premature deaths, suicides, addictions, eating disorders, abortions, barrenness, finances, poverty, occult involvement, other religions, secret societies, new age, accidents, untimely deaths, traumas, emotional traumas, hurts, sins, inner vows, soul ties, unforgiveness, bitterness, etc. Salvation, religious affiliation, knowledge of the scriptures, praise, worship, Holy Ghost, ministries, etc. We get as much information as possible so we can obtain understanding of what needs healing and locate demonic entry points. We want to always be under the eyes and direction of the Holy Spirit.

Max did not seem to have significant information of any problem in the generations except that he was told that his grandfather drank too much. This was very significant as when we investigated his relationship to his father we found severe emotional traumas. His now deceased father had been an alcoholic and would beat him up during his binges. In the area of sin there were marked issues of unforgiveness and bitter root judgments. When I asked him have you forgiven your father he immediately said no, why would I forgive that so and so.

Because of the abuse suffered he reacted: he judged, condemned, blamed, hated, cursed, and dishonored his father. He vowed never to drink alcohol and never to hit his children and he never drank, but he states that at times he would loose control at home with his boys and would scream and even did pushed them a couple of times. This really affected his wife who was always intervening and had asked him to get help with his anger.

Obviously there was also the compulsive sin of adultery. He states that he had a normal sexual development having his first real sexual encounter "late" when he was 18 years-old with a young woman at college. There were no homosexual encounters, sexual abuses, pornography, drugs or alcohol addiction. There was no history of occultism, other religion, etc. He states that he never received real Christian education, never read the bible etc. He thinks that he was baptized as an infant but he had no idea of salvation or Jesus.

Max mentioned something very important. He said, I have never been loved by anyone in my whole life. This was a major destructive ungodly belief and a stronghold in his being. This is not an uncommon ungodly belief in persons afflicted with sexual addictions. It creates inner vows and deeply entrenched demonized compulsive behaviors.

It's the unmet need syndrome. The unfillable hole syndrome. It is a powerful survival mechanism that says I have to find love or I'll die. We bound lying and deceiving demons and he had to agree that his terrified and wounded mother had loved him and tried to protect him, that his wife really loved him, and we found several people including his business partner that loves him. He cried when we dismantled the lies of the devil.

The soul tie area was a major source of demonic infestation. This was serial adultery. This was the time when he manifested the most during the deliverance part of the session. There were all kinds of stuff from everybody that he had been with. It came out through deliverance. We will discuss soul ties next.

Max received salvation as he accepted Jesus as his Lord and savior. We did a long salvation prayer involving a lot of his issues. The exchange at the cross involved all hurt, shame, anger, sins, betrayal, loneliness, depression. Jesus gave him a new life. The Lord took all his stuff and gave him all His goodness. Max repented of the sins of the generations, of his sexual sins, anger, unforgiveness, betrayal, hurting his wife and children, of ungodly beliefs and inner vows, of sexual addiction. He renounced sexual addiction. He had a lot of trouble forgiving his father but we explained that it was a choice and a process.

We reminded him of the forgiveness accomplished at the cross and that it is God's will for us that we forgive. We bound demons of unforgiveness. He declared his willingness to forgive his father. We cast out demons of hurt, rejection, shame, anger, unforgiveness, betrayal, lust, fantasy lust, rebellion, control, seduction and bondage. One of his sexual partners still had a hold over him and we broke the hold of the spirit of witchcraft: control over him. When we prayed for inner healing: the presence of Jesus at the time of the woundings, he rested in the spirit for about one hour.

I had laid hands on him and prayed in tongues over him during that time. When he came out he was like another person. He seemed a bit confused but he said, "I have been blessed." We also prayed for his wife and children. The next step is the most important step to maintain freedom. To live the Christian life: Jesus' way. All of this was new to Max. I gave him directions regarding the Christian community, scriptures, the Holy Spirit, temptation, etc. I had to be very honest with him and I told him that if he did not do anything else in his new walk there was a high possibility of relapse into his old behaviors. Thank you Jesus. We pray that Max walks in your way: freedom's way, amen.

V- Soul ties

Before salvation I had no defenses against intimate sexual relationships that would soon become destructive. They became destructive because right from the start they were wrong. I was totally aware of: repetition compulsion in hell and that soul mates become hate mates. I had no discrimination, discernment, boundaries or will. I had obsessions, cravings and endless desires. I had something established in my belly that I was not really aware of. Always ready to attach to something that had been established in certain women's bellies.

I now know that "these energies" were evil sexual spirits in the belly. I was a puppet of those spirits. Many times my conscious will would say I am not going to get involved, but the demonic realm had other plans and I would get involved.

The origin of such bondage is in general like all bondages:

a.) Ungodliness.

b.) Generational sin- freemasonry in my family.

c.) Trauma- rejection real or perceived.

d.) Sin- unforgiveness, rebellion, sexual sin.

For example: sex with prostitutes early on, not uncommon in certain societies.

e.) Ungodly belief- no one can love me.

f.) Demonization.

There was a major deception regarding falling in love, soul mate, the woman of my life, I give my life for you, obsessions, dependency, passion, intensity, needs, wants, desires. I believe all these areas had demonic infestations. There were cords, conduits, tentacles, ropes, shackles, attachments, binding my partner and me together in a sinful ungodly relationship.

I believe that there is a strongman even above both partners directing the show. This one has to be bound and his control broken Matthew 12:29.

All the ties have to be severed in the name of Jesus.

We know that there can be a definite transference of evil spirits as you become one flesh with another person 1 Corinthians 6:16. I believe that there can be also transference of soul fragments between two bound persons. For example: a child fragment desperately seeking love can be taken captive into the other person. There is usually bilateral transfer of fragments, Ezekiel 13:17-23.

Ezekiel 13:20
A hunting of the souls to make them fly.

Isaiah 61:1
The spirit of the Lord is upon me to... proclaim liberty to the
captives, and the opening of the prison to them that are bound.

Also we can have parts of the other in us that needs to be sent
back. Often there is the issue of the wounded inner child that needs inner
healing. When Jesus and His Spirit came into my life I was healed and
delivered. No demon controls my life now.

Repent and renounce the ungodly relationship and any sin. Repent
from judgments. Forgive and receive forgiveness. Bind the strongman that
directs the other spirits involved in the bondage. Cut all cords in the name
of Jesus. Ask the Father to release angels to help in the process of
retrieving your migrated fragment of the soul, and release what is not
yours that is of the other person. Invite Jesus to do the healing of wounded
parts: rejection, shame, fear, loneliness. Cast out all evil spirits: lust,
dependency, attachment, needs, wants, desires, false love, obsession,
compulsion. Be filled by the Holy Spirit and the love of God.

Just like bitter roots Hebrews 12:15 defile many, any hidden
unhealed infected wound inside a person can attach or attack spiritually
another susceptible person- a person with a complementary lesion. We
have already discussed the sexual soul ties. I definitely know several very
intelligent people who whenever they start working at a place there is
conflict and strife. They perceive unprovoked attacks from others. The
truth is that they have an ongoing demonically induced system of
rejection, self-hate, judgment, bitterness that induces the attacks from
other.

Simply stating it- demons of rejection inside seek demons of
rejection outside (this is mostly unconscious). The only solution is healing
and deliverance that can only be accomplished by our Lord and savior
Jesus Christ- He did it all at the cross.

A man by the name of Raoul was referred to me by his wife Sarah
with the diagnosis of manic depression-bipolar disorder- mood disorder.
Raoul had been on multiple medicines including Lithium and Bupropion

HCL. He reluctantly came to see me, because he wanted to have children, but Sarah was afraid because of "the way I am."

Sarah had told me on our telephone conversation that her husband was very angry and controlling, and that he could explode because of insignificant circumstances. She wanted him to get better before they would have children. She said that she really loves Raoul, and that he had a good heart but that she "did not want the children to be defiled."

I am going to summarize Raoul's history. Raoul suffered rejection and humiliation in early childhood. His parents had been very immature and had been ungodly and involved in drug and alcohol addiction, sexual immorality, new age practices and got divorced when he was about 5 years of age. He had to survive and developed powerful defense mechanisms around his woundings: control, anger, domination, intimidation. He developed powerful ungodly believes and inner vows: if I am not in control I will die.

He had profound bitter root judgments against his parents. It is true that both of his parents neglected him and deeply hurt him, but his judgments and unforgiveness became a stronghold and a deep seated pattern in his life. What we sow we reap. It is a law. His life was marred by anger, bitterness and unforgiveness. He had classical bitter root expectancies. His wife who is an able professional, intelligent Holy Spirit filled Christian woman, often makes mistakes in the simplest of things, and that hits a sour spot in him in which he feels a deep rejection and reacts violently to it.

The power of the ungodly hidden expectations makes his wife act at times contrary to her own nature. It is true that Sarah has codependent issues, but Raoul's issues are overwhelmingly more powerful than Sarah's issues. Raoul himself before his marriage had been involved in sexual immorality, alcohol and drug addiction and new age practices, but he had repented and had accepted Jesus as Lord and savior. He was now an avid Church go-er. As I interviewed Raoul there was clear evidence of a tongue out of control. On our first meeting he cursed himself and everyone else. We discussed his panorama of healing:

    1.) Repentance, renunciation and forgiveness of the sins of the generations.

    2.) Forgiveness of his parents.

3.) Inner healing of the deeply hurt child, rejection, abandonment, neglect, shame, humiliation, fear, betrayal.

4.) Repentance, renunciation, forgiveness of , major sins of: judgment, unforgiveness, bitterness, anger, rage, hate, resentment, accusation, condemnation, power, control, domination, intimidation, tongue out of control.

5.) Repentance and renunciation of severe inner vows and ungodly beliefs, I have to be in control, I am unlovable, I'm not open to what God says we are.

6.) Deliverance and healing of the heart of stone from which the tongue was out of control.

The heart of stone that was developed, created as a survival protective defense mechanism, was now a major rigid enemy stronghold. It is the waxed and rebellious heart that prevents the knowledge, healing and love of God.

On our first session Raoul began to manifest evil spirits and they came out through the mouth: spirits of anger, rage, accusation, condemnation, etc. We commanded them never to return in the name of Jesus. I really recommended Raoul to begin associating with Holy Spirit filled Christians, receiving the gifts of the spirit, training in the things of the kingdom of God, learning the scriptures. I strongly urged Raoul to receive inner healing, but he seemed resistant in getting involved in that are of healing.

A month after our session, Sarah called me to thank me. She said that Raoul had a dramatic change, that he had become normal. She said that she was very happy, because if we did deliverance and he changed so much it was a matter of demonization and not just mental illness.

I loved what she said, and what she implied: that she rather have him demonized and healed through deliverance than just mental illness and then what. Mental illness is one of the areas that we need to press through and obtain major increments in healing as Jesus would do.

About three months later Sarah called me again and said that Raoul was beginning to act out again with anger, bitterness, control, etc. I talked to Raoul and again recommended what we never really did: inner healing. I told him about different places,

CHM (Christian Healing Ministries) Francis and Judith

MacNutt.

Restoring the Foundations with the Kylstras.

Elijah House with the Sandfords.

I explained to him that he needed to be involved in a place in which his deep hidden core would be exposed and healed. That he needed to let his guard down, to become vulnerable in a place that he would trust, that he really needed to heal that childhood hurt, so that the demonic would not have legal rights or a place where to land. He understood it in his mind. I prayed that the Lord would guide him to the best place for him.

Types of Demonic Spirits[39]

We have already described many types of spirits in the previous chapters. In the chapter of Curses we studied generational demonic transferences, the occult, other religions, cults, etc. In the chapter of Inner Healing we discussed spirits of emotional trauma. In the chapter of Healing and throughout the book we have discussed demons of illness and infirmity.

We have seen how these categories are often interrelated, for example: a Masonic generational curse can cause sexual immorality in the descendants, manic depressive disorder, strokes, new age involvement, etc.

Here we will go in a deeper and more extensive ways into new arenas, for example: religious spirits and territorial spirits.

1.) Generational curses and demonization: (See chapter on curses).
Spirits transferred through generational sin.

2.) Demonization through other curses: (See chapter on curses).
For example: the cursing tongue. Witchcraft curses while ministering in the nations: a witchdoctor in Africa, Santeria in Cuba, voodoo in Haiti.

3.) Spirits of the occult, other religions, cults: (See chapter on curses).

The toughest to deal with are people who have made a blood pact with Satan. I have seen two individuals in this category who came for prayer. One adult man received deliverance after prolonged prayer in which he needed to be held and controlled by several mature and experienced ministers.

The other was an adolescent who was in a coven in which they drank blood, drew pentagrams, called upon the devil, did mirror witching, offered their soul to the devil, hanged out in the cemetery, did blood pacts, drank his own blood that he sucked from his arm, spoke in tongues from "down under". This man was confronted by his family and I don't think that he wanted to be free.

We did several sessions in which different defiant and hostile voices came out of him, he spit, growled, fought, he did seem to get better but would rapidly relapse into severe demonizations. He did not want to get rid of all kinds of objects and escaped his house to hang out with his coven. His parents sent him away for control and treatment of his condition.

4.) Spirits of emotional trauma and reactions to trauma:
abuses, abandonment, rejection, losses. See chapter on inner healing.

5.) Spirits of sin:
For example: sexual sins, lust, greed, unresolved anger, pride, fear, control, judgment, bitterness, rebellion, unforgiveness, jealousy, etc.

6.) Spirits entering through accidents.

7.) Spirits related to illnesses:
This is a complex area-to start with, illnesses appeared after we broke covenant at the garden and Satan got a hold of the world. In the simplest ways illnesses are related to evil.

Isaiah 53:4, 5, Matthew 8:17, 1 Peter 2:24: Show us that Jesus accomplished our healing at the cross.

I believe illnesses are often related to demonization from any type of demon. With the power, discernment and knowledge of the Holy Spirit we cast them all out including the demon of the specific illness and proclaim healing. All over the gospels we see that those possessed with devils were healed.

Acts 10:38 (A.B)
How God anointed and consecrated Jesus of Nazareth with the [Holy] Spirit and with strength and ability and power; how He went about doing good and, in particular, curing all who were harassed and oppressed by [the power of] the devil, for God was with Him.

At times specific demons were cast out.

Matthew 9:32, 33
A dumb demon. When the demon was cast out the dumb spake.

Matthew 12:22
Blind and dumb demon.

Mark 9:17-29
A deaf and dumb spirit that wanted to destroy the boy by casting him into the fire or into the water.

Luke 13:11-13, spirit of infirmity.

I commonly see in my office generational spirits, occultic spirits, other religion spirits, spirits of the cults, emotional trauma spirits, spirits of sin and spirits of illnesses. These are much easier to control and cast out if the patient wants to. We have already discussed a lot about such spirits.

As I am writing about deliverance, all that I seem to be doing at the office is deliverance. Its like our Father is showing that He just heals, that's His nature and that He heals through many different ways and right now He is healing physical illnesses mainly through the deliverance prayer.

A woman came to see me at the office. She had a right frozen elbow, a left frozen shoulder, and a weak right leg. She had an undefined collagen vascular disorder. She was followed by a neurologist and an orthopedist, had received injections in the joints, and taken multiple medicines. She was receiving rehabilitation therapy without effects. I had to preach and teach. She was willing to get healed by the casting out of evil spirits. She received salvation and without any extensive history I submitted and yielded to the Holy Spirit inviting him to bring words of knowledge and discernment regarding the spirits afflicting her. I interceded for her, repented and renounced the sins of the generations and repented for her sins.

I began to cast out spirits of spiritism and witchcraft. When I mentioned freemasonry she closed her eyes and began shaking, her neck turned to one side and she began suffocating. I bound the freemasonry spirit and told her to open her eyes, then we kept casting all spirits out: freemasonry, collagen vascular disease, infirmity, fear, death, pain, frozen parts, shortness of breath, arthritis, etc. Her elbow got loosed, her shoulder got loosed, and her leg got strengthened. It was marvelous and wonderful. Our Jesus is extraordinary.

My patient then said that when she was about 9 years old, her grandfather who was a freemason got sick and was dying, called her, and held her hand as he died. She admits to being very affected since that time, even having the chills when she thought of that event. She did not know anything about freemasonry and had been confused about the whole event. I explained to her about freemason curses and demonization, and that in her case I believed spirits were transferred into her at the time of her grandfather's death and that all her ailments were related to demonic infestation as when we cast out the freemason demons she was physically healed. Hallelujah.

I saw that same day two patients with severe persistent asthma on full treatment who needed hospitalization but were healed through deliverance. I saw a very interesting elderly man with chronic intractable constipation since childhood. There was discernment that this was spiritually controlled. The Lord showed me the face of such demon: stubborn, controlling, proud, rebellious, self righteous, resistant, and defiant. I felt I needed to tell him that this spiritual condition could also be transferred to his descendants. He seemed very affected when he emotionally said my grandchildren are affected by it and my daughter is very worried. We prayed for healing and deliverance and cut the generational curse. I will see him in a week.

In my office when praying for illnesses I always include a prayer of deliverance. In illnesses one way or another there might really be a demon under most bushes.

8.) Spirits of places and objects:

Many places can be demonized including any non-Christian worship area, temples and mountains. I always protect myself when I go to hospitals, nursing homes, etc. At times you can sense spirits of death and other spirits. It is very common to have demonized objects in the house like statues, objects from India, South America, Africa, Tibet, New Age objects, crystals, books, paintings, etc. These are demonic entry points and can bring curses and problems. We ask the Holy Ghost to show us what we need to get rid of.

9.) Religious Spirits[40]:

They are very common in all the churches. There are many varieties. Just think of denominationalism. I was once praising the Lord at a Catholic charismatic conference in New Orleans attempting to follow the ways of David without inhibitions while dancing for the Lord, and a woman comes and says, "I don't think that you are Catholic", and I said, "Why?" She says that uninhibited jumping and swirling does not seem proper for a Catholic. I told her to read 2 Samuel 6:14-23. David danced before the Lord with all his might. His wife Michal saw David leaping and dancing before the Lord and she despised him in her heart... Therefore Michal the daughter of Saul had no children unto the day of her death. I told her, "I love you and I bless you. Come lets dance like David". She just turned and walked away.

Once I was in a nondenominational Church where a prophet was going to teach, and a woman comes and asks me what Church do I belong to. I said, "St. Louis Catholic Church" and she said, "Oh my God, what are you doing here, are you one of those that worships saints?" etc etc. I really felt this woman needed deliverance and I offered it to her. This one didn't walk away, but ran away. God bless her.

In Cuba I was baptized as an infant and did confirmation. It would have been just great if the Holy Ghost had just taken over then in 1959, but the Holy Ghost fell on the Catholic Church in 1967. I was one that needed the power of God to get healed. It happens that the Holy Ghost took over my life in a nontraditional mass in the yard of a private house in 2003. The Lord did not tell me to leave the Catholic Church.

As I lived the new age movement I just knew certain aspects of the dark years of the Church. I just rattled all the negatives like a parrot, the inquisition, the bad popes, the murder of the natives, etc.

I love the knowledge of God. The supernatural realms of God. I have been at Patricia King's Growing in the Supernatural I and II and her Glory School. I have been at Abbotsford to receive an impartation from Todd Bentley. I have been at Randy Clark's School of Healing and Impartation. I love Heidy Baker and many other saints. I love the presence of God.

Last year while in a Catholic Charismatic conference when the bishops and the dancers were coming in, the presence of the Lord was totally powerful. The Holy Ghost fell on the place. I wept as I felt the love of God endlessly pouring over us. I asked God, please Father, many people judge us but you are here just like you are at Patricia's or Todd's or Randy Clark's. God said to me- "this group loved me since the beginning. Many died for me. When all was dark a few kept the faith. I am a faithful God. There has always been a remnant in this Church that loves me above all things. I see the whole picture. That's why the Holy Ghost is in this Church".

That made totally spiritual sense to me. I began to learn a bit about the Fathers of the Church, the powerful first 300 years, there are volumes written about it.

In St. Louis Catholic Church we have a great pastor Father Fetscher. We have bible classes, Emmaus retreats where people learn about having a relationship with Jesus, life in the spirit seminars where you can again get baptized with the Holy Ghost with evidence of speaking in tongues, prayer for healing, trainings, healing services, a room for healing, charismatic meetings, praise and worship, training and equipping plus all the other regular activities of the Church.

At the Azusa Street revival 100 year celebration convention we came from all churches. Our identity was only in the Father, Son, and Holy Ghost. We were celebrating the spirit of God. We were together with one accord, no divisions, denominations, strife, judgments, accusations, etc. It was awesome.

At the last day at the convention center all the Churches were called and the Catholics were a very large group. Our Lord wants to return to a unified body.

A classical religious spirit is the pharisaical spirit. As soon as Jesus began ministering the confrontation began.

In Luke 4:29 they wanted to cast him down headlong from a hill. These religious people were so entrenched in their beliefs and their traditions that there was no place for the revelation of God.

Matthew 15

3- Why do ye also transgress the commandments of God by your tradition?

6b- you have made the commandment of God of none effect by your tradition.

8- This people draweth nigh unto me with their mouth, and honoureth me with their lips; but their heart is far from me.

9- But in vain they do worship me, teaching for doctrines the commandments of men.

13- Every plant, which my heavenly Father hath not planted, shall be rooted up.

14- Let them alone: they be blind leaders of the blind. And if the blind lead the blind, both shall fall into the ditch. (See also Mark 7:5-13).

Matthew 23 exposes further this spirit.

The basic problem is an opposition to the spirit of God and a quenching of the spirit of God. Mark 3:29, 1 Thessalonians 5:19.

The pharisaical spirit is still attempting to murder Jesus- the spirit of God, the Holy Ghost, Mark 14:1. One of his major characteristics is envy, Mark 15:10.

The father of the spirit of the Pharisees is the devil, John 8:37-59

The pharisaical spirit- the spirit of the traditions of man that opposes the activities, power, and gifts of the Holy Spirit is a major demonic stronghold that lives in our Churches.

It is a legalistic spirit, John 9:30.

It loves the praise of men more than the praise of God, John 12:43.

This is the classical deaf dumb waxed heart spirit, John 12:40.

We see that Nicodemus, a Pharisee ruler of the Jews, John 3:1-12 could not understand Jesus.

The pharisaical religious traditional legalistic spirit cannot know Jesus. The real Christian life is all about knowing Jesus FROM THE HEART.

I never knew you, depart from me, Matthew 7:21-23.

The most important thing I do everyday is to lie down early in the morning and call for my Lord. He loves me and visits me, and gives me experiences of Him and His kingdom, and my whole day is set up for the scriptures, praise and worship, tongues, ministering, salvation, healing and deliverance.

I tell you of a simple experience with the religious spirit. I went to church one Sunday and a group who had been with an elder leader of the church came to see me to tell me that this famous leader told them that he did not think that he needed to speak in tongues and that many of the saints of the church never spoke in tongues. Then they said in an accusing way that I was a double dipper. I said, "Wow, what is that, which I have become". They said you mingle with all the denominations. I was really happy with that accusation. I love to be with all the children of God that really love God.

The religious spirit goes against, Acts 1:8, Acts 2, Acts 4:31, Acts 10:46, Acts 19:6, Mark 6:17, etc.

The spirit of the Pharisees has a form of godliness, but denies the power. This spirit even opposes the leader of the Catholic Church who exhorts us about the importance of the Holy Spirit, fighting the devil and being ecumenical. The pharisaical spirit can ally itself with the political spirit that lives under fear of man and compromises. Pilate had Jesus- the Truth- right in front of him and said unto Him, what is the truth? This is such a powerful encounter exposing the ignorance from which people perish. The religious and political spirit accuses and condemns the spirit of God. Satan is the accuser of the brethren.

Some possible signs of demonization in the Churches

1.) Lack of deep-heart-vital relationship with Jesus above all things. This is the immunity and antidote against the spirit of religion. God searches the heart. We need to know God's word, His heart and His character.
The letter kills, but the spirit gives life, 2 Corinthians 3:6b.
No one knows the things of God except the spirit of God, 1 Corinthians 2:11-16.
2.) Placing religion above the scriptures or our relationship with the Holy Spirit. Pharisaical law vs. God's law.
Traditions of man and man's law:
Legalism, salvation by works, rituals, dogmas, theologies, denominations, actions above an intimate relationship with Jesus Christ our Lord and savior, being so entrenched in beliefs that there is no place for revelation.
3.) Unbelief.
4.) Cessasionism, heresies, universalism...
5.) Mechanical rigid compulsive religiosity.
6.) Outward appearance more important than the kingdom within.
7.) No Holy Ghost power, opposition to the gifts of the spirit
8.) Negative tongue, cursing tongue, gossiping tongue.
9.) Unresolved emotional woundings.

Shame	⟹	Pride	⟹	Religious
Rejection		Bitterness		Spirit of
Hurt				Control

10.) Wrong identity, extreme redemptive suffering philosophies, victim, martyr, self pity, false pride.
One of the reasons people seem unable to move from rigid religion to spiritual victory is unresolved hurts as in #9. When God says we are

more than conquerors, we are more than conquerors. It is not just an idea or an intellectual assent.

Romans 8:37
Nay, in all there things we are more than conquerors, through Him that loved us.
WE HAVE THE POWER OF GOD THROUGH THE HOLY GHOST THAT LIVES IN US.
I am who the scriptures: God says I am. Wow, hallelujah. Amen.

11.) Witchcraft in the Church often born through the door of reactions and defenses to hurts plus demonization.

Bitterness, judgment, accusation, condemnation, control, manipulation, intimidation, domination, self righteousness, guilt, shame, anger, resentment, violence, attack, murder.

12.) Rigid wine skins.
13.) Need to maintain status quo.
14.) Fear and pride.
15.) Idolatry to leaders, priests, ministers, pastors, prophets, denominations, saints.
16.) Cultism.
17.) Wrong knowledge regarding:
  a.) Salvation: I am saved because I am a good person, do
  not hurt anybody and help others.
  b.) Healing: God gave me this illness. It is His will and I
  will bear my cross. We need to be humble and suffer.
  c.) Deliverance: Demons can't affect Christians.
18.) Politics.
19.) Rejection of Halal praise.
20.) Lack of joy.
21.) No revelation, knowledge, or real awareness of the love of the Father.
22.) Contamination with new age, other religions and practices, certain alternative medical practices.

23.) False prophet syndrome. Balaam's syndrome: anointed but wrong heart.
24.) Looking for father's syndrome, unmet needs, idealization, deceptions, cults, abuses.
25.) Roles: hero, scapegoat, etc.

We must repent and renounce the religious spirit, and be specific about which manifestation has taken hold of you. There might be generational agendas and even a generational familial religious spirit that we need to renounce. Check the list of signs of demonization. For example: pride, control, shame, fear, avoiding the power of the Holy Spirit, wrong theologies, etc.

There's usually the need for inner healing and breaking of ungodly beliefs. We repent and renounce all our pharisaical agendas. Most specifically how we have rejected and not known the love of the Father- what heals all. We receive the forgiveness accomplished at the cross, forgive the church and break our relationship to the religious spirit and cast it out with all of His tentacles and agendas. We get filled by the Holy Spirit and live the life of Jesus. We become who Jesus says we are- only through the sanctification and power of the Holy Spirit.

10.) Territorial Spirits
The Church without power and the hypocrisy of man.
To play a part.
Falseness.
Pretend.

Some people have a need to find the real. Some people get fed up and rebel against powerlessness and hypocrisy.

Jesus is the road to the real and the real.

I am the way the truth and the life.

Other roads lead to counterfeit real (alternative spirituality). It boils down that if we Christians don't have an active Holy Ghost which is the power of God, we have a Church without power and we are hypocrites.

Hypocrites: The practice of professing believes, feelings or virtues one does not possess. We cannot possess true life with our carnal minds and our flesh.

The world is not The Life.

There is a world-flesh-evil complex that wants to take our life away. The world and the flesh oppose true life. They are in opposition. They oppose each other. There is a war for our souls. The spirit of seduction wants us to become children of deception.

The war is for our wholeness. Maybe you are saved. Because of his grace you said a prayer and you are saved, but if that is all that happened, as far as kingdom living is concerned, it is powerless Christianity.

Now some say that we need more than a prayer to be saved. Jesus implied that He needs to know you. This probably means: relationship, communion, connection, association, involvement, communication, obedience. He said if you love me you obey me. If you believe in me...

How do we obey Jesus? What does He want you to do? He says my sheep hear my voice. Do we hear what He is telling us? Remember, he violently fought the religious spirit of the Pharisees. It is about knowing Him, and by knowing Him His kingdom is exposed.

Even as a child I tried to find God in the Church, but for me He wasn't there. The Holy Ghost was not actively there. It had not fallen in the Church at that time: Cuba in the 1950's. That set up the rest of my life: God, power, truth, life, wholeness, holiness, righteousness, healing, deliverance, and salvation were not in the Church.

A powerless Church is a hypocritical Church. We are the Church- we have to look at ourselves. A powerless Church is following his own tradition. God's tradition is the gift of the Father: the revelation of God: the spirit of God active in us. Please look at the message of the Holy Father Benedict XVI. To the young people of the world on the occasion of the XXIII World Youth Day, 2008:[41]

Acts 1:8
You will receive power when the Holy Spirit has come upon you; and you will be my witness.

Even while fully participating in the new age movement I tried to read the scriptures, but it did not mean too much to me. The day the Holy Ghost began to live and be active in me I began to really read the scriptures and to receive revelation. There is not one day that goes by that I don't fill myself with the word of God.

Thank you Holy Spirit, welcome Holy Spirit.

Why am I writing about all of this under territorial demons? Because in my generation there were millions of young people who got fed up with powerless superficial life and hypocrisy and a revolution began.

1967:

1.) The Jesus Movement began.

2.) The hippie and the new age movement began

3.) The Catholic charismatic movement began.

4.) The church of Satan began.

I ended up in the hippie-new age death movement. I recently looked at the Rolling Stone Magazine "The 40th Anniversary, Summer of Love 1967". I got angry and then wept. Oh how I would have rather been in the Jesus Movement. Many young people were rebelling to hypocrisy, social, political, familial, church-dishonesty, superficial life, facade, persona, masks, social graces, unreal false selves, role playing, unreal personalities, false identities, superficial identities, images, correctness, the world, nice-good-hero roles, religiosity, nice Christian selves hiding hell, pleasers, dishonesty, hidden agendas, no inner self, no inner life, no inner substance, false security and image, role playing.

Christianity was in many places:

A social Christianity,

A superficial Christianity,

A weak Christianity,

A demonized Christianity.

A pharisaical Christianity.

I rebelled and went the wrong way; maybe rebellion is always sin, but some went to Jesus. Superficial life did not work for me. I wasn't going to go with a God that was just like society, social, superficial and dishonest.

It was an issue of power and freedom. THE CAPTAIN OF THE HOSTS IS ALWAYS AROUND, but territorial spirits are always ready to deceive and take you to their hell. I went into a counterfeit alternative spirituality that offered me power, knowledge and freedom.

Genesis 3
The Fall: you will be as God, you'll know good and evil.

What I got was besetting sin, captivity and slavery. God does not bring us into His kingdom for a purely social and superficial life. We rebelled against deadening status quo, but got infected. We looked for the real in places that smelled like real, but there was NO REAL.

I want to be like you Jesus, loving, powerful, righteous, forgiving, convicting, not permitting sin to rule or remain hidden.

Lord, all is really dung. I trust you above all things. Thank you Lord for the only sword that divides real from unreal. You are a God of depth and deep calleth unto deep. You have now shown me the deep and powerful things of God, supernatural realms, warrying angels, the throne room, the Holy Ghost, true healing.

30 years of searching for God lead me to write a book, "Seeds of Enlightment- Death Rebirth and Transformation through Imagery". It is about a very personal unfolding drama of trying to find the truth in places where there is no truth. JESUS IS THE ONLY TRUTH. It is a book about rebellion against status quo, but how do we rebel against such an enemy without the Holy Ghost. (Christianity is an upward supernatural movement)

I had good intentions, but that did not stop the hellish contaminations. There was poetry and incredible insights, but I remained bound. How many times did I died but was never truly born again. This is a true new age book. It is a rebellion against superficial reality, masks, false identities, hypocrisy. There are truths in it mixed with untruths.

This is the New Age.

The Great Deceiver.

Our adversary is always ready to influence us.

Lots of poetry, truths, insights, transformations, issues of the true self, and ways to God-BUT NO SALVATION OR TRUE BIRTH THAT COMES ONLY THROUGH JESUS- The summer of love 1967 degenerated into sex, drugs and rock and roll, sexual immorality, drug addiction, abortions, deaths, broken families, demonically contaminated music, eastern mysticism, Hinduism, Buddhism, gurus, yoga, meditation, native American spirituality, psycho spiritual psychologies, alternative healing, psychic healing, enlightenment, unity, cosmic consciousness, reincarnation, past life therapies, higher consciousness, karma, reiki, shamanism, Silva mind control, Taoism, spirit guides, guided imagery, transcendental meditation, course in miracles, Ouija board, astrology, pendulum, chakras, aura, iridology, horoscopes, etc, etc, etc.

-The fatherless generation was born.

- Millions rebelling and looking for God.

-Many curses fell upon America.

Thank God for intercessors Lou Engle, Mike Bickle, Che Ann, Dutch Sheets and many others. The call Nashville 07, 07, 07; tens of thousands of young people from across America gathered to fast, pray, and cry out to God for a massive youth revival, even greater than the Jesus movement. Something supernaturally happens when we collectively repent and renounce our sins and the sins of the generations. True intercession is keeping America afloat and pushing for a breakthrough.

Hell suffered a major defeat. The demonic portals opened in 1967 are shattered and destroyed. Godly portals opened wide. Revival comes. True revival is nothing less than an inescapable downpour of the Holy Spirit that drenches the Church and washes away our apathy, supernaturally empowering us to preach the gospel and transform society. Thank you Lord that I fought it for many years, but I have finally become a Jesus freak.

Jesus brought His revolution-

Revolution of the power of God-

Revolution of the kingdom of God-

Revolution of bringing heaven into earth-

Revolution of the will of God-

Revolution of the Holy Spirit living in us-

-Status quo; surface life, appearances, activities, world-society-things of man: Matthew 23:27: Woe to you scribes and Pharisees; hypocrites! For you are like whitewashed tombs which indeed appear beautiful outwardly, but inside are full of dead men's bones and all uncleanness.

Jesus was radical:

Let the dead bury their dead. Martha and Mary. Conviction fell upon the earth. There is something wrong in the way I'm living, there is something wrong with society and the world, there is something wrong in the generations of the families. How are we going to change? Surface life, social life, worldly life, purely intellectual life is missing something.

1967- Many doors were opened to search for what was missing. Jesus was so radical that He was the first born from the dead.

Counter culture 1967, polarization, protests, demonstrations, scandals, radical minority, riots, civil rights, feminist movements, Roe vs. Wade, social movements, gay and lesbian movements, silent majority, environment, etc.

True Christianity is radical. It moves out of the streams of regular living. We cannot just be politically correct. JESUS WAS NOT POLITICALLY CORRECT. The king of truth went for the heart; the king of truth went for the depth.

There is a river of death:

Same old, status quo, the dead with their dead, purely Martha's.
He came to bring life and life more abundantly.
Revolution 1967-
Conviction of something wrong.
Hell sucked in millions of unprepared warriors.
Crocodiles grabbing unsuspecting preys.
We have a way to God, and a way to freedom ways.

I was sucked in into other rivers of different kinds of death. It wasn't the status quo death, but a rebellion that went the wrong way. I cry out in pain remembering how deep I went into hell. For rebels there are two depths, the kingdom of heaven and the kingdom of hell. Counterfeit freedom. The kingdom of Satan is a kingdom of pride. Submit to God. Desire Him above all things. Give Him your heart. He will turn your life around. He will turn the world around.

Repent workers of iniquity, surface dwellers. Deep calleth unto deep. Life calls, truth calls, love calls, Jesus calls, Jesus call 1967, no ears to hear, territorial deaf dumb blind waxed heart spirits, witchcraft and iniquity, Mount Carmel conflicts.

Leviathan swallowed me. The Lord gave me His sword and I opened the belly of the beast and came out of the beast. It was all darkness. Then I saw His light. The light of my savior. I sense somehow that I was fighting a war since 1967 being beaten up round after round until the power of God came into my life, then I punched hell out of me.

He is a victorious Lord. We are to conquer the world for Him. Arise wounded, victims, children of the wounded, arise, shine; for your light has come! And the glory of the Lord is risen upon you. For behold, the darkness shall cover the earth, and deep darkness the people; but the Lord will arise over you and His glory will be seen upon you, Isaiah 60:1-2.

In my family we were Catholics, and we are still Catholics, but we were all saved here in the USA. My father, my mother, my brother, my sisters, myself, and our offspring. How come we were not saved there and we were saved here, BECAUSE HERE WE GOT JESUS, a relationship with Jesus. Walking in the ways of Jesus. We had none of that in Cuba. Even though we lost our land and our possessions in Cuba, we got something beyond compare: our Lord and Savior and His kingdom.

As a collective group, territorial spirits followed us: idolatry, greed, sexual immorality, abortions, addictions, freemasonry, witchcraft, Santeria. Santeria did come to America. The Supreme Court of the United States decided on June 11, 1993 that such religion had the right to sacrifice animals.

There are many thousands of followers of Santeria in Miami alone. The International Journal of Urban and Regional Research had a symposium on space and religion. One of the articles discussed RETERRITORIALIZATION of the Orisha religion: Nigeria, Cuba, and The United States.

There is even a course in Santeria Religion at a local university in Miami, FL.

These are all territorial, second heaven agendas. A darkened atmosphere moved over Miami. The cursed brought the curses with them. We are generally passive about it. Corporately we need to intercede and destroy all strongholds that prevent the kingdom of God to move on. Miami needs the power of God to bring salvation, deliverance, life and blessings instead of courses, demonization, sin, and death.

Scriptures We Can Use In Deliverance

1 John 4:4
Ye are of God, little children, and have overcome them: because greater is He that is in you, than he that is in the world.

Luke 10:19
Behold, I give unto you power to tread on serpents and scorpions, and over all the power of the enemy: and nothing shall by any means hurt you.

Colossians 2
13- And you, being dead in your sins and the uncircumcision of your flesh, hath he quickened together with Him, having forgiven you all trespasses.
14- Blotting out the handwriting of ordinances that was against us, which was contrary to us, and took it out of the way, nailing it to His cross.
15- And having spoiled principalities and powers, he made a show of them openly, triumphing over them in it.

Philippians 2
9- Wherefore God also hath highly exalted him, and given him a name which is above every name:
10-That at the name of Jesus every knee should bow, of things in heaven, and things in earth, and things under earth.
11-And that every tongue should confess Jesus Christ is Lord, to the glory of God the Father.

Romans 8:31b
If God be for us, who can be against us?

James 4:7
Submit yourselves therefore to God. Resist the devil, and he will

flee from you.

2 Timothy 1:7
For God hath not given us the spirit of fear; but of power, and of love, and of a sound mind.

Job 22:28
Thou shalt also decree a thing, and it shall be established unto thee.

Isaiah 54:17
No weapon that is formed against thee shall prosper; and every tongue that shall rise against thee in judgment thou shalt condemn. This is the heritage of the servants of the Lord, and their righteousness is of me, saith the Lord.

Proverbs 26:2
The curse causeless shall not come.

Isaiah 55:11
So shall my word be that goeth forth out of my mouth: it shall not return to me void, but shall accomplish that which I please, and it shall prosper in the thing whereto I sent it.

Romans 8:1, 2
Ephesians 1:20-23
Galatians 3:13
Revelation 12:11
1 John 3:8
Hebrews 2:14-15
Luke 11:20
Mark 16:17
2 Corinthians 10:3-5
Ephesians 6:10-18

Kings David's Method of Warfare[42]

We focus on the evil spirits not on the person. We decree the warfare Psalms. There are over 50 warfare verses. For example: Psalm 3:7- Arise, O Lord; save me, O my God: for thou hast smitten all mine enemies upon the cheek bone; thou hast broken the teeth of the ungodly.

Psalm 5:10
Destroy thou them, O God; let them fall by their own counsels; cast them out in the multitude of their transgressions.

Psalms 10:15
Break thou the arm of the wicked.

Psalm 11:6
Upon the wicked he shall rain snares, fire and brimstone, and an horrible tempest: this shall be the portion of their cup.

Psalm 18:14
Yea, he sent out his arrows, and scattered them; and he shot out lightnings, and discomfited them.

Psalm 18:48
He delivereth me from mine enemies: yea, thou liftests me up above those that rise up against me: thou hast delivered me from the violent man.

Psalm 35:5
Let them be as chaff before the wind: and let the angel of the Lord chase them.

Psalm 59:13a
Consume them in wrath, consume them, that they may not be.

Psalm 68:1a
Let God arise, let His enemies be scattered.

Psalm 71:13
Let them be confounded and consumed that are adversaries to my soul.

Psalm 72:4
Break in pieces the oppressor.
9- let the enemies lick the dust.

Psalm 74:14a
Thou brakest the heads of Leviathan in pieces.

Psalm 76:12
He shall cut off the spirit of princes: He is terrible to the kings of the earth.

Psalm 89:40
Thou has broken down all his hedges; thou hast brought his strongholds to ruin.

Psalm 94:23
He shall cut them off in their own wickedness.

Psalm 107:40
He poureth contempt upon princes, and causeth them to wander in the wilderness, where there is no way.

Psalm 112:10
The wicked shall melt away.

Psalm 129:4
He cuts asunder the cords of the wicked.

Psalm 149
6- Let the high praises of God be in their mouth, and a two-edged sword in their hand;
7- To execute vengeance upon the heathen, and punishment upon

the people;

8- To bind their kings with chains, and their nobles with fetters of iron;

9- To execute upon them the judgment written: this honour have all his saints. Praise ye the Lord.

The practices of this Psalm can free us from evil spirits. We use warfare by the Halal praise and the high praises. I love to praise as indicated in the scriptures. I want to focus in the Halal praise which is the most common praise method in the scriptures. See Strong's concordance 1984 (Hebrew).

Give God a bright shinning celebration with ranting and raving, boasting and bragging, clamorously foolish, stultified, willing to appear as one of an unsound mind; like those who have had too much to drink and have temporarily lost their senses while praising God. (Covenant Ministries)

Other important scriptures we will use are Psalm 100:4. Enter into His gates with thanksgiving and into His courts with praise.

Psalm 22:3
O thou that inhabitest the praises of your people.

Psalm 16:11
In thy presence is fullness of joy.

Nehemiah 8:10
The joy of the Lord is your strength.

If we are scriptural out of our bellies shall flow rivers of living water John 7:38.

This is a vital God pattern of praise, bringing God's presence into our situation, out of us into our environment. Under Randy Lechner at the school of the prophets we trained to build endurance to Halal.

<u>Hebrews 5:14</u>
But strong meat belongeth to them that are of full age, even those who by reason of use have their senses exercised to discern both good and evil.

The Spirit of God is in us.
The Kingdom is within.
Stir it up; let Him out into our environment.

We can develop a skill and a strength to release Him in our hearts, to release His presence, power and voice in our situation. Lets praise Him for who He is and what He did for us. Lets dance for the Lord with all our might. Let's shout. Let's leap and dance before our Lord.

Getting Ready For Deliverance

This chapter is a comprehensive view on deliverance; in reality we are always ready: the Holy Spirit is always ready to destroy the works of the devil: in a prayer line in conferences there's commonly a rapid activity of the Holy Ghost with power, discernment, words of knowledge that can deliver the people from Satan's grip. We can also have rapid deliverances in the medical office.

Today I saw a new patient with the complaint of severe pain in the back of her head and jaw for over a year! She was wearing a specialized brace and had seen many specialists, orthopedics, neurologists, neurosurgeons, and had all the available diagnostic tests. Nobody knew what she had; also her affect was consumed by her condition. She could only talk about it. She had the appearance of an afflicted, powerless, victim and martyr.

I listened to her stories for a long while. My first impression was that this was a very hard rock to break. That I would get in trouble if I was going to try to help her spiritually. Thank the Holy Ghost that He thinks different than me. I explained to her that after listening to her story my diagnosis was that this was a spiritually induced illness. She said that she belonged to a certain Christian denomination and with a demeanor of depression, pain, and defeat said that she had great faith!

She had never read the bible and did not know Jesus or the Holy Spirit. I always need a lot of patience, tolerance and compassion. She became willing to receive prayer. I explained to her that nobody had been able to heal, cure, or change her pain, because her pain needed to come out. We did a powerful prayer of salvation and did not mention the demonic, but I kept telling her, do you understand: the pain needs to come out of you, it needs to leave you in the name of Jesus. We command it to leave you.

We also commanded other spirits to leave her: hurt, woundings, affliction, depression, wanting to die, anger, and declared all those tissues healed in the name of Jesus. She was released of oppression and pain and felt much relaxed and stronger with great diminishment of the pain. We commanded the spirits that came out never to return, and prayed for the infillment of the Spirit of God. I told her to come everyday for prayer: the Lord wants her totally healed and without a neck, jaw, or head brace.

I have several patients with terminal metastatic cancer and I pray for them, but I found that I have kept from confronting them about sins like fornicating, unmarried sexual relationships, alcoholism, etc.

After Jesus confronted the man at the pool of Bethesda He told him in John 5:14, Behold, thou art made whole; sin no more, lest a worse thing come unto thee.

Also I believe these terminal people need to be baptized with the Holy Ghost with the evidence of speaking in tongues and today I did just that with a man that is dying and that I love. He repented and renounced sexual sins and received the Holy Ghost with the gift of tongues. I am pressing through for miracles of healing in metastatic terminal cancer. God already gave us Jesus and His healing cross, but the manifestations must fall. Let the kingdom come and His will be done on earth as it is in heaven.

Always remember the key of healing: forgiveness- that's how we all got healed. The forgiveness of the cross.

Today a woman came to my office as a guest of a nurse. She had an endless recurrent cold. She said that she went to Church regularly, was married, had a good business, and that her life was fine. I told her that I sensed emotional woundings that had affected her immune system. After breaking through defenses, resistance and rationalizations she shared how her mother had been extremely controlling and preferred the sons over the daughters. She admitted longstanding feelings of rejection and bitterness and that she left the house early and got married to a man that soon would abuse her physically. She finally divorced him and was now remarried to a good man.

She admitted that she could not forgive her mother and that man. We did the prayer of salvation and she wept when the presence of the Lord came upon her. She felt the forgiveness of Jesus and repented of judging her mother and her ex husband. She became willing to forgive them and declared it. We cast out spirits of hurt, trauma, anger, resentment, bitterness, unforgiveness, judgments.

The Holy Ghost strengthen her whole system and she felt the love, joy and healing of God. She was born again, healed and delivered. She did look like another person. Thank you Lord.

Deliverance Proper

In the elective setting of the prayer room in my house after I have taken notes of the chief complaint: why are you here, what troubles you, etc? And the whole history which includes generational issues, sins, curses, woundings, illnesses, relationships, emotional or mental issues, etc. I have a good idea of which demons are involved. We always call upon the Holy Spirit and during the deliverance session we keep receiving more revelation, guidance and direction from the Holy Spirit.

I- Be sure the person is born again and do a prayer of confession of faith. Be ready to start taking control as demons can manifest at any time. Recently we helped a man with the diagnosis of schizophrenia that as soon as he sat down he began shrieking in a bothersome way. We always do a complete prayer of protection before any ministry. I use Francis MacNutt's prayer that you can get from Christian Healing Ministries Inc. (http://www.christianhealingmin.org/), a prayer of protection and a prayer to be set free. Demons can manifest in multiple ways: shakings, twisting, trembling, pains, headaches, traveling pain, abdominal pain, panic, palpitations, suffocation, fainting, unresponsiveness, yelling, screaming, running away, falling in the floor, abnormal movements, abnormal sounds, coughing, vomiting, yawning, burping, passing gas trough the rectum, rinorrhea, demonic tongues, aggressiveness, hostility, insults, swearing, stares, eye signs like pupils disappearing upwards, etc, etc. We are always in control with the power of the Holy Spirit. Take authority over the spirit. Command it to be quiet and to submit in the name of Jesus. Repeat the commands as often as necessary. Establish and maintain communication with the prayee. Have eye contact as much as possible. In a general way we do several prayers.

II- Repentance and renunciation of the sins of the generations.

III- Renunciation of Satan and all evil involvement. Renunciation of specific sins, for example: occultic-sexual.

IV- Prayer of healing of emotional woundings and memories. Forgiving others.

V- Repentance and renunciation of ungodly believes and inner vows, and receiving Godly believes and the saint's identity in Christ.

VI- Prayer of repentance and renunciation and breaking of soul ties.

VII- Prayer of physical healing.

We want to destroy all of Satan's legal rights and deliverance will be much easier. As I move through the different areas of ministry I command demons to leave in the name of Jesus. A demon is a spirit. The Greek word for spirit, pneuma, also means breath. When a demon comes out of a person, it normally comes out through his mouth and there is usually some manifestation like coughing, burping, yawning, spitting, vomiting.

We have had prayees that kept speaking in tongues or quoting scriptures as we were praying for their deliverance, and it was only when we guided them to stop praying in tongues, quoting scriptures or talking, and to just breathe in and out through the mouth, that evil spirits began to come out. So as a prayee, expel the demons and pray only if you are guided to pray by the team leader.

We do want the prayee to declare his confession of faith, his forgiveness prayers, his repentance and renunciation of evil etc. but at the moment of expelling demons just expel.

We always consider the complete picture: the organized and hierarchical kingdom of Satan.

We have power over all the power of the enemy,
Luke 10:19.

The devils are subject unto us through the name of Jesus,
Luke 10:17.

We have power and authority over all devils,
Luke 9:1.

We can bind the powers of darkness,
Matthew 16:17.

We are supposed to cast out devils,
Mark 16:17.

We have mighty weapons through God,
II Corinthians 10:3, 4.

The Holy Spirit and the gifts of the spirit, 1 Corinthians 12:7-11 and Acts 1:8. The Cross, Father God, The Word of God, the Blood of the Lamb, The Name above all Names, the angels, the armor of God, Ephesians 6. Victory has been assured. Satan is a defeated foe.

In Ephesians 6:12 we learn what we wrestle against:
1- Principalities: Territorial and ruling spirits over nations, cities, areas, like the prince of the kingdom of Persia in Daniel 10.
2- Powers: Demons have been given authority and power from Satan to carry on their assignments.
Demons have to bow at the name of Jesus, Philippians 2:10.

He is far above all principality and power... and all things are under his feet. Ephesians 1:21, 22.

3- The rulers of the darkness of this world.
The world rulers. Demons in charge of controlling the world.
4- Spiritual wickedness in high places. All kinds of attacks coming from the heavenlies.

I like to prepare myself with prayer and fasting. I don't want to eat too much the day I have an appointment for deliverance. We pray in tongues, praise and worship, anoint the room with oil, do the prayer of protection in the name of Jesus and by the power of His Cross and His blood we bind up the power of all evil spirit involved here today and command them not to block our prayers.

We break all curses and declare them null and void. We break the assignments of any spirit and we command them to leave in the name of Jesus. We bind all interaction and communication in the world of spirits as it affects us and our ministry. We ask for the protection of the shed blood of Jesus Christ over all the ministers present, over their families, over the prayee and his family. Thank you Lord for your protection and please send your angels to help us win this battle today.

We submit and yield to the Holy Spirit and we go for the victory. We first take authority over the enemy by using the keys of the kingdom of heaven. The gates of hell shall not prevail against us, the church, Matthew 16:18, 19. We bind Satan first, then every principality, power, ruler of darkness, wicked spirits in high places, the strongman, Matthew 12:29, and every involved spirit.

We already know who we are dealing with from the history and discernment and we keep yielding and submitting to the Holy Spirit who will also show you the strongman and the other spirits.

Engaging the Enemy

Satan, I bind you in the name of Jesus Christ. I bind every principality, power, ruler of darkness, wicked spirits in high places, the strongman, and any and all other spirit involved. In the name of Jesus Christ I separate and isolate each of you and command you not to connect, communicate, reinforce, or empower each other.

I declare you bound, isolated, impotent and powerless. I command you to cause no harm or retaliate. I break all of your powers in the name of Jesus and loose (the prayee).

We go now more directly against the strongman and his associates. Strongman I bind you in the name of Jesus and separate and isolate you from Satan and any other evil spirit. In the name of Jesus I brake and destroy all your plans, assignments, curses, and all that is not of God our Father.

(We break the power of whatever we are dealing with: occultic, curses, new age, witchcraft, etc.)

In the name of Jesus Christ I loose you (Prayee) from the (for example) spirit of Kundalini yoga, and I command the spirit of Kundalini yoga to come out of you now in the name of Jesus without harming anybody. You keep repeating the commands for the spirit to leave now in Jesus name and to never return.

At Francis MacNutt ministries the spirits are commanded to go to the feet of Jesus where the Lord will decide what to do with them. Jesus just cast them out; once they went into pigs. At Bern Zumpano's ministries they are commanded to go wandering in dry places never to return. At Frank Marzullo's ministries they are just cast out never to return.

I have heard other commandments, for example: Sheol, hades, hell, the pit, the abyss, dessert arid lands, etc. I cast them out and commanded them never to return. Then we bind the rest of the spirits and kindred spirits individually. We name them according to their function, what they do, and cast them out in the name of Jesus. For example: divorce, fear, control, jealousy, addictions, panic, depression, lying, lust, bitterness, etc.

In deliverance we are persistent in commanding demons out and are always ready to receive input from the Holy Spirit. At Frank Marzullo's ministries we ask the prayee to take a deep breath and exhale them out. At times that seems to help or precipitate the process of expelling the demons.

I personally like that practice too and do it all the time in my office. How do we know when the person is free (delivered) from the spirits?

1.) Our spiritual discernment.
2.) The prayee's discernment.
3.) Simple observation and communication with the prayee.
4.) The fruit of deliverance is change.

Sometimes we need more sessions. Always fill up the house with the Holy Spirit. This might be a good time for the patient to be filled and baptized with the Holy Spirit with the evidence of speaking in tongues. Sometimes we prophesy over the prayee filling him in a deeper way. Do the setting free prayer:

Lord Jesus thank you for your ministry of healing and deliverance, cleanse us Lord from whatever we might have picked up, if any evil spirit have attached to us or affected us in any way we command them in the name of Jesus to leave right now and never to return. We call for an infilling of the Holy Spirit. We call for angels to minister to us and our families and to give us a safe trip home, we praise and thank, Father, Son, and Holy Ghost. We command no retaliation, counter attacks or revenge upon ourselves, our families or any area of our lives.

We always give a plan to maintain the deliverance.
(A manual for the Deliverance worker by Frank Marzullo)[43]
Total commitment to Christ, Matthew 22:37, John 12:26.
Unless a person is totally surrendered to Christ as Lord, he will continue to experience problems due to being led by his flesh. Demons prey upon such people who fail to deny their self life. Those who embrace the cross, considering their sinful nature dead with Christ, defeat the power of sin and mental problems. Matthew 10:38, Matthew 16:24, Luke 9:23, Luke 14:26, Phillatians 3:17-19, Romans 5:10.
Know your position in Christ, Galatians 2:20. Know that you are in Him

and He is in you.

Obedience is better than sacrifice.

Stay in the word of God. Regularly study and draw life from the word of God. Psalm 1:1-3, Psalm 119:9, 11, 105, 165, Joshua 1:8.

Praise and worship, Psalm 100, 149, 150.

Thanksgiving, 1 Thessalonians 5:18.

Pray in all circumstances 1 Thessalonians 5:17.

Pray in the spirit, Romans 8:26, 27, Ephesians 6:18.

Make positive confessions.

Deal promptly with sin, 1 John 1:9, Isaiah 59:2.

Live a life of forgiving.

Crucify the flesh, Romans 6, Galatians 5:24-25.

Do self deliverance and spiritual warfare when needed, James 4:7, Luke 10:19.

Put the whole armor of God, Ephesians 6:10-18.

Be accountable, Hebrews 13:17.

Don't be yoked with unbelievers.

Keep in fellowship, Hebrews 10:24, 25.

Keep home life in order, 1 Timothy 3:3-13, Ephesians 5:18-33, Ephesians 6:1-4.

As I was moving into the next chapter "Dreaming of God," which is the most mystical chapter of the book, I gave a teaching on deliverance at a local Church and I was guided to touch on certain important areas that I did not address in the Deliverance chapter. So I am adding the summarized teaching and it is really a beachhead into the more supernatural last chapter.

Before we came to Jesus we had different degrees of demonization. In the ministry of Phillip in Samaria Acts 8:5-13, it seems unclean spirits came out before Baptism. I believe this was a pattern in the early Church. People still ask can a Christian have a demon. We come to Christ with demons that can stay and we can get them after receiving Jesus as Lord and savior.

We all had generational curses and childhood traumas. We all sinned and had ungodly believes and inner vows, all causes of demonization.

John 1:11-13
Being the sons of God we have power and authority over all the
enemy.

Luke 10:17-19
The Lord gives us power and authority over the enemy.

How are we using the power? Just the sacraments do not eliminate
the demons. Just going to Church does not eliminate the demons. Just
hearing good preaching does not eliminate the demons. We have to
exercise the authority.

1 Peter 5:8
Be sober, be vigilant, because your adversary the devil, as a
roaring lion, walketh about, seeking whom he may devour.

A Christian can have a part of their being infested with evil spirits.

John 13:27
As soon as Judas took the bread, Satan entered into him.

We have seen Christians, even leaders committing major sins.
Some place within was controlled by evil spirits. Jesus tells us to cast out
devils. Mark 16:17, Matthew 10:1, 8, Luke 4:35.
There are different levels of oppression and infestation[44].
A.) Demonic activity from outside: Temptation, physical attacks,
oppression, heaviness, depression.
We use: James 4:7, 8:
7- Submit yourselves therefore to God. Resist the devil, and he will
flee from you.
8- draw nigh to God, and He will draw nigh to you, Cleanse your
hands, ye sinners; and purify your hearts, ye double minded.
We use Ephesians 6:10-18 and many other victory scriptures,
praise and worship, tongues, etc.
B.) Demonic activity from within. Demonization.

<u>Acts 5:3</u>
But Peter said to Ananias, why hath Satan filled thine Heart to lie to the Holy Ghost.

Possession: The Gadarene demoniac would be an example of severe possession.

We will discuss that a true Christian has a place within that the devil cannot touch. Demons entice, harass, torture, compel, enslave, cause addictions, defile, deceive, attack the physical body- in the areas of the emotions and attitudes, the mind, the tongue, sex, physical appetites, the body, etc.

I will describe demonization in different ways to increase our understanding.

Many Christians have evil induced problems. There could be an area of the person under the influence of a demon, for example: a spirit of jealousy. A demon can occupy a part of a person, for example: a spirit of unforgiveness, bitterness, resentments, a neoplasia, a spirit of infirmity.

A Christian can have a stronghold: an area dominated or occupied by enemy forces, for example: ungodly believes: God gave me this cancer because of my previous sins and He is punishing me.

We as Christians can have something damaging in us that is in control of a certain area- mental emotional physical- that is not of God and that it needs to be cast out.

What places in us can a demon invade and what places are off limits to demons:

After we are born of the spirit there is a place in the spirit that is an impregnable fortress: The holy of holiest. The glory of God. The secret place of the most high. The place without yokes. The place of El Elyon and El Shadday and El Shammah. The most high all powerful supreme God.

<u>Psalm 91:1-15</u>
He that dwellest in the secret place of the most high shall abide under the shadow of the almighty.

That's where Jesus was in the boat in Matthew 8:24. In the midst

218

of the storm He was asleep at the secret place of the most high. See also Psalm 27:4, 5, and Psalm 31:20, 21.

We will now look as man as a spirit soul and body. In the spirit there is the most sacred place, the untouchable place where the Lord abides, but there might be parts of the spirit that can get contaminated.

2 Corinthians 7:1
Having therefore these promises, dearly beloved, let us cleanse ourselves from all filthiness of the flesh and spirit, perfecting holiness in the fear of God.

1 Thessalonians 5:23
And the very God of peace sanctify you wholly; and I pray God your whole spirit and soul and body be preserved blameless unto the coming of our Lord Jesus Christ.

Jeremiah 51:51
We are confounded, because we have heard reproach: shame hath covered our faces: for strangers are come into the sanctuaries of the Lord's House.

We also have the soul composed of the mind, the will and the emotions.

We have the carnal mind which is enmity against God, Romans 8:7.

We could be in the flesh and unable to please God, Romans 8:8.

We could love the world and the things of the world and the love of the Father is not in us, 1 John 2:15, 16.

We need to walk in the spirit and not fulfill the lusts of the flesh, Galatians 5:16-21.

We can have areas of carnal mind, world mind, afflicted emotions, places in the flesh, a will with loss of control, a sickened body, all fertile grounds for the demonic.

Man as Spirit Soul and Body

In the experience of the glory (I)
In the realization of the glory there are no demons

I. Spirit Core
God Most High
Secret Place
The Glory
Total Freedom
2 Chronicle 5:13, 14
Colossians 1:27
Hebrews 2:10

II. Place of Potential Filthiness
Of the Human
Spirit that
Needs Cleansing

III. Soul= Emotions,
Afflicted Emotions, Mind,
Carnal Mind, Flesh, The
World, Needs Sanctification

IV. The Body

All other areas except I could be demonized.

Man as the Temple Of God

Where Do You Live?

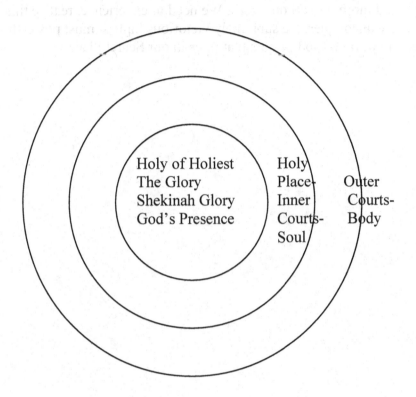

Holy of Holiest
The Glory
Shekinah Glory
God's Presence

Holy
Place-
Inner
Courts-
Soul

Outer
Courts-
Body

The Lord cleansed the temple: drove out, expelled thieves and money changers from soul and body, inner courts and outer courts.

Review these scriptures:

Luke 1:71-75, Galatians 3:29, Galatians 5:25, 2 Corinthians 3:17, Romans 8, Hebrews 2:10, Phil 2:15, Colossians 1:27.

I don't think that we can escape demonization. There is too much sin, defilement and contamination in the earth. It is very hard to serve God and live in victory if we are not delivered. We have a covenant, we are the sons of God, we live and walk in the Spirit, we carry the Glory, there is liberty in our midst, we serve the Lord in a mighty way. We need deliverance, sanctification and holiness. We need The Presence, The Glory, The Holy of Holiest, Elohim, El Shadday, The Anointing to expand more and more into all our areas. We need to experience, realize this almighty unconquerable supremely victorious highest most powerful Creator Glorious God of ours that lives in our Secret Place.

Chapter Seven

"DREAMING OF GOD AND HOLY VISITATIONS"

Getting rid of the harness of the past
Then a precipice
Deep trust
Only Him
I fall- am taken away
I can fly in new places.
There are eyes in the sky.
Winds take me.
No place to hold on.
Only Him.
Only Your will Lord.
A Blast from the sky.
Rays of Light.
Sun of Righteousness with healing in His wings.
I am equipped with wings-
for the dance in the sky.
There's a swirling and the sound of many waters.
His voice rises up.
Thundering and Lightning.
A Roar
The King of Kings.
My Savior.
Heavens appear.
Extreme angelic realms.
In their midst is the King.
Glory Himself appears.
My consciousness is gone and I swirl in the air in the presence of
His Majesty.
The shower of manifestation begins:
Gold, diamonds, rubies, emeralds, pearls, sapphires, water, fire,
clouds, smoke, sounds from heaven, Spirit of Revelation.

His Love makes it all manifest.
He plays with his children.
Joy invades.
Love abounds.
Healing appears.
Spirit of Healing right from the Heart of the Father.
It is His will that we are healed and made holy.
The incense of Praise comes up to the throne.
He loves the aroma.
Hallelujah.
A shower of blessings falls on the children.
We are further anointed.
He imparts eyes of revelation.
The creatures soar.
The wheels turn.
Heaven cracks open.
We swallow golden liquid.
Love deepens in us.
The past is far away.
We move deep into the Kingdom.
We get anchored in the new.
God blows His power upon us and we get it!
We are able to love and to heal without any limitations.
We partake of the throne and of the things of heaven.
God is in our midst.
And God is within.
We manifest Kingdom explosion.
And decree His Word.
Thank you Jesus.
Hallelujah and Amen.
Give a shout of Praise.

In this chapter we are shifting modes a bit. We are wearing the hat of visions, dreams, revelations, poetry, and the presence of God, heavenly downloads and more. All good things come from above and this is another very good thing.

Here we will briefly expose supernatural realms of the Kingdom of God. It is not the purpose of this book to do an extensive profound study. There are saints like Patricia King, Todd Bentley, Jim Goll, Joshua Mills, and many others that have been dwelling in these realms for many years. I will describe some of my experiences from the early morning seeking of the Lord.

Without vision I perish.
I want to have all that God wants me to have.
I believe in heavenly things, John 3:12.
I believe in the word of God:
It is written in 1 Corinthians 2:9: But as it is written, Eye hath not seen, nor ear heard, neither have entered into the heart of man, the things which God hath prepared for them that love Him.
-I am seeking the things above where Christ sitteth on the right hand of God, Colossians 3:1, 2.
-God hath raised us up together, and made us sit together in heavenly places in Christ Jesus, Ephesians 2:6.
-The Father has given us the kingdom, Luke 12:32.

One way that I seek the kingdom is from 4-7 am when I lay down in the sofa in my prayer room and yield and submit to the Holy Spirit and really go for the presence of God.

Luke 11:9-13
And I say unto you, Ask, and it shall be given to you; seek, and ye shall find; knock, and it shall be opened unto you.
10- for everyone that asketh receiveth; and he that seeketh findeth; and to him that knocketh it shall be opened.
11- If a son shall ask bread of any of you that is a father, will he give him a stone? Or if he ask a fish. Will he for a fish give him a serpent?
12- Or if he shall ask an egg, will he offer him a scorpion?

13- If ye then, being evil, know how to give good gifts unto your children; how much more shall your heavenly Father give the Holy Spirit to them that ask Him?

I rarely know what God will do. I invite the wind to take me wherever it wishes.
It is an experience without words when Jesus comes and I am undone, Isaiah 6:5.
The spirit of glory and of God resteth upon us, 1 Peter 4:14.

I cant breath, I weep, I explode, I am renewed.

The inward man is renewed day by day, 2 Corinthians 4:16.

Isaiah 40:31
But they that wait upon the Lord shall renew their strength; they shall mount up with wings as eagles; they shall run, and not be weary; and they shall walk, and not faint.

These are not just ethereal inconsequently experiences.

2 Corinthians 4
17- For our light affliction, which is but for a moment, worketh for us a far more exceeding and eternal weight of glory.
18- While we look not at the things which are seen, but at the things which are not seen: for the things that are seen are temporal; but the things which are not seen are eternal.

They are vital experiences to bring the active presence of God with us into our daily ministry. I didn't know what to call my early morning experiences. I know that they are related to visions, dreams, and the prophetic. The scriptures came from the revelatory realms of heaven. The prophets received heavenly downloads. They were seers and hearers of the word.
We know that the devil has counterfeits for every good thing. This is evident in the multiple new age systems, other religions, and

psychospiritual psychologies that use diverse types of imagery, visualization, oracles, intuitions, psychic abilities, divination, spiritual guides, etc.

Our God is the true God and higher than any God. Christians are taking back what belongs to us. We become mature in Christ and the Word and get involved in the deep things of God. We are not stopped by fear filled controlling cessationist or the devil. We submit and yield to the Holy Ghost and we don't get snakes, scorpions, or rocks. Anyway we are to walk in power, authority and discerning good and evil.

I took Patricia King's six day Glory School[45] and it was an extraordinary experience: supernatural! Patricia is gifted by the Lord to connect heaven and earth. In the Glory School manual we get scripturally convicted that our God wants us to be involved in His supernatural life: God encounters and places in the kingdom, appearances of Jesus and our Father, Third Heaven and Throne Room visitations, the Glory, manifestation of the glory, places in the kingdom and abodes of God, open heavens, angelic visitations, traveling in the realm of the spirit, divine revelation, dreams, visions, signs, wonders, miracles, etc, etc.

I have also been with Todd Bentley and read his also extraordinary book "The Reality of the Supernatural World" that shows us how to be caught up into heavenly realms[46].

There are many scriptures showing us that we have access to the supernatural realms of the kingdom of God and many scriptures revealing this hidden world with its different areas, structures, aspects, beings, etc. I will enumerate some of these scriptures and then describe several of the holy visitations and experiences that have occurred to me in early morning soaking sessions.

Colossians 3:1-4, Jeremiah 33:3, 2 Corinthians 4:16-18, Ephesians 2:6, Luke 17:21, Hebrews 4:16, Ephesians 1:17-18, 1 John 1:1-4, Isaiah 6, Isaiah 11:2, 1 Corinthians 2:9-16, Hebrews 11:16, Matthew 6:9-10, John 3:8-12, Colossians 1:26-27, 2 Corinthians 12:1-4, Mark 15:37-38, Isaiah 4:1-4. Matthew 3:16-17, John 1:49-51, Psalm 78:23-25, Deuteronomy 28:12, Ezekiel 1:1-28, Ezekiel 10, Ezekiel 43, Daniel 7, Daniel 10, Revelations 1, Revelations 4, Revelations 19, Revelations 21, Revelations 22.

1- I Want To See You Father

You that took me away from sin. You took away the occult. You took away sexual sin. You opened me to supernatural living. Jesus is about supernatural living, not just my limited human agendas. We have access to heaven's resources. How did He take away my cocaine addiction; how did He take away my occult involvement; how did He take away my sexual bondage.

Of course God is supernatural. He wants us to know Him supernaturally, spirit to spirit; not limited carnal mind to limited concepts, intellectualizations, ideas. The Holy Spirit is supernatural. The fire of God is supernatural. Signs, wonders, miracles are supernatural. The word of God from beginning to end is about things from heaven. Genesis, Exodus, all the heroes, Abraham, Joseph, Moses, Joshua, Elijah, Elisha, Isaiah, Jeremiah, Ezekiel, Daniel, the apostles, the saints.

Jesus- the most supernatural who told us you will do what I do. I am sending one like me who will live in you. The devil blinds. There are alliances with flesh-world systems. God is supernatural. He wants to give us eyes to the supernatural, Ephesians 1:17, 18. He wants us to experience the things from above, heavens, the throne, Revelations 4:, kingdom realms, angels, visions and revelations.

Hell wants to limit us from the full knowledge of God. God wants us to know Him with our mind, our heart, our strength, our intuition, our vision, our imagination, our feelings. Spirit to spirit not just an intellectual limited knowing. We need to exercise, activate and open our spiritual senses. Fear, control, pride, and limitations be gone.

Let's break the bondage of the limited mind. The world belief system is in alliance with the anti-Christ, anti-anointing system. We have the same Father, the same Jesus, the same Holy Ghost, the same kingdom than from the beginning.

Evil decreed that all has ended. There is still the same devil that comes to steal, kill, and destroy the truth. The truth is Jesus, the same yesterday, today and forever.

The truth is indestructible and the demon's destiny is the lake of fire. Let's move into the supernatural. Let's bring forth the victory of heaven. When the Holy Ghost settled in me, became established in me, became activated and alive in me, when the power of God became part of my will I was free.

The years of besetting major sin that would separate me from God and cause havoc in my life: divorces, drug addiction, sexual addiction, loss of jobs, separation from family, poverty, illnesses have ended. I can choose blessings today. I want your love Lord. I want to love you more. I want to visit the throne. You said ask and you shall receive. At this moment the presence and the glory of God overwhelmed me, tears began to flow and I just received……

A while later I see my heart flying up and entering the heart of the Father, then a young powerful eagle with large eyes comes out of the Father's heart and comes into my heart.

The Lord said: nurture the prophetic. The next day while praising the Lord at a charismatic prayer meeting the eagle suddenly peaked out of my heart and said, what, you are not going to use me. I had to bend over with holy laughter and joy. The prophetic anointing was released right then and there, and I prophesied collectively and individually with precise healing words of knowledge, and words of edification, exhortation, and comfort.

There were open heavens and a heavenly atmosphere touched everybody. I had visited heaven and received a gift that I brought back to earth. Visiting supernatural realms is not an ethereal inconsequential event, but an empowering glorious activity of God.

2- How Good Are You My Lord

I came late into your kingdom and you have given me many coins.
There is the coin of the Throne.
Your presence abounds in your Throne.
Oh Holy Father.
Thunder, lightning, darkness.
Don't hide from me Oh King.
Let me see you.
I feel you very deep within me.
Your joy is such pleasure.
Your flowing too good for words.
Your power glorious.
Your wings are overwhelming.

I want to fly Lord; I want to fly with your flock.

We follow the leader, the captain of the army. Jesus, Lord of all.

We are like arrows inundating the world. We bring the latter rain. Everywhere grace appears. Glory clouds all over the world.

An annunciation. The King is moving into our arena. Raise your voices, shout, the King is coming, the King is here. Bow your heads. The lover of your soul is here. He made us holy for Him. The bridegroom is here. Let no speck of the old remain.

In this dance hall only the truth prevails.

Dance, rejoice, shout, and move in all ways. Expose, express, jump and swirl in the air. Feel His presence. Become His presence. Jump in the ocean.

River, river where are you taking us? The Father is joyfully waiting at the end of the runway. It came from Him and is taking us back to Him. He wants to candidly converse with us. This is the day of love. There is love going back and forth between you and the Father, be filled, relax, let go, explode. Be in the language of love.

Today we celebrate creation. We have taken over all gardens. Goodness spreads. Jesus is our lover. The conquering giant over all universes. The Name above all Names is our lover. Feel this in your gut. Yes, be in love with the creator. That's why He made you: for love. Be free, fly with the flock. Be a spear for the Lord. Bring His goodness and love. Change the world.

Lets enforce the original plan: intimacy, relationship, communication, visions, dreams, prophetic, healing, peace shalom, abundance, multiplication, dominion, love. Go for it, that's what He wants. That's why He made you. Clouds of presence, clouds of glory, gold dust, signs and wonders, eyes of heart opening, revelation after revelation, total salvation.

The army brings a contagious Holy Ghost. Every step we take brings a mile for God. There is no stopping us. The lion of Judah directs our march. Each step is a glorious step. The river of confidence, boldness, signs, wonders, love, flows within us. Angels play large trumpets. The atmosphere is ours. The Lord reigns, Father rejoices.

Yes, I made my children like me. I give you all says the Father. I trust you. My goodness thrives in you. Keep on trucking. Go and go beyond. You have the word with you. What can stop you? everything old is shattered. It already happened at the cross. All deception is gone. I have given you my eyes, see clearly. Move on. March faster. Take it all. I am with you to the end of times. We reign together forever and ever.

3- Serving The King

Papa come.

A sheep running in deadly mazes and shrubs. Barb wire of the enemy lacerate my skin. A tempest in our midst. The boat is about to sink. Father where are thou. A heavy burden is on me, but Lord you said: my yoke is easy. Days of heaviness prevail. Despair afflicts me. Pricking thistles go into the sheep. Helpless, the sheep calls upon the Shepherd. A dark night that persists.

I am lost and I can't see. There is no light at the end of the tunnel. The tunnel has been blocked by unbelief. Roots of bitterness suffocate me. I am entrenched in a bunker of hell. Negativity is all I see. Holy Spirit were are thou. Am I not the temple of the Holy Ghost? Is there a sin that I cant see. Has a curse fallen on me? Are there any open doors for the demonic? Is there a sin of omission? Am I not praising enough or speaking in tongues for hours? Am I not going to the right church? Is it you Lord that has gone away from me.

It is time to change skins.

To enter a new garment there is the need to grow.

Life in the Spirit is different than life in the flesh. In the Spirit you are supposed to grow. Dark nights are for growth. The seed has to die for life to come on. Growing pains are the standard rule. The mind has to change. Supernatural belief has to rule. Crack open the shell.

Personality after personality has to go. This is not one old self that died, but the daily self needs to die. This is not about sin, but about serving the King. All I want is to serve the King, well, whole, complete, all of me. Have no fear.

There is a new river, a new Jordan. I lay across. The old me has been the bridge. I lay my life on the line to find the King. I am into a new land of the giants. With a new ministry come new giants. You have the power and authority to cut the head of any giant: despair, unbelief, impasse, seeing failure and death, seeing hell arise, anger, frustration, overwhelmed. Will I proclaim I am a grasshopper, or will I go forth like Joshua and Caleb? This is the time for the different spirit, new spirit of power and faith. Lord I call upon your name. Help my unbelief. Help me be born again. Help me go through this death.

It was all about His ministry. Coming out of an old structure of death. A tendency not to want to grow. A deadly status quo. I call upon the true revolution, the true rebellion. Messiah come. Emmanuel I welcome you. Holy Spirit take over. Father I need your powerful love. Let the Lord arise and His enemies be scattered. What are the enemies of grouth: unbelief, lack of vision, bondage and captivity, stagnation, fear, rigidity, old self unwilling to die, stuck in maze, helplessness, powerlessness, deception, blindness, deafness, waxing of the heart, looking back, man thing, a back bone thing. Stand firm, move across in faith, there are not only giants in hell; be a giant of the faith. You gave us the Holy Spirit.

So I have the Holy Spirit. It is a relationship. We submit to each other. A life giving relationship; the power of God. I am burning the thistles, the thorns, and the maze. Nothing is to quench the Holy Ghost. Sheep you are free to roam in the new land. There is an enemy of failure and defeat, frustration and bitterness, pride and self pity. Break the casket, let dead bones arise. Be filled up. Arise and shine. Corruption is the old. I am in the last pages of an old book. It is not a new chapter of the old book. But an all together new book; a new vision. Thank you Jesus.

4- The Seed

The deep things of God are not black and white. The rational mind sees all white and black. Papa, help me care only for your opinion. Rational mind- prideful mind- self-righteous mind- limited mind-controlling mind- bitter mind- contaminated mind-. Then there is an inner world. The eyes of the heart. The fear of the Lord is the beginning of wisdom. The surface of the iceberg, controlling mind.

I want to be who you want me to be. Sowing in dead lands. Raising my voice where no one can hear. No response, no reaping. Standing on dead lands. The land says: your anger and your rage finished me off. Your need to control separated us from God. Thinking that I know what's right, even saying: that's what the Bible says. There is a better way. Through the ages, controlling people used the Bible. The devil knows the Bible. It is about the heart. People killed quoting the Bible. It is the heart that sees the things of God.

Heart of revelation.
Eyes of revelation.
Lord I give you my heart.
The heart is a spirit.
The heart is the Holy Spirit.
Heart with wings.
Judgment and bitterness have killed the land.
Defeat, despair, depression;
Hell covers me and I can't see.
The canopy of hell obscures the eyes of the heart.
Who can see?
Rebel against the things of hell.
Breakthrough.
Hands pull us down.
Lord you are the only hope of glory.
I had a hope for the things of the earth, the things of this life,
hidden hopes in me, longings, and desires. I blame you God that
you took it all away from me.
Another level of intimacy. There is an outer façade and an inner
world. There are mixtures in the inner world: fantasy,
relationships, and bondages. How do I live Lord? Ask and you
shall receive.
I don't want to be in this desert. Transplant me into the good land.
Lord, I surrender.
I am blind, deaf, and mute. My heart is waxed.
I am done for. I fell into my pit. My limited identity has destroyed
me. I want the identity of Christ. Rescue me Lord.
Out of the mound of mud a shoot. I am the dying seed. The death
of the seed. The process of the death of the seed. Dying ain't easy.
If there is no death, there is no birth, only a lingering, an evasion,
distractions in the name of God. God wants our death. The death of
our limitations. Hard and confusing. "Who am I" thing. Can't be in
control. Have to let go of all. I am the seed. Times of darkness.
Cocoon time. All gets dissolved before any growth.

Trust. Trust you God. Dying before the new season. Seasons of God. Reckon myself dead and wait on the Lord. Lord let this be the time to birth. What is God's will is the first thing. We are learning about death so we can live.

5- The Abiding Presence

Don't hide from me my God.
I am desperate without you.
You are the only one I love.
Come Lord Jesus, come.
I look up.
I ask for the abiding presence.
The kingdom of God and joys forevermore.
The mysteries of God.
We have the spirit that knows it all.
There is a wall that prevents the knowledge of God.
The limitations of the human mind.
Spiritual knowledge comes through the Spirit.
I am the weapon of war.
The violent take the kingdom by force.
Attitude and positioning.
Character.
I can't wait on the Lord in a passive deadly hopelessness.
I can't wait on the Lord full of devils.
He gave me power and authority to destroy all walls and
  strongholds.
On the other side lay the riches of the seven spirits of God.
I run and crash into the demonic wall.
A stronghold of limitations.
Emotional creepy crawlers of the inner life.
We have yielded to the emotions but no more.
We are raising a stand and here Jesus is the only one.
Jesus, Jesus, Jesus: all is Jesus.
I want the mind of Christ.
I throw whatever gets in the way into the cross and command evil
  to flee.

There is a roaring lion in me.
The Captain of the hosts of heaven lives in me.
Enough is enough.
Self pity demons I hammer you out of existence.
Let the Lord arise and His enemies be scattered.
I don't care about the life that is away from God.
What I care is God's life in me.
Come Lord Jesus, come.
I fight to the death for Christ in me.
I command the mountain of the limitations to be removed in the name of Jesus.
The massive hammer of the Lord breaks such fortresses.
The fire of the King burns such things to ashes.
The brilliant sword of the spirit slashes evil to insignificant pieces.
The light shatters darkness.
Ruler, Creator, King, Messiah, Emmanuel, Lion, Lamb.
That blood covered body who resurrected accomplished it all. I receive the blood of the lamb that touches all my body. There is suffering in this world. We have the suffering servant who guides us out of the maze. The Lord sets my personality on fire. I go into the cross. Who would I be without me? I look more and more like Him. Freedom based being. I depend on you Lord for each breath I take.
Sanctify the will so it looks only upwards.
Even in transitory captivities we look-up.
Character formation.
Structuralization.
Moving into the rock.
Established in the rock.
I am the rock: abiding in the presence.
Tests and tribulations to remove the dross.
Moving up: let things behind, things that hold you down.
The limitations.
I am the limitations.
So die daily.
So He can live.

So He can manifest.
So He can arise and shine in you.
Let the glory come.
I need more, Lord.
I don't want just to see.
I want to be.
Harness of heaven to be upward minded and less world- afflicted.
Lord impart on me your reality in a progressively deeper way.
The Lord says: you are in my image, activate your spiritual senses.
Lord, remove scales off the eyes and ear plugs.
Remove the wax off my heart.
I want to be healed.
I want to see.
You healed my heart of stone at the cross.
There was an exchange.
You have given me a heart that sees.
The spirit of revelation.
I want to see your mysteries.
I want to walk in your mysteries.
I want to partake of the mysteries.
I want to be with you.
I come out of hidden places, and sit at a higher place.
It is the doings of my Lord.
The Lord keeps lifting me up.
I am in His River on my way to bless.
I flow as He flows and go where He goes.
A new voice comes out of the water and expresses through me.
I have a little piece of His crown on my head.
He is happy and rejoices and I hold on to Him.
My Jesus you are my need.
I feel such fullness holding on to you.
In an instant I am transformed.
A further cleansing happens and evil comes out of me.
There are banners and eyes everywhere in me.
An experience of being.
An experience of seeing.

The lion roars and chains shatter.
I am on top of Mount Zion and the breezes of the Lord caress my body.
My skin is activated to sense His presence.
Angels swirl and sing: Holy is the lamb.
In His presence I am free and full of joy.
The place under His wings is fantastic, majestic, glorious.
I swallow His breath.
My cells raise little hands and praise.
This is a new wine that I had never tasted.
In the cellars of the Lord there are endless bottles of newer and newer supernaturally aged wines.
The Father appears and blesses me.
I weep.
Such love.
I am further liberated.
Father, Father, Father.
Papa, you came to visit.
Glory, glory, glory.
Love, love, love.
Life, life, life.
Pleasures forevermore.
Father, Jesus, Holy Ghost.
Creatures soar around the throne.
Sea of glass all around.
Elders throw their crowns.
There is thunder and lightning.
Praise and worship.
The power of God is being released for the sons of God to manifest His Kingdom.
I have given you all, says the Lamb of God.
Go and take over.
Every circumstance.
Every area, every agenda.
I have given you all power and authority to do my will over yourselves, over your families, over the world.

The mountain and strongholds of the limitations have been shattered under our feet.
Go forth.
Move on.
This is the year of the blessings.

6- I Need To See God

God I need to see you.
I need to be with you.
You are my deepest longing.
My soul cries for you.
Life without you is not worth living.
God I want to experience you.
My Jesus, come.
Holy Ghost open heavens doors.
Outpour, my God.
Fill me with your presence.
Lord let me be a sacrifice in your altar.
Come, Lord Jesus, come.
I wait on you Lord.
An outcast in dessert lands.
I make an altar and remember my Lord.
I remember you Lord, how we walked hand in hand until the fall.
Fullness of life was then.
Now is a longing and a guilt and a shame.
Hopelessness and despair.
Closed heavens.
But I keep the fire going and I do want you Lord.
Bygones be bygones.
I accept my mistakes.
I walked away from you.
I burn my hand in the fire; maybe you'll smell my burning flesh.
My whole being burns for you Lord.
I am on fire for you.
I am alone in an empty dessert with my fire burning for you.
Suddenly, streams come from all angles and now I am stranded on

a mound in the midst of a lake.
A voice says come, come ye to the waters.
You who are thirsty enter these waters.
I flow in the river.
Angels sing on the banks of the river.
Come up, rise up.
Come up, rise up.
An eagle comes out of the water and it gets hit by the light.
The eagle sings, arise and shine.
Arise and shine.
Sleeper wake up.
God has made His abode in your heart.
I had been soaking in the waters and the waters are now in me.
God flows through my veins.
God flows through me.
Come up you who carry God.
Come up.
What is in me is of the same substance of what is in heaven.
Heaven did invade the earth.
Jesus came.
I hold on to His blood.
There is a new covenant.
I can boldly enter the throne.
I have my passport: the Blood of the Son.
I see the Father of glory and I am small.
He says come on, come in.
Partake of the glory.
I scream and open my arms: Father!
Angels come and I fall.
Swirl in golden floors.
I am full of gold.
The Father says gold man we love for you to visit.
You are an heir.
You are part of our Kingdom.
Come, enjoy, fly around.
Meet heaven's members.

Father.
Jesus.
Holy Ghost in me.
Angels.
The creatures.
Scrolls I eat.
Streets of gold.
The marvelous throne.
Sea of glass.
Rainbows.
Lightning and thundering.
Millions of saints filled with love.
Praising and worshiping.
Intercessors.
Our high priest leads intercession.
He is always thinking of us.
Oh my God and my Lord.
I am filled by your love.
Mansions and rooms in heaven.
Mountains of praise.
Songs never heard.
Gold storms.
Fire of God always burning.
Angels throwing diamonds into the earth.
A joy that never ends.
God is love.
I am embedded in heavenly love.
Nothing can separate me from the love of Jesus.
I engorge myself with emerald fruit.
My whole body shines from the glory.
The holy of holiest has taken over.
There are rivers in the sky and I have glimpses of still higher
 places in heaven.
I am that I am appears and I experience eternity and timelessness.
A vastness nature of God.
All knowing omniscient Father.

All is in you He says.
Ever particle of me He made.
He heals me.
I am taken into the heart of hearts.
As we are born again He places a part of His heart into our hearts.
Spirit to spirit.
Heart to heart.
Deep to deep.
He craves that connection.
The highest human need:
Intimacy with God.
Emmanuel: God with us, God in us.
We are sons of God.
Heirs to the kingdom.
Priests and Kings.
Friends and lovers.
He gives us The Kingdom.
He gives us all blessings in heavenly places.
We sit with Christ at the throne.
We have access to heaven now.
It is raining now in heaven.
Rays of light come down.
We get pierced by the light.
Remnant stains of darkness in the outer courts are driven out.
I love shinning for you Lord.
I remember how you took me out of my pig pen.
Your brillo pad really worked out.
It's dancing time in heaven.
Everybody dances like David.
Jesus leads a whole entourage.
Whirlwinds of joy and love erupt.
I have a body of joy.
Strength comes.
Peace shalom pervades the atmosphere.
Absolutely all was achieved at the cross.
I touch Jesus' hands, feet, and His side.

I touch the wounds.
I look in His eyes…
Power and love.
He is truly the King of the universe.
All knees bow to His name.
We bow in reverence and awe.
His love created us.
I don't want to go away.
There is no other place to go.
I eat a scroll to bring His presence, to bring heaven, to bring the glory down.
Everything is in us.
The kingdom and the Spirit of God.
So we go forth releasing the kingdom of God and the things of God until we move permanently up.
Hallelujah.
Praise you God.

I have been praying for very sick people with cancer. On one occasion I prayed for a man whose bone marrow had been invaded by cancer cells and he developed a very significant bleeding through his nose due to very low platelets (cells that come out of the bone marrow to clot the blood). He eventually stopped, but then I began to bleed. I always cover myself everyday with the blood of the lamb and bind the demons before praying and command no retaliation, revenge, or counterattacks, but I guess something jumped on me. I rejected the insinuations of the devil that I had whatever, and commanded the bleeding to stop in the name of Jesus and it stopped.

Then I prayed intensively with a man with cancerous ulcers of the buccal mucosa. Using gloves I placed sanctified oil upon the ulcers in his mouth and the pain stopped. He was supposed to have major disfiguring surgery but the surgeons were surprised when they went in and only had to do much less surgery.

Then I developed an ulcer in my upper palate similar to this man's ulcer. I never had such ulcers. I knew that it was another attack. I prayed against it. I went to the throne and my Father said it is not cancer. This was in February and with the ulcer I went to Patricia King's "Raising the Dead" conference. All her conferences are at least 100%.

We had Sunday morning off and the Lord suggested for me to stay in my room at the Grace Inn Hotel and pray. I prayed and wrote from 6am-3pm. I am including this prayer in this chapter, because it came as a heavenly revelatory download rhema prayer for victory over cancer. I had the ulcer for weeks, but when the kingdom did invade the place of the ulcer, the ulcer began to shrink. Thank you, Jesus.

Something happened to me after that day of prayer in my room. All happens together for good. My prayer tent enlarged. I pray now with increased intensity, power, authority and persistence. I am not backing away from what I see. I pray that I always see with the eyes of the Father. Thank you Jesus. I believe.

There is a cancer room, a chemotherapy room in my office and the Lord had guided me to bring his kingdom there and I was ready, then the ulcer came. I know evil did not want the light to push away death and darkness out of that room. It was good when I decided that I would go into the room of cancer no matter what. Never a dull moment in our kingdom. King, you rule.

7- Victory Over Cancer=The Revelation of Jesus (Long Prayer For Healing Of Cancer)

Job 22:28
Thou shall also decree a thing, and it shall be established unto thee: and the light shall shine upon thy ways.

What I am seeing, Jesus can destroy; a so called cancer.
Yes He can destroy cancer.
Fear is the enemy of life.
There is no fear in love.
Cancer: cells out of control.
Stubborn self will. An army.
The strongman: spirit of death.
Prayer of deliverance: repentance, renunciation of sin.
Bind the strong man: the spirit of death.

Command lesser spirits to leave in the name of Jesus.
Demons you have no legal rights.

Romans 6:23
For the wages of sin is death: but the gift of God is eternal life
through Jesus Christ our Lord.

2 Corinthians 5:21
For he hath made him to be sin for us, who knew no sin; that we
might be made the righteousness of God in him.

1 Peter 2:24
Who his own self bare our sins in his own body on the tree, that
we, being dead to sins, should live unto righteousness: by whose
stripes ye were healed.

I will not fail thee nor forsake thee.
Be strong and of a good courage.
The book of the Lord shall not depart out of thy mouth.
The Lord thy God is with thee whitsoever thou goest.
Sanctify yourselves.
Know that the living God is among you and that He without fail
drive out from before you the inhabitants of the land.
We have a memorial for the victory.
The Lord said this day I rolled away the reproach of Egypt from
off you.
The captain of the host of the Lord comes and gives us the strategy
for the victory. He is the victorious one and we cleave unto Him.
For me and my house we will serve the Lord. Amen.

Romans 8:2
For the law of the Spirit of life in Christ Jesus hath made me free
 from the law of sin and death.

Roman 8:14
I am lead by the Spirit of God. I am a son of God.

Romans 8:11
The Spirit of resurrection dwells in me.

Romans 8:15
I have not received the spirit of bondage again to fear, but I have received the Spirit of adoption, whereby I cry, Abba, Father.

Papa, send me a ministering angel.
Angel tells me, you are going to go through it in a victorious way.

1 John 5:4
For whatsoever is born of God overcometh the world: and this is the victory that overcometh the world, even our faith.

Romans 8:37
Nay, in all these things we are more than conquerors through Him that loved us.

There are millions with cancer consumed by darkness.
I see a huge wall.
The city of cancer.
Millions of captives behind the wall.

Deuteronomy 28: consumption, can't be healed, oppression and crushing, inflammation, devastation, downtrodden, the stranger within shall get up above thee very high, accused and consumed by torturers: we must forgive!
Curses shall pursue and overtake thee until thou be destroyed.
We must break all curses.
Generational, witchcraft over us, words from others, words from ourselves.
I am the head and not the tail. I am above and not below.
I am healed.
I have been fighting the city of cancer: there is backlash and retaliation.
I break the power of backlash and retaliation in the name of Jesus.

Ephesians 6:12
For we wrestle not against flesh and blood, but against
principalities, against powers, against the rulers of the darkness of
this world, against spiritual wickedness in high places.

Ephesians 6:12 (A.B)
For we are not wrestling with the flesh and blood [contending only
with physical opponents], but against the despotisms, against the
powers, against [the master spirits who are], the world rulers of
this present darkness, against the spirit forces of wickedness in the
heavenly (supernatural) sphere.

We are to take the territory of cancer in the name of Jesus.
The land of cancer.

Deuteronomy 7
1- When the Lord thy God shall bring thee into the land wither
thou goest to posses it, and hath cast out many nations before
thee...
2- and when the Lord thy God shall deliver them before thou; thou
shall smite then, and utterly destroy them...
I smite you and utterly destroy you- cancer- in the name of Jesus. I
curse your roots and totally dry you in the name of Jesus. Cancer
you are no more. Amen.
6- for thou art an holy people unto the Lord thy God...
8- but because the Lord loved you, and because He would keep the
oath...
9- know therefore that the Lord thy God, He is God, The faithful
God, which keepeth covenant and mercy with them that love Him
 and keep His commandments to a thousand generations.
14- Thou shalt be blessed above all people.
Thank you Lord, I receive your blessing.
15-and the Lord shall take away from thee all sickness, and will
put none of the evil diseases of Egypt...
17- If thou shall say in thine heart, These nations are more than I;
how can I dispossess them?

21- Thou shall not be affrighted at them: for the Lord thy God is among you, a mighty God and terrible.

24- and He shall deliver their kings into thine hand, and thou shall destroy their name from under heaven...

I sever and hold the head of the king over death and cancer in the name of Jesus just as David did with Goliath and the demonic army involved in cancer flees. Lord I came to you. I believe. Help my unbelief. Fear go. Doubt go. Gift of faith arise. I touch the hem of your garment Lord and I am healed.

Deuteronomy 8

3- ... We live by every word that proceedeth out of the mouth of the Lord...

14- He brought me out of the house of bondage.

House of bondage. House of cancer. Territory of cancer. Captivity of cancer. The land of cancer. Living as a prisoner of cancer, darkness, death.

Jeremiah 51

51- We are confounded, because we have heard reproach: shame hath covered our faces: for strangers are come into the sanctuaries of the Lord's house.

53- Though Babylon should mount up to heaven, and though she should fortify the height of her strength, yet from me shall spoilers come unto her, saith the Lord. So, spoilers come from the Lord to destroy Babylon.

Jeremiah 23:29

Is not my word like as fire? saith the Lord; and like a hammer that breaketh the rock in pieces?

Jeremiah 51:20

Thou art my battle axe and weapons of war: for with thee will I break in pieces the nations, and with thee will I destroy kingdoms.

2 Corinthians 10
3- For though we walk in the flesh, we do not war after the flesh:
4- For the weapons of our warfare are not carnal, but mighty
through God to the pulling down of strongholds;
5- Casting down imaginations, and every high thing that exalteth
itself against the knowledge of God, and bringing into captivity
every thought to the obedience of Christ;

Romans 12:2
Be transformed by the renewing of your mind, that ye may prove
what is that good, and acceptable, and perfect, will of God.

I am to prove the will of God for me.
The army of cancer in the city of cancer.
The stronghold of cancer.
The territory of cancer.
The power of cancer.
The strongman of death.
Rebelling cells.
Sins, traumas, curses, ungodly believes, inner vows, fear.
I bind all such spirits from top to bottom and command them to
leave in the name of Jesus. I loose myself from any evil grip in the name
of Jesus. I call upon ministering angels from my Father to help me defeat
cancer. Today I break the power of cancer over me in the name of Jesus.

Jeremiah 1:10
See, I have this day set thee over the nations and over the
kingdoms, to root out, and to pull down, and to destroy, and to
throw down, to build, and to plant. Thank you Jesus.

Luke 12:32
Fear not little flock, for it is your Father's good pleasure to give
you the kingdom.

See Ephesians 1:17-23, Ephesians 2:6, Ephesians1:3, Romans

8:31, 1 John 4:4, Psalm 68:1.

Jeremiah 10:7
Who would not fear thee, O king of nations? For to thee doth it appertain: forasmuch as among all the wise men of the nations, and in all their kingdoms, there is none like unto thee.

Isaiah 26:3
Thou wilt keep him in perfect peace, whose mind is stayed on thee: because he trusteth in thee.

Luke 12:29b
Neither be ye of doubtful mind.

Demons infuse fear and doubt. I bind you in the name of Jesus.

2 Timothy 1:7
For God hath not given us the spirit of fear; but of power, and of love, and of a sound mind.

Psalm 31
15- My times are in thy hands: deliver me from the hand of my enemies, and from them that persecute me.
21- Blessed be the Lord: for he hath showed me his marvelous kindness in a strong city.
23a- O love the Lord, all ye his saints: for the Lord preserveth the faithful...
24- Be of a good courage, and he shall strengthen your heart, all ye that hope in the Lord.

I see blazing arrows of fire falling on the city of cancer, the cancer ward, Psalm 3:7, Psalm 11:6, Psalm 7:13, Psalm 18:47-48.

Kingdom invasion. The kingdom invades all lesions. The love of God is upon us. Dunamis power and exousia authority. He gave us all to conquer the cancer ward. Hallelujah, praise the Lord, Psalm 150.

2 Chronicles 20

6- And Jehoshaphat said, O Lord God of our fathers, are not thou God in heaven? and rulest not thou over all the kingdoms of the heathen? and in thine hand is there not power and might, so that none is able to withstand thee?

7-Are not thou our God, who didst drive out the inhabitants of this land before thy people Israel, and gave it to the seed of Abraham thy friend for ever?

9- If, when evil cometh upon us, as the sword, judgment, or pestilence, or cancer, or famine, we stand before this house, and in thy presence, (for thy name is in this house,) and cry unto thee in our affliction, then thou wilt hear and help.

12- Oh our God, will thou not judge them? for we have no might against this great company that cometh against us; neither know we what to do: but our eyes are upon thee.

15- And the Spirit of the Lord said, Hearken ye, all Judah, and ye inhabitants of Jerusalem, and thou king Jehoshaphat, Thus saith the Lord unto you, be not afraid or dismayed by reason of this great multitude; for the battle is not yours, but God's.

20- And they rose early in the morning, and went forth into the wilderness of Tekoa: and as they went forth, Jehoshaphat stood and said, Hear me, O Judah, and ye inhabitants of Jerusalem; Believe in the LORD your God, so shall ye be established; believe His prophets, so shall ye prosper.

21- And when he had consulted with the people, he appointed singers unto the LORD, and that should praise the beauty of holiness, as they went out before the army, and to say, Praise the LORD; for his mercy endureth for ever.

22- And when they began to sing and to praise, the Lord sent ambushments against the children of Ammon, Moab, and mount Seir, which were come against Judah; and they were smitten.

27b- And the Lord made them rejoice over their enemies.

Psalm 149

6- Let the high praises of God be in their mouth, and a two-edged sword in their hand;

7- To execute vengeance upon the heathen, and punishments upon the people;

8- To bind their kings with chains, and their nobles with fetters of iron;

9- To execute upon them the judgment written: this honour have all his saints. Praise ye the LORD.

I execute upon you demons of cancer the judgment written. This honor have all His saints. Praise ye the Lord.

Don't look at your circumstance look up at the King of Glory.

Colossians 3

2- Set your affection on things above...

10-put on the new man...

24- Thank you Lord that you have given me the reward of the inheritance for I serve the Lord Jesus Christ.

The fire of God and the sword of the spirit are falling on the city of cancer. Lot and his family left. All else will perish. Evil parts of me are taken out by the army of the Lord.

Be sanctified by the Holy Ghost, Romans 15:16.

Be baptized with fire, Luke 3:16.

Like a refiner's fire, Malachi 3:2.

Like gold tried with fire, 1 Peter 1:7.

He comes with fire, Isaiah 66:15.

Zachariah's prophecy, Luke 1:67-79.

Be holy as I am holy. God reigneth over the heathens: God sitteth upon the throne of His holiness, Psalm 47:8.

2- He is a great King over all the earth.

3- He shall subdue the people under us, and the nations under our feet.

Philippians 2

5- Let this mind be in you, which was also in Christ Jesus:

10- That at the name of Jesus every knee should bow, of things in heaven, and things in earth, and things under the earth;

11- And that every tongue should confess that Jesus Christ is Lord, to the glory of God the Father.

16- I hold forth the word of life...

Cancer bow and confess Jesus Christ as Lord and Savior, deliverer and healer. The gates of hell shall not prevail, Matthew 16:18.

Revelations 1:18

The Lord has the keys of death and of hell.

Matthew 16:19

I give you the keys of the kingdom of heaven.

Psalm 23

Psalm 107

10- such as sit in darkness and in the shadow of death, being bound in affliction and iron (the city of cancer)

13- Then they cried unto the Lord in their trouble, and he saved them out of their distresses.

14- He brought them out of darkness and the shadow of death, and break their bands in sunder.

15- Oh that men would praise the Lord for his goodness, and for his wonderful works to the children of men!

16- For he hath broken the gates of brass, and cut the bars of iron in sunder.

19- Then they cry unto the Lord...

20- He sent his word, and healed them, and delivered them from their destructions.

Thank you Lord that you brought me out of darkness and the shadow of death. Thank you Lord that you have sent your word and healed me. Thank you Lord that you have poureth contempt upon princess and causeth them to wander in the wilderness where there is no way. The Lord is destroying the city of darkness, the house of death, the place of cancer. Fire is upon it, Psalm 18:13. Arrows are falling upon the persecutors, Psalm 7:13.

Psalm 18:14
Send more arrows Lord. Shoot out lightnings. Discomfit my enemies.

Hebrews 11:7 Send your angels Father; let them be flames of fire. Thank you Lord, you did cast out my enemies as the dirt in the streets, Psalm18:42. Hallelujah.

Thou hast delivered me from the violent man, Psalm 18:48, from the strongman, from the tyrant, from the king and his kingdom of darkness. So we first bind the strongman and then ransack his house, Mark 3:27.

Cancer be gone.
Death go.
Darkness flee.

Psalm 27
Psalm 35
27- Let them shout for joy, and be glad, that favour my righteous cause: yea, let them say continually, Let the LORD be magnified, which hath pleasure in the prosperity of his servant.
28- and my tongue shall speak of thy righteousness and of thy praise all the day long.

Thank you Lord that we have proclaimed liberty to the captives and the opening of the prison to them that are bound. Thank you Lord that we have repaired the desolations of many generations. There are only ashes at the city of cancer. The old is gone. Evil was defeated at the cross. The violent take the kingdom by force. He gave us power and authority over all evil. Power over unclean spirits- to cast them out, and to heal all manner of sickness and all manner of disease.

We put the full armor of God, Ephesians 6:12.
We were healed, 1 Peter 2:24.

Isaiah 55:11
So shall my word be that goeth forth out of my mouth: it shall not return unto me void, but it shall accomplish that which I please, and it shall prosper in the thing whereto I sent it.

Exodus 15:26
I am the Lord that healeth thee.

Isaiah 54:17
No weapon that is formed against thee shall prosper; and every tongue that shall rise against thee in judgment thou shalt condemn. This is the heritage of the servants of the Lord, and their righteousness is of me, saith the LORD.

Isaiah 60:1
Arise, shine; for the light is come, and the glory of the LORD is risen upon thee.

Again, be transformed by the renewing of you mind.

1 Corinthians 2:16
But we have the mind of Christ.

Light is coming down from heaven to enlighten, to light up the city of death. Ashes only remain after warfare, but we are to take full dominion.

All has been given to us; we have a pact, a covenant, a commission. We are to bring our light and our salt into the world. Out of our inner temples comes out the Holy Ghost. We take over the lands. We take over the land of cancer. The sun of righteousness comes with us with healing in His wings.

I am born of God.
I am a son of God.
The true light is in me.
Healing come.
Light arise.

There is a highway of holiness entering the wasted place.
Holy, holy, holy is the Lord of hosts.
Enlarge the place of thy tent, Isaiah 54:2 for thou shall break forth.
All the walls of the stronghold fall.
Ashes are filled with light and dead bones begin to rise.
Prophesy: life, life, life,
Breathe life into dead bones.

Ezekiel 37:14
And I shall put my spirit in you, and ye shall live

In John 11:25, 26 Jesus said:
I am the resurrection, and the life: he that believeth in me, though
he were dead, yet shall he live: and whosoever liveth and believeth
in me shall never die. Believeth thou this?

There is a tree of life in the place where cancer was. The mustard
seed of the kingdom gave forth a humongous tree. Eagles perch at
the branches. It is all I can see. It reaches the heavens.
There is an open portal and the house of God. Angels go back and
forth. I see Jesus as this tree of life pouring His blood and His
blessings upon all the lands. That's why He died: to give us Life.
Jesus, Jesus, Jesus.
My God and my Lord.
I raise holy arms to you.
I hear the lion roar.
My messiah, my Emmanuel.
God is in me, God with me.
Your Holy Spirit dwells in me.
Hallelujah my Lord.
Miracles of healing.
Miracles of love.

Psalm 1
My delight is in the law of the Lord and I am planted by the rivers
of waters, my leaf shall not wither.

Isaiah 55

Everyone that thirsteth come ye to the waters... Incline your ear and come unto me: hear and your soul shall live; and I will make an everlasting covenant with you.

He healed all that were sick:
Matthew 8:17

That it might be fulfilled which was spoken by Esaias the prophet, saying, Himself took our infirmities, and bare our sicknesses.

Revelations 22

And he showed me a pure river of water of life… and the tree of life and the leaves of the tree were for the healing of the nations.

Isaiah 28:17b

The waters shall overflow the hiding place.

Isaiah 35:6

… In the wilderness shall waters break out, and streams in the desserts.

Psalm 29:3

The voice of the Lord is upon the waters: the God of glory thundereth: the Lord is upon many waters.

Hebrews 4

12- For the word of God is quick, and powerful, and sharper than any two-edged sword, piercing even into the dividing asunder of soul and spirit, and of the joints and marrow, and is a discerner of thoughts and intents of the heart.
13- Neither is there any creature that is not manifest in his sight: but all things are naked and opened unto the eyes of him with whom we have to do.
14- Seeing then that we have a great high priest, that is passed into the heavens, Jesus the Son of God, let us hold fast our profession.
15- For we have not an high priest which cannot be touched with

the feeling of our infirmities; but was in all points tempted like as we are, yet without sin.

16- Let us therefore come boldly unto the throne of grace, that we may obtain mercy, and find grace to help in time of need.

Proverbs 4

20- My son attended to my words; incline thine ear unto my sayings.

21- Let them not depart from thine eyes; keep them in the midst of thine heart.

22- For they are life unto those that find them, and health to all their flesh.

23- Keep thy heart with all diligence; for out of it are the issues of life.

24- Put away from thee a froward mouth, and perverse lips put far from thee.

25- Let thine eyes look right on, and let thine eyelids look straight before thee.

26- Ponder the path of thy feet, and let all thy ways be established.

27- Turn not to the right hand nor to the left: remove thy foot from evil.

John 6:63

It is the spirit that quickeneth; the flesh profiteth nothing: the words that I speak unto you, they are spirit, and they are life.

John 7:38

He that believeth on me, as the scripture hath said, out of his belly shall flow rivers of living water.

Isaiah 43

19- Behold, I will do a new thing; now it shall spring forth; shall ye not know it? I will even make a way in the wilderness, and rivers in the dessert.

21- I have formed you for myself; show forth my praise.

<u>Ezekiel 47:9</u>
… Every thing that liveth, which moveth, withersoever the rivers shall come, shall live…

<u>Hebrews 1:9, Psalm 45:7</u>
God hath anointed me with the oil of gladness.

<u>Psalm 92:10</u>
I am anointed with fresh oil.

James 5:14-19, thank you Jesus. Isaiah 53:4-5, thank you Jesus that you have chosen me into your royal priesthood, 1 Peter 2:9.

Isaiah 61: Thank you Jesus that you have given me beauty for ashes, the oil of joy for mourning, the garment of praise for the spirit of heaviness.

I am called a tree of righteousness. The planting of the Lord, that He might be glorified. Amen.

I am healed of cancer.

Thank you Jesus that you have appeared unto me, Acts 26:8, Psalm 27:1.

The true light of the world.

Thank you Lord that you shine in dark places and that the day star has risen in my heart 2 Peter 1:19.

Thank you Jesus that you turn us from darkness into light and that you are our fountain of life.

In thy light shall we see light, Psalm 36:9.

I believe in the light and prophesy the light to shine into the city of cancer..

He called us out of darkness into His wonderful light.

We now have obtained mercy, 1 Peter 2: 9-10.

God is light and in him there is no darkness at all 1 John 1:5.

The darkness is past.

The old has died.

The new is here.

The true light now shineth.

<u>Luke 20:36</u>- We are the children of the resurrection.

<u>1 Thessalonians 5:5</u>
We are the children of light, and the children of the day: We are not of the night, nor of darkness.

Jesus is the God of the living.
He satisfies me with long life, Psalm 91:16.
He is the bread of life, John 6.
He gives me life.
We have passed from death unto life.
We love the brethren, 1 John 3:14.
God is love, 1 John 4:8.
And he loves me with an everlasting love, Jeremiah 31:3.
Captivity has been taken captive.
Jesus has set me free.
I am free indeed.
Amen.

<u>Prayer Of Deliverance Of Cancer</u>

I repent and renounce all sin known and unknown and receive the forgiveness accomplished by Jesus at the cross. I break the power of rebellion and witchcraft in the name of Jesus. I break the power of curses in the name of Jesus. I break the power of ungodly believes and ungodly alliances in the name of Jesus. I bind Satan in the name of Jesus. I bind the spirit of death and all spirits related to cancer in the name of Jesus. I bind the strongman of cancer in the name of Jesus. I bind up the strongman of rebellion in the name of Jesus. I curse the root of cancer in the name of Jesus. I command all rebellious cells to submit to the power of the blood of Christ; to submit to the power of the cross of Christ. To submit to the power of the name of Jesus. We ask the Father to release mighty warfare angels to eradicate the stronghold of cancer. I loose myself from cancer and all spirits related to cancer. I command out of me all spirits related to cancer. I command out of me spirits of illness and infirmity. We command all that is not of God to come out now in the name of Jesus and never to return. We declare total healing in the name of Jesus. We call upon the Holy Ghost to totally fill my house and seal off all entrance doors to the demonic. Thank you Lord that in the cross you accomplished all.

We release the resurrection power of God over all tissues.
Death be gone.
Life arise.
Fullness of life be established in Jesus most holy name.
I release the DNA from the blood of Jesus to all my tissues.
Thank you Lord that you made me an heir and a son.
What is not of God is no more.
Only Jesus is in me.
Thank you Father, Son, Holy Ghost.
I am healed of cancer.
Amen.

God in Nature. The Nature of God.

I had been at a prophetic healing meeting with a minister that, through words of knowledge, knew everybody's names and there were many signs and wonders, but my spirit grieved and that evening I asked God to give me a dream because I was not sure what was going on in that ministry.

This is the dream:

I am walking in the evening asking where is the beautiful, where is the poetic, where is nature? It is like I miss something of the natural, something of the intensely poetic, something of the beautiful. I look up and I see God in the stars and I wake up. I then asked God if He could give me more revelation about His dream. God said, I created the stars, that's why you see me in the stars. I asked the Holy Spirit to take me deeper into the truth of God in nature. I see a fast river with wild white waters, and the sun sparkling on the foam. There are sparkles everywhere. Sounds intense. Like a whoosh and a hum, and a roar, and a lion majestic stands erect watching his creation. Out of the sparkles arise little rainbows, moderate rainbows, large rainbows, sparkles and light give birth to rainbows. Rainbows give birth to rainbows.

I am going to have two grandchildren. God said let there be light and there is the light. Brilliant light hits the rapid waters. The salmon come to spawn. The bear eat the salmon. The bear give birth. I give birth to the things of God.

It is not just intellect, but the deep things of God. My heart is not just a factory of whatever, even words of knowledge, but a place in which He abides and He is love, He is creation, He is resurrection. He is not rigid or constricted. He is not just intellectual, oppressed, or in need of money. He is God and He created all. I am birthing life, love, miracles, and more love.

The sun of righteousness covers the earth and our healing is in His wings. I colabor with my God, but I need to get into the spring. Out of a little hole high in the mountain He begins to trickle and He is happy; each drop of water is filled with light. The light of the creator. Let there be light and all else followed.

Each drop of water has God in it.
Each drop of water has light in it.
Each drop of water has love in it.
Each drop of water has life in it.
Each drop of water has miracles in it, and I am full of water.
I am mostly water. Lord let this be your water, your light, your love, your life.
Lord I am your miracle.
You created me and filled me with you.
If there is anything dead in me come alive now in the name of my love Jesus.
The water trickles.
It birthes in the mountain.
Mount Zion exudes water.
Many springs merge.
There are sounds everywhere.
The elephants trumpet.
The monkeys howl.
The shofars reverberate throughout the land.
The wind brings a loud sound.

Eagles and angel's wings make a new shhhs and shurrrs.
The wind hits the mulberry trees and different shhhs come forth .
High pitch, low pitch, all the pitches.
Holy Ghost.
Intellect, rigidity, dryness, oppression, deadness all bow.
The name of God is everywhere.
The rocks sing songs.
The birds sing songs.
The crickets sing.
The humans shout and the rains come.
Truly all is God.
The rains come and the trickle that is born out of the mountain becomes a mighty spring.
Everything gets out of the way and watches in awe.
A few drops is now a mighty waterfall.
Oh God you are so beautiful.
Oh God you are so mighty.
Oh God you are so strong.
Show me your face oh King of Kings.
I flow in the moving waters.
My skin falls.
My issues are taken away.
My head, my heart, and my belly are opened.
I don't care about myself.
I care about my God.
Lord I want you issues.
I am bare and exposed.
Open and vulnerable like a little child who just learned how to walk.
Running to hug my Father.
Running towards my Father.
Without any agendas.
There is nothing in my mind.
There is nothing in my heart.
There is nothing in my belly.
I am running, tumbling, falling, getting up, happy, happy, happy,

free, without any agendas.
Just running to hug my Father.
I melt in the arms of my Father.
The earthen vessel rests, and the spirit soars.
My spirit is full of the Holy Ghost.
The golden eagle flies.
Light shines upon the eagle.
The eagle's eyes are God's eyes.
Sees far.
Sees deep.
Sees wide.
It grabs its fish.
I preach salvation out of the depth of my heart.
Out of the depth of the heart of God.
The word is made flesh and abides in me.
God is love.
All is out of love.
If I become rigid, judgmental, oppressive, stonehearted, dry, dead
bones, I have to die again and be born again.
I don't want to live without God.
I don't want to live without love.
I don't want to live without light.
I don't want to live without the river.
I don't want to live in my head only.
I am the eagle going 100 miles an hour into a deep dive and
suddenly I turn up.
Hallelujah.
Oh, space is mine.
Heavens are available.
You are my treasure, not my ministry, or my giftings, or my needs,
or my money, or my agendas.
You are my treasure.
Lord I give you my heart.
The trickle is now a mighty river,
It is moving, advancing, going forward, and it has a name.
The unstoppable river of God.

There were dead dry desserts, unreachable lands, but the river advances.
Nothing can get in His way.
It is the River of God.
Life, resurrection, creation, live in it.
There were old deadened places in me that are now alive.
I am the river.
I am the eagle.
I have the eye of God.
My heart has been touched.
God owns my heart.
He is the treasure that made His house in my heart.
Bethel, house of God, open heavens, Jacob's ladder, angels going up and down, down and up.
What goes up must come down.
Now a company of eagles take over the sky.
All creation groans and looks upwards.
Shouts of praise overwhelm the whole earth.
The King is about to return.
Hearts are being invaded by God.
Hail the King of Kings.
Lord of Lords.
Messiah.
Jeshua.
Emmanuel.
The creatures soar.
Holy, holy, holy.
The elders throw their crowns.
The Lord reigns over all the earth.
His glory is everywhere.
Hallelujah.
Oh that I am taken totally by my maker.
Away from stuff into His Kingdom.
The kingdom of God is with me.
The kingdom of God is with me.
The kingdom of God is with me.

There are no words.
There is the kingdom of God in me.
The unstoppable river advances.
The entourage of heaven flies all around the river.
All creatures sing, chirp, crick, howl, make sounds.
The wind has a voice, and there is a voice in the waters.
The Lord proclaims the Truth.
The word of God erupts out of the water.
Rhema.
Prophetic.
Mighty words of knowledge.
Drops, sprinkles, showers, waterfalls fall on everybody.
We get soaked by the word of God.
Christ dances unimpeded.
There's a whirlwind in our midst.
The Lion roars his message.
Repent because I am coming.
Love because I am coming.
Minister because I am coming.
Fly high because I am coming.
Die to self because I am coming.
Put your garments, shake loose.
Heavens have invaded the earth.
The Kingdom is in our midst.
The King is shaking all loose.
So we be holy as He is holy.
The river of holiness has invaded the unreachable dead places.
It is the river of miracles.
God is the River.
It is the river out of Mount Zion.
God has enthroned Himself in our praises.
Glory is in our midst.
It is the river from the throne.
It is the river of His heart. Grab on, do not let go, hold on to your
bucket and drink-drink-drink.
Drink the waters from the throne.

This is the time of birthing.
Enlarge you tents.
Open up to the impossible.
Faith is not what we see.
Grab the unseen.
Live in the supernatural.
Bring the things of heaven into the earth.
God is with us.
God is within us.
Praise and release Him and arrange the atmospheres.
Interceed and change the nations.
That is His will.
The river is now in new old places.
Uncharted territories.
Lands that were dead.
It is us and it is the world.
Seeds sprout all over the earth.
There is not a place that God is not touching.
This is a real sweet water.
A water that brings life.
All hunger for the water of God.
You that hunger and thirst come to the waters.
He has released the river.
Life, love, light.
He has released His goodness.
Become a sponge and be filled.
Dead bones have become a mighty army.
Stone hearts are hearts of flesh.
Captives are set free.
Broken hearts healed.
Dead raised.
Blind see.
Cripples walk.
Deaf hear.
Prisoners jump like wild calf out of the barn as they are set free.
Yes, He is the Messiah and He is in our midst.

The river now covers the whole earth.
Small beginnings.
God in a manger.
Now He rules.
Flush gardens being raised on old crooked dried skeletal ridden lands.
This is called renewal of the mind.
This is the new heart of flesh.
This is the tabernacle in the belly.
I do love high praises that bind kings and nobles.
Hallelujah.
Oh what beautiful mustard tress are covering the old lands.
Trees of life everywhere.
We are the army of the Lord, planted in the flowing river, being fed constantly.
Always with green leaves.
Always with mighty fruit.
Give-give-give.
It is better to give than to receive.
We stampede and run to the altar to give.
I give you me, Lord.
I give you all I have King.
I am honest Lord, I need to have you.
I need more of you.
I cant live an instant without you.
You are all I want.
You are all I need.
You are my desire.
Come come He says, sit in the throne, accompany me.
Lets talk, lets ponder, lets converse, lets relate, lets have communication.
Lets love, lets plan.
Millions of creatures are praising in heaven and interceding for us that are running the good race here in earth.
There is the cloud of witnesses rooting for us.
Many blessings are pouring from heaven.

God intimately knows about the war.
Inner wars.
Outer wars.
The conquering of His earth.
He knows.
Do you understand.
He totally knows our struggles and our conflicts.
At times He suffers with us and it is not only my tears, but our tears.
Lord you are showing me your glory and your goodness.
Oh mighty God of Mercy, Grace, Compassion, Love.
So I sit with my Lord at the throne, blessing the whole earth, preparing the way of the Lord. Justice and tribulation will come. But we are on His side. He is established in us. I trust you my Lord. Amen.

Chapter Eight

"THE LAKELAND, FLORIDA OUTPOURING HEALING REVIVAL"

After I finished the supposedly last chapter of the book "Holy Visitations", THE MOST HOLY VISITATION surprised us at Lakeland, Florida on April 2008. While driving to the Church of Auburnsdale on Highway 4 I saw eight nests on the telephone poles. There were young ospreys moving their wings getting ready to fly. These are fish hawks that always get their fish, and the Lord again told me, there is a new brand of doctors no matter the age that will give Jesus to the patients at the office. Hallelujah.

The Lakeland outpouring revival seems to be a major revival- The Biggest Yet? If 600 million people were influenced by the Azusa street revival of 1904, many more will be influenced by this revival. As soon as I began watching Todd Bentley in the internet I began to receive impartation. The presence of God and the healing anointing increased in my office. Faith, boldness, and power increased, but the biggest gift was the falling of the Healing Glory on the office.

Why did that happen so soon in my office? Even before visiting Lakeland.

1- I had been waking up early in the morning seeking God for five years.

2- I knew that the spirit of God could arise in me through the airways.

Several years ago I received a direct healing, faith, boldness, anointing while watching Todd Bentley healing people through the cell phone. I became intensely activated and healed seven patients through the cell phone.

3- I became a partner of Fresh Fire Ministries.

4- I went to the impartation conference at Abbotsford on November 2007 where Todd laid hands on me and gave me a double anointing. When I got back to my office in Miami the number of patients waiting for me had doubled. That day I saw forty patients. Many were saved, healed and delivered. So, there had been a preparation. God planted seeds in me through Todd Bentley. A way had been opened. So, when the Lakeland outpouring began it fell in my office. This is the e-mail I sent to Ignited Church 4/16/08:

Testimony from Miami Beach of Lakeland Healing Revival

I am a medical doctor and a partner with Fresh Fire Ministries. Impartation and anointing came from Lakeland and revival fell in my office. The presence of God and angels are lingering in the office, even in the parking lot.

Today an 85 year old woman was totally healed of a hip fracture. Endstage knees, sciatic pains, rotator cuffs, fibromalgia are rapidly healed. Many childhood hurts have been healed. The love of the Father is breaking forth and many weep. Many people rest in the Spirit. Some are baptized with the Holy Ghost and speak in tongues. Words of knowledge and prophetic words just flow from the heart of God. All kinds of spirits of death, infirmity, and depression are cast out. This is ongoing, day after day, just as Lakeland. It fell here!

A cesarean scar disappeared from a patient. Another patient was lifted up and visited rooms in heaven and received a crown. All of this and more is happening at the doctor's office. Bless you. Keep revival on. Thank you Jesus.

I visited the Lakeland outpouring and went to the two original Churches, The Ignited Church and The Auburnsdale Church. I didn't want to leave. I had an awesome time in the Glory. After I left, the revival moved to the Lakeland Civic Center and now 5/03/08 is at Tiger Stadium due to the increasing number of visitors and lack of space.

I was there from 4/23/08-4/27/08. What a blessing. Todd laid hands on everybody. He laid hands on me eight times. Completion and New Beginnings!

This week in my office 4/28/08-5/02/08, the Presence of God and His Healing Glory pushed through. God is into healing. He is in pursuit. I began to record testimonies in a notebook. In five days there were over fifty people saved, healed and delivered in my little room at the doctor's office. God loves the sick and wounded. I don't fully understand it. I am in awe and fear of the Lord. Lord, never leave me or my patients.

Oh my God I become so humbled as you keep showing up when we call upon your name. Oh my King I cannot not cry. I'm feeling your goodness deep within me. I praise you Lord that you have also invaded my patients and they are being blessed.

I am preparing to go back to Lakeland or wherever the wind takes Todd and his team. Something absolutely new is happening. We had a healing in the Glory meeting in my house with amazing deliverances. Thank you Lord.

A new ministry was born from the revival. In November I am going to Uganda to train, equip and impart "Jesus in the medical office" to doctors there. Isn't that marvelous? Millions will be saved, healed and delivered at many doctor's offices.

As the days go by more and more people are healed. There are many salvations, healings and deliverances. These are some of the testimonies of instantaneous healings in The Presence: Hepatitis C, carotid stenosis, severe cervical and lumbar spine disease, herniated discs, radiculitis and raduculopathies, canal stenosis, nerve damage, peripheral neuropathies, sciatic pains, arm and leg pains, bronchitis, asthma, manic depression, facial rash, crippled hands, abdominal pains, epilepsy, vascular disease, fibromyalgia, osteoarthritis, knees, shingles, neuralgia, tinnitus, throat ulcer, sinusitis, depression, bleeding from bladder cancer, severe foot pain, gastrointestinal bleeding, insomnia, headache, right arm numbness from stroke, vertigo, baker's cyst, trigeminal neuralgia, deafness, allergies, dizziness, acute trauma and many deliverances of spirits of witchcraft, freemasonry, infirmity, deaf, suicide, spiritism, the occult, new age, pain, etc.

Many people were healed by simply becoming quite and resting in The Presence.

A lady that was healed of severe fibromyalgia and major clinical depression described what she felt: immense joy, incredible satisfaction, tenderness and peace in the heart, tears of happiness, something wonderful. Oh how wonderful is our God.

I will end the book with five essays in relationship to the beginning of the Florida Revival.

1.) Rooms in Heaven

The only important thing is Your Presence Lord.

Do whatever you need to do in me so you can fully come.

It's more than being eager. I can't exist without you.

Lord, I am hurt and broken. Dismantle me. Make me in your ways.

Lord, I want to see your Glory. Finish me off. Come, Lord Jesus.

Open my eyes Lord. Give me revelation of you. Give me new eyes of revelation. Let me see your face Lord. You said ask and you shall receive.

Holy Spirit show me Jesus.

Angels take me to my Lord.

Roaring waters, a waterfall, The Presence.

Two waterfalls filling the wells. The gifts are in the well.

I grab a sword and go up and enter the Heart of God.

I receive hope and healing and eat emerald fruit of the rainbow of heaven.

I am full of green and dance for Jesus.

I see the throne of David.

I hold on to The Lamb. I hold on to The Lion.

Gifts of power and love fill me up. I look up to Jesus.

Change my eyes Lord so I can see the things of heaven. Give me new eyes of revelation Lord. You said, "I give you anything you ask for."

I Believe: I Receive.

Gift of faith, gift of seeing, gift of revelation, gifts of power and love, revelatory gifts of heaven. Gifts of the Holy Ghost.

To serve. For the Glory of God.

Father says: when are you going to act in ways according to what I have given you?

The Lion and The Lamb. Power evangelism. Moving in the gifts.

Jesus pushes me into my room of the heart in heaven. The room of the circumcision. Fear and weakness are taken out. Self pity, paralysis, unbelief, inferiority, age, no, are taken out too. Yes is poured in. Stand firm is established. An eye that sees is placed in. The goodness of God is installed in me. Justice. Righteousness. Conviction. Attributes of God. Act like God. Behave like God. The

Throne. Judgment. The love of the Father. The power of God. The eyes of Jesus. Faith to hold on to what has been given. Act out your faith. The faith of God. Go forth.

Barriers, walls, impediments. All evil is under our feet. We trample on serpents and scorpions.

It all began with two waterfalls filling up the wells of salvation. Holy Ghost in me, Jesus in me, Father in me, God in me. An outpouring that shoots out. Fountain of God, Holy Ghost, things of heaven, keys of the kingdom of God, hold on, truth of Spirit. Open the wells Lord. Depths inside of the maker. The Word. Let there be Light. Power of creation, power of resurrection, power of life.

He is the life and the resurrection.

Jesus is Lord. I die Lord, I live in you Jesus. I'm coming forth. The ministry of Jesus. And you will do greater things. I give you the Holy Ghost. And He blew on them. Fruit, fruit, fruit. Fruit from the Glory. I eat of you and I become your fruit. Out of the vine I move on. I am intimately and permanently connected. I glorify my Father. Fruit and more fruit. Holy Ghost. Shaba. Life erupts. A volcano of the love. Rooms in heaven where I get fixed up. Oh I am getting my make-up. Eyes of revelation. Mouth from which His word flows. Ears to hear His word. Heart of the Father. Wings and the sun of righteousness. I am filled up. Shoes of the gospel. Helmet of salvation and hope. Breastplate of righteousness. Belt of truth. Shield of faith. Major sword of the spirit. Tongues and more tongues. Shababababa. I am ready. Equipped in heaven. Now I can minister in the earth. My belly groans. The Lion roars. The river flows. The kingdom marches on. The King is in our midst. He directs our march. Strategies from heaven fall in our midst. The circle within the circle. Jacob's Ladder. Angels move up and down. Angels for every issue. Angels over cancer. The healing revival angel. New spine to stand firm. New back bone. Strength and the power of God. Holy Ghost. I go forth.

Amen my Lord.

2.) Prayer of Impartation of the Healing Anointing in the Medical Office

Let me see what you are doing Father. I want to know what you are doing.

I want more of all of you Lord. Blast me with your presence Lord. Invade me Jesus. Cleanse my heart so you can come in. You made me like you so we could know each other. I want to know you Lord. I want to know you at the depth. Heart to heart, spirit to spirit. The anointing is the presence. How does the presence come. Seek God with all your heart.

Persona, masks, bitterness, rigidity, false selves, unbelief, woundings, spirit of judgment, go, in The Name of Jesus.

Seek God with childhood innocence. I seek the anointing. I seek the presence. I come with an open heart. I surrender, Lord Jesus. Image. What is my image of me. Carnal image. Demonic image. Ungodly beliefs. Identities. Feelings. Emotions. States of mind. Conditions. Circumstances. Robbers of the Glory. Looking at myself vs. looking at God.

Colossians 3. No matter what, I have my affections on you.

How do we break through collective atmospheres. Atmospheres that oppose the Glory. The Glory, The Presence, The Anointing. Bronze heavens of unbelief. Unbelief in the Church. A controlling curse. Chains of hell.

Psalm 149: warfare. We chain hell.

Open heavens. Jacob's ladder. Angels going up and down. I see the creatures carrying the throne. The Glory fell upon the house and we could not walk or talk. Heaven entered earth. Life support. A new awareness of The Silent Awesome Presence. If you don't come Lord, it would be a dead day at the office. I can't bare that. You know how much pain and suffering is in the sick. You are always moved with compassion. You always heal the ones that come to you. No matter what, you healed. You are Mr. Healing Lord. That's who you are. You are just like your Father Jehova Rapha. It is your character Lord. It is your nature. I want you Jehova Rapha. You that live in me. Come out, come out into the environment. Do not remain hidden Lord. Change atmospheres.

Release healing. Presence come. Power of God come. Fully equip me Father. Anoint me Lord. Jesus come. Holy Ghost come. Let me be one with you and heal, heal, heal, love, love, love. Bring the Kingdom on. Fully manifest Lord- Jesus in the office. The Healer in the office. Notable signs, wonders, and miracles. Open eyes today Lord. Heal cancer today Lord. Raise the dead Lord. Bring salvation on.

The Kingdom is about Sozo salvation. The Presence is about Sozo salvation. The Anointing is about Sozo salvation. Break the yoke in my office Lord. Release the anointing. I receive You King of Kings, Lord of Lords. The knee of illness bows to your name. Father let me see what you do. Open my eyes Lord. I want all of you Lord, not a partial you Lord, but all of you. give me your eyes Lord so I can see what you see. Release all the types of healing angels specific for each disease. Open heaven's doors. Open the rooms of the organs. Give me the key of creative miracles. I know your heart Father. Heart of compassion of my Father. Circumcise me to the end Lord. let me not be. You be. You are the Glory. Come Lord. release yourself. Don't hold back. Release the gifts. You are the gift. I seek you Lord. I seek you above all things. Come Lord Jesus. Welcome Holy Ghost. I yield. I submit. Take over the atmosphere of the office. We bind and expel evil from the office. We bind the territories of illness, disease, infirmity over the office. We anoint the office. We declare the office sacred territory. We call upon the blood of the Lamb upon the office. We slay all giants that oppose the anointing. You rule King. Lion roar upon the office. We are taking the land. You gave us the land. You go before us and take over. Faith walks before me. Faith invades the office. Seeds sprout in my office. New highways are established in the office. The highway of healing. The river from The Throne. It is the office of Jesus. He rules in the office. Take over Lord. do your thing. I get out of my way and get in your way.

Healer, lover come. Inundate my heart. Inundate my office. Inundate my patients. All is yours. I bow to the King. Name above all Names. Ruler of the Universe. The Presence of God in the medical office. I prophesy millions will be saved, healed and delivered in the medical offices. Life has come into medicine. The wings of healing now guide the direction of medicine. Name above all names, King of Kings, Messiah, Emmanuel, Jeshua has risen in my office. That's what I am doing says the Lord.

3.) Anointed

Oh my Lord, give me more of you, stay, let your Presence linger. There is such emptiness, despair and deadness without you.
Lord Jesus, I lived most of my life without you; of course there is regret. Angel says, do not look back. He took you out. He gives you now. Open to receive. Open your heart for your Father. There are specific fruits for each of us in heaven.
Father, I want the healing anointing. Throne of Faith. Substance of things hoped for. Evidence of things not seen.
Father says, what you want is more, right?
Father, I am new, my time is short. Zap me to do the activities of your Kingdom in the medical office. Blindness and cancer go.
I receive a large key chain with multiple keys. I put it around my neck. The Word around my neck. Keys to unlock the mysteries.
Lupus: self hate.
Emerald fruit is the substance. I have the evidence. The evidence is in me. Act out the evidence. Produce the evidence. Manifest the evidence. I have given you the Kingdom little children.
I am small, I am a newcomer, I am a little child. I call upon the Kingdom to manifest In The Name of Jesus. The spirit of God abides in me. I have all power and authority to cast out devils and to cure illnesses and diseases through Christ Jesus.
The spirit of the Lord is upon me, because HE HAS ANOINTED ME....
I have to proclaim the Kingdom. Heal the sick....
I sit in heavenly places. I am a king and a priest.
He has released angels for me.
The evidence is His Word. The evidence are His promises. The evidence is what my Lord did at the cross. I have the evidence.
How do I manifest such awesome evidence?
Believe, and whatever you ask will be given unto you.

I accept the healing anointing to open blind eyes and to cure all kinds of cancer.

Room of the circumcision. Surgery for unbelief. Renewal of the mind- for what He has for me. Take away fear, unbelief, doubt, weakness, self-pity, inferiority, old age, language.

Receive the power of God you who believe.

I had a sinful life, but He made me new. Shame be gone, guilt go, fear go.

The Anointing to manifest The Presence of God. The tangible, contagious, transferable, manifest Presence of God in me manifests around me.

Bring the people into the Kingdom radius. More, Lord, more manifest Presence. Heart to heart. Spirit to spirit.

Transferable Presence. There is an explosion of faith. Contagious faith. Anointed to impart faith. Faith faith faith that sees the impossible happen. Nothing is impossible to God. For God all things are possible.

Anointed to see the things of God. Anointed to speak what we see. Seeing in the Spirit. Bringing the things of heaven into the earth.

Substance of miracles. I hope for miracles. There is an expectation for miracles. I see miracles above- bring them down. Act out your faith. Faith of God. Holy Ghost.

Winds of change manufactured in heaven reaching the earth. Faith pulls them down. Faith opens the doors of heaven. Outpouring. Raining gold.

The King reigns over our agendas. We are sons and heirs.

My identity is in Him: Him alone.

Lord, you rescued me and got me involved in all of this.

Let me see you. Oh how I love you. My affections are on you. Change me, mold me, embrace me, let me look like you.

If I behold your face I am changed from Glory to Glory. Let me peek Lord. Open the door. I knock. You knock too. I open the door of my heart. We both open the doors of our hearts. We commune. Deep to deep. Heart to heart. Spirit to sprit. Come Lord. You who are worthy come. I call upon your name. I bow. Come Lord. Jesus places His hands upon my head. The Lion roars. Angels put a Fire in me. I am on Fire. I burn for you Lord. There is a heavenly Fire. The baptism of Fire. Faith and Fire. Anointed to see. Taking keys out of my bag in heaven and placing them in my key chain around my neck.

4.) Necessary

To meet God in the early morning. The intimate connection from where my soul grows. The spirit wants to soar. That's the nature of the born again spirit- to soar, to sit in heavenly places.
Earth is a Patmos, so come up.
I groan and grieve for Michael Ann. Oh do I have a broken heart. I trust you Lord, but I must ask why. I love you Lord, but I must ask why.
Silence.
One running from his destiny. It jumps to his death, but is paralyzed in mid air. It takes off his garment of hell and there is a shoot. Milk honey substance from the Glory feeds it. A fat infant is at a black nest of hell in mid air. Old roots have to be taken out.
Old nests discarded. Roots to the beginning. Adamic nature. Roots to the world. Roots to flesh. Conceived in sin. Rooted to sin. The hoodwink.
Blind deaf waxed hearts can't be healed. The hoodwink and old roots.
Do you love Jesus above all things.
Do you love Jesus above yourself.
Do you love Jesus above your issues.
Do you love Jesus above sin.
The baby tries to move his wings, but there are strong roots to the old.
Roots that bind. Adam-flesh-the world. Roots that suck the life out of you. Roots of defeat.
Roots, ropes, shackles, cords. An umbilical cord that depletes.
All evil forces mount an attack against growth.
Father of lies has established deception as a root.
Roots of deception. Blinding deception. Veils, scales, wax, ear plugs.

Captivity. Can't see, hear, understand.

Depleted in the old nest. Defeated in the old nest.

Disease, illness, infirmity: ruling of death. Gasping for breath.

Generational imprinting has taken over. Life of curse.

Hopeless suffocation makes you hold on to flesh and the world. A deadly empty heart needs to be fed. The infant was thrown out of the garden into barren lands. Evil grabbed the infant in mid air. The grip of death.

Evil blinds and suffocates. The grip of death.

Shells, masks, personas, wrong identities, lies, walking around dead. They have not been truly born again.

Limited facades live lives of death.

Empty shells roam the world.

The child gasps in the nest.

Transitions. Places of choice. A war for our souls. What way would I go. Life vs. death. Blessing vs. curses.

The honey Glory cloud is always present. God is always pursuing us. Which offer are we going to take. Heaven or hell. Christ or devil. Life or death. We have been sentenced and are already dying. But there is one hope. JESUS THE HOPE OF GLORY.

From the nest of death I choose to abandon all that is not of God and I am all that is not of God.

I choose to die today so Christ can live in me.

The old nest crumbles.

The Adamic nature is destroyed.

The blood of the Lamb falls on me.

Angels hold me.

I am an infant renewed.

I have been born of the Spirit.

I am a new creation.

The old has passed away.

Now I can look up to Him and set my affections on Him.

I have passed from death to life, from darkness into His Wonderful Light.

I call the Father Abba. Abba empowers me to do His will.

Abba says, I give you power and authority to do my will.

I am a king, a priest and a prophet and I have the Sword of the Spirit.

The Word of God is established in my heart.

I live for you Lord. The old structures crumble. All that is not of the King goes.

There is a destiny and a purpose and the full equipping to fulfill the destiny and the purpose.

I work for the Kingdom of God. I have all blessings in heavenly places.

I sit at the Throne. I rule and reign with my King.

We have the keys of the house of David. We open and close doors. We take dominion. I move under the wings of the most high. If God is for me who can be against me. I am purified, sanctified, and made holy. Evil has no hold on me. My affections are on Him. I have new eyes that look at the goal: Jesus and only Jesus.

Jesus releases the anointing. I am going to Africa to impart the anointing for praying at the doctor's office. The anointing to bring the Presence and the healing Glory into the medical office. Spirit of revelation and the seer anointing to receive downloads from the Spirit for healing of specific illnesses. Dunamis and Exousia to conquer illnesses. Gift of faith and boldness. Impartation to establish the Kingdom of God in the office. Power of God to transform lives in the office visit.

Thank you God, the old has passed away. The new shines forth.

Doctors arise and shine for the Glory of the Lord is upon you.

I stand on the firm and settled ground of the Word. I am in the rock, my Jesus.

All stronghold have been rooted out and destroyed.

The mustard seed has become a tree.

I am planted in new ground. A ground that gives 100 fold.

I am planted on the river that constantly nourishes me. The river of life.

God is in me and I worship Him.

Let me feel you Jesus. Come Glory. Fill this house.

A new ministry is born out of the Glory to equip and train physicians to bring the healing Glory into their offices.

Jesus is Healing the Broken Heart of Medicine
(Patients come in and they get a pill but they don't get Jesus).
NOW THEY WILL GET JESUS. You came today Lord. Oh
faithful God. I worship you. Everlasting love. You give so much.
Oh my Jesus you know me; how I want to take you everywhere.
Keep me in the grip of holiness Lord. You transferred me Lord. Oh
Lord don't let me veer right or left.
Keep me established in you for the rest of my days. Amen, Jesus.

5.) Emmanuel in our Midst

You made me holy. You separated me for you.
How can that be?
That God took me out of the pit and became loving to me.
Evil wants to separate us also to itself.
A war for our souls.
Love never fails.
We were born to love our God.
My main problem is me. What do I do with me?
Fears, tremblings, shakings. I just want to hide.
But I was called for the breakthrough.
This is the Time of the Breakthrough.
Times of Revival.
Times of Holy Visitations.
Times of Empowerment.
Time to do the things of the Kingdom of God.
Fears go. Trust arise.
I see new shoes, reddish shoes that point outward.
Kingdom radius: expansion, multiplication, dominion.
He is giving us all.
The King is empowering us with all blessings in heavenly places.
He gives each of us a scepter of His Kingdom.
We are to carry on His agendas with all power and authority.
Out of the works of holiness we receive a new authority.
Out of relationship and intimacy we receive: keys over cancer,
keys of provision, and many keys.
Jesus did come and He is here and He is a rewarder of all who

diligently seek Him. So choose today. His agendas or my agendas. Blessings or curses. Life or death.

I see flags. Dominion over finances. Dominion over the city of cancer.

Ask and you shall receive. Seek and you shall find. Knock and it will be opened.

Lord I want you. Holy Visitation.

Fiery hot coals for the nations.

I see the eagle wet from the afterbirth.

Wow, birth is tough. I was really born again. My wings have been trimmed for trips into heaven and trips into the earth. I have even visited hell and proclaimed the dominion of my King.

I am a carrier of the Kingdom and of Heavenly Glory. Isn't that awesome.

The King majestic stands dressed in white. Glory rays are on His Face. He smiles.

We have arrived at a most special time- a kayros time of taking over.

New territories have been opened right in front of our eyes.

Move on, move in, and take over for The King. He is in our midst and nothing can stop us.

It is the unstoppable river of God that flows from the Throne.

Leaves of heaven and glorious water come with us.

Glory to glory. Everlasting to everlasting. We are becoming like our King.

The King of Glory is in our midst and He says rejoice.

The Glory of the Lord is covering the earth.

Arise and shine you all that love me.

I am commissioning you to go and to go beyond where you have been before.

This is the Time of the Increase.

The Increase of heaven in the earth.

As it is in heaven let it be in the earth.

Enlarge your tent.

Be ye holy as I am holy.

I have captured you and made you holy.

I have captured your hearts says the King and I wont let go, so come with me.
I am opening the doors of the darkest places.
I am the Lord that opens prison doors and set the captives free.
I decree that the end of captivity is in our midst.
Rejoice and go forth. Spread the good news. The miracle of salvation has inundated the earth: blind eyes are being opened, deaf ears unplugged, wax in the heart removed.
I proclaim that the new is in our midst. A time of change.
A Time of Turning.
A time to see the light. The light came to the world. The time to recognize the light of the world.
Shine forth the light of the Christ. The Messiah is exposing Himself everywhere. The lover of our soul is increasing so much that He is all we see.
The old has really passed away. New, new, new is moving forth. Strongholds are falling down. Lies are being shattered.
The need for God is unquenchable. A new hunger for God is exposing itself everywhere.
Grace, grace, grace and more grace.
Extraordinary miracles, signs and wonders in every marketplace. The Church has invaded the streets.
Everybody knows something wonderful is happening.
Emmanuel is in our midst.
He took over my heart and I take over other hearts for Him. Amen.

This is one of the last patients that I recently saw with the following problems:

1.) Persistent trigeminal neuralgia for twenty years with constant pain in the face.

2.) An atypical seizure disorder.

3.) Transient ischemic attacks with numbness in parts of the body, slurred speech etc.

4.) A recent brain hemorrhage with severe headaches proven by MRI and CT.

There was discernment of a definite spiritually induced illness. Upon taking a very detailed history he admitted to keeping the ashes of a family member who had been a priest in the Santeria Caribbean witchcraft tradition. He also had kept statues, collars, pendants, medallions, wrist bands etc. All witchcraft paraphernalia. All demonic contact points.

This patient accepted Jesus as Lord and Savior, repented of his sins, renounced satan and witchcraft, forgave, received prayer of healing and deliverance and when he threw away every demonic object, he received total healing: no pain, no bleeding, no stroke, no seizure. A repeat scan of the brain was totally within normal limits. Hallelujah. Thank you Jesus.

This is an example of an illness secondary to occultic open doors to the demonic- possession of cursed objects that are spiritual contact points- there can be transference of evil spirits through these objects that can cause curses and illnesses.

Numbers 6: 24-27

24- The Lord bless thee, and keep thee:
25- The Lord make His Face shine upon thee, and be gracious unto thee:
26- The Lord lift up His countenance upon thee, and give thee peace.
27- And they shall put my name upon the children of Israel; and I will bless them.

2 Corinthians 13:14

The Grace of the Lord Jesus Christ, and the love of God, and the communion and fellowship of the Holy Spirit be with you all. Amen.

Endnotes & References

[1] Norma Dearing, "Salvation," in Francis and Judith MacNutt's, *School of Healing Prayer: Level I Facilitator's Manual* (Florida: Christian Healing Ministries, Inc., 1999), 93.

[2] Greg Trainor, Holy Spirit Missionary Association Conference.

[3] Bill Bright, *The Holy Spirit: The Key to Supernatural Living* (Florida: New Life Publications, 1980), 266.

[4] Randy Clark, *Ministry Training Manual* (Pennsylvania: Global Awakening, 2002), E-1.

[5] Derek Prince, *The Gifts of the Spirit* (Pennsylvania: Whitaker House, 2007), 10.

[6] Randy Clark, H-1.

[7] Gordon Lindsay, *Commissioned with Power: An Overview of the Gifts of the Spirit* (Texas, Christ for the Nations, Inc., 2001).

[8] Derek Prince, 85.

[9] Bill Johnson, *The Supernatural Power of a Transformed Mind: Access to a Life of Miracles* (Pennsylvania: Destiny Image Publishers, Inc., 2005).

[10] Francis MacNutt, Ph.D., *Healing: Revised and Expanded – The Bestselling Classic* (Indiana: Ave Maria Press, 1999) 133.

[11] Chester and Betsy Kylstra, *Restoring the Foundations: A Integrated Approach to Healing Ministry, 2nd Edition* (Florida: Proclaiming His Word Publications, 2003).

[12] John and Paula Sandford, *The Transformation of the Inner Man* (Oklahoma: Victory House, Inc., 1982).

[13] Joan Hunter, *Healing the Whole Man Handbook: Effective Prayers for the Body, Soul, and Spirit Revised Edition* (Pennsylvania: Whitaker House, 2006).

[14] Henry W. Wright, *A More Excellent Way* (Georgia: Pleasant Valley Church, Inc., 2005).

[15] *Healing Room Ministries: How to Minister to Specific Diseases* (Washington: Healing Room Ministries, 2003).

[16] Randy Clark

[17] Judith MacNutt, "Inner or Emotional Healing," in Francis and Judith MacNutt's, *School of Healing Prayer: Level I Facilitator's Manual* (Florida: Christian Healing Ministries, Inc., 1999), 57.

[18] John Sandford, *Biblical Basis of Elijah House Ministries, Elijah House School for Prayer Ministry* (Idaho: Elijah House) CD01, Basic I Audio CD.

[19] ibid

[20] John Loren, Paula Sandford, and Lee Bowman, *Choosing Forgiveness: Turning from Guilt, Bitterness, and Resentment Toward a Life of Wholeness and Peace* (Florida: Charisma House, A Strang Company, 2007).

[21] Stephen Seamands, *Wounds That Heal: Bringing Our Hurts to the Cross* (Illinois: InterVarsity Press, 2003).

[22] Judith MacNutt and Norma Dearing, "Inner Healing and Forgiveness," in Francis and Judith MacNutt's, *School of Healing Prayer: Level I Facilitator's Manual* (Florida: Christian Healing Ministries, Inc., 1999), 75.

[23] Kylstra, 81.

[24] Tom Wilkerson, "Bitter Roots and Inner Vows," in Francis and Judith MacNutt's, *School of Healing Prayer: Level II Facilitator's Manual* (Florida: Christian Healing Ministries, Inc., 1999), 70.

[25] John and Paula Sandford, 237.

[26] Maria Vadia, *There is Power in Your Tongue* (California: Queenship Publishing Company, 2002).

[27] Todd Bentley, "Tearing Down Strongholds: Seven Giants," from *Open Heavens Bible* (Canada: Fresh Fire Ministries, 2006).

[28] Francis and Judith MacNutt, "The Occult Sheet," in Francis and Judith MacNutt's, *School of Healing Prayer: Level I Facilitator's Manual* (Florida: Christian Healing Ministries, Inc., 1999), 179.

[29] Selwyn Stevens, *Unmasking Freemasonry: Removing the Hoodwink* (New Zealand: Jubilee Resources, 2004).

[30] Francis and Judith MacNutt, "Preparation of a Family Tree," in Francis and Judith MacNutt's, *School of Healing Prayer: Level I Facilitator's Manual* (Florida: Christian Healing Ministries, Inc., 1999), 210.

[31] Frank Marzullo, *Breaking the Curses of Deuteronomy 27 & 28* (Florida: Christian Covenant Fellowship, 1995).

[32] Randy Lechner, "Confession of the Saints" (Covenant Ministries), prayer sheet.

[33] Derek Prince, *They Shall Expel Demons: What you Need to Know About Demons – Your Invisible Enemies* (Michigan: Chosen Books, 1998).

[34] Francis MacNutt, *Deliverance from Evil Spirits: A Practical Manual* (Michigan: Chosen Books, 1995).

[35] Peter Horrobin, *Healing through Deliverance Volume 2: The Practice of Deliverance Ministry*(Michigan: Chosen Books, 2003).

[36] Frank Marzullo and Tom Snyder, *A Manual for the Deliverance Worker* (Florida: Frank Marzullo, 2006).

[37] John Loren Sandford and Mark Sandford, *A Comprehensive Guide to Deliverance and Inner Healing* (Michigan: Chosen Books, 1992).

[38] Chester and Betsy Kysltra, *Biblical Healing and Deliverance: A Guide to Experiencing Freedom from Sins of the Past, Destructive Beliefs, Emotional and Spiritual Pain, Curses and Oppression* (Michigan: Chosen Books, 2005).

[39] see notes 33-38

[40] C. Peter Wagner, *Freedom from the Religious Spirit* (California: Regal Books, 2005).

[41] Message of the Holy Father Benedict XVI to the young people of the world on occasion of the XXIII World Youth Day, 2008: (Acts 1:8) http://ww.vatican.va/holy_father.com

[42] Frank Marzullo Jr., "King David's Method of Warfare"(Florida: Christian Covenant Fellowship, 2003-2008) http://www.frankmarzullo.com

[43] Frank Marzullo and Tom Snyder, 97.

[44] Francis MacNutt, *Deliverance from Evil Spirits: A Practical Manual*, 69.

[45] Patricia King, *The Glory School with Patricia King* (Arizona: Extreme Prophetic, Inc., 2005).

[46] Todd Bentley, *The Reality of the Supernatural World: Exploring Heavenly Realms and Prophetic Experiences* (Canada: Sound of Fire Productions, 2005).

Other References:

Divinum Illud Munus, Encyclical of Pope Leo XIII on the Holy Spirit, May 9, 1897 http://www.papalencyclicals.net.

Confronting the devil's power, Address of Pope Paul VI to a general audience, November 15, 1972 http://www.papalencyclicals.net.

Todd Bentley, *Christ's Healing Touch Volume I: Understanding How to Take God's Healing Power to the World* (Canada: Fresh Fire Ministries, 2005).

Derek Prince, *Blessing or Curse: You Can Choose* (Michigan: Chosen Books, 1990).

Maria Vadia, *Healing is for You!* (California: Queenship Publishing, 2007)

Bern Zumpano, "On-Site Deliverance Workshop" from Word of Faith Ministries International (Florida: Harbor Light Publishers)

Dr. Rene Pelleya-Kouri was born in Havana, Cuba on May 12, 1946, to Rene Pelleya, and attorney, and Josephine Kouri, a physician. In 1960, Dr. Pelleya-Kouri, then 14 years old, came to the USA.

In 1982 he graduated from the University Of Miami School Of Medicine with degrees in Internal Medicine and Nephrology. For several years he was also involved in the fields of Addiction medicine and Alternative medicine. He investigated many psychological and spiritual modalities of healing.

In 2002, Dr. Pelleya-Kouri received Jesus as Lord and Savior, and in 2003, received the Baptism in the Holy Spirit.

Dr. Pelleya-Kouri now practices Internal Medicine in Miami, Florida.

Praying Doctors was born from a progressive commitment to Jesus Christ.